Introduction to
Soviet National Bibliography

Introduction to
Soviet National Bibliography

Thomas J. Whitby
and
Tanja Lorković

Libraries Unlimited, Inc.-Littleton, Colorado
1979

LIBRARIES UNLIMITED, INC.
P.O. Box 263
Littleton, Colorado 80160

Library of Congress Cataloging in Publication Data

Whitby, Thomas Joseph.
    Introduction to Soviet national bibliography.

    Includes translation of Gosudarstvennaía bibliog-
rafiía SSSR, by I. B. Gracheva and V. N. Franĭskevich.
    Bibliography: p. 211
    1. Bibliography, National—Russia. I. Lorković,
Tanja, joint author. II. Gracheva, Iía Borisovna
Gosudarstvennaía bibliografiía SSSR. English.
1979. III. Title.
Z2492.5.W47   015'.47   79-4112
ISBN 0-87287-128-2

To provide society as a whole and each of its citizens with information about publications issued within the country, to guide the reader in the wide stream of domestic publication, helping him find what he needs, and at the same time to promote the book as one of the powerful means of satisfying the educational, professional, and aesthetic requirements of man—such is the chief aim of national bibliography.

IU. I. Fartunin
Director,
All-Union Book Chamber

PREFACE

Bibliographic control has once again become an important issue at both the national and international levels. To be sure, the desire for effective bibliographic control has motivated the thinking of individuals and organizations before, as witnessed in the last century in the endeavors of the International Institute of Bibliography in Brussels, the Concilium Bibliographicum in Zurich, and the Royal Society of London. Other organizations, such as Unesco, the International Federation of Library Associations and Institutions (IFLA), the International Federation for Documentation (FID), the International Organization for Standardization (ISO), the International Council of Scientific Unions (ICSU), and the International Translations Centre (ITC), have for some years been engaged in the organization of bibliography internationally. Recently, several comprehensive programs, including the National Information Systems (NATIS), the Universal System for Information in Science and Technology (UNISIST), and the International Serials Data System (ISDS), have been successfully launched and, although greater program coordination is desirable, seem to be providing the kinds of approaches to bibliographic control that have been lacking for some time. Each of these organizations and programs is concerned with one or more facets of bibliographic control: cataloging, classification, abstracting, indexing, standardization, networking, computerized data bases, serials control, and translations. Pondering the activities of such broad-based organizations and programs as a whole, one cannot help feeling that something is taking place on a scale hitherto unknown in the bibliographic world.

National bibliography is currently one of the vital areas of concern. Its importance lies in its function as a building block of Universal Bibliographic Control, that ambitious program established in 1974 to bring together through cooperation and coordination the many disparate efforts in national bibliographic control. While some countries, like Great Britain, the United States, and the Soviet Union, do have well-established national bibliographies, many countries, especially the developing ones, have no program whatsoever for developing a comprehensive national bibliography.

There are, of course, variations in the scope, organization, and methods of national bibliography from country to country. It is obvious that in some countries national bibliography is a *de facto* predicament, while in others it is carefully planned and organized. An example of this is the stark contrast between the fragmented system that exists in the United States and the highly organized system of the Soviet Union. In the United States, many organizations, governmental and private, contribute to the national bibliography. In the USSR, a single organization, the All-Union Book Chamber (with its republic affiliates), has been designated the center of national bibliography. No law underlies national bibliography in the United States; and there is no national bibliographic center, unless one recognizes the Library of Congress as such. In the USSR, a legal basis has existed since before the revolution. Since its inception, Soviet national bibliography has been characterized as complete and current, terms that no longer apply to the U.S. system.

The core of a national bibliographic system is, of course, a publication (or family of publications) which attempts to list (i.e., register) on a current basis everything that is published within a country. While there may be other important features of such a system, the publication program is of primary concern. Complete coverage is dependent upon a strong legal foundation, either in the form of a copyright law or a legal deposit system. Due to its voluntary nature both in publication and deposit, copyright cannot ensure the collection of all published materials. Legal deposit, on the other hand, seems to be highly effective, especially in the USSR, where printers rather than publishers are responsible for delivery of publications to a national center.

At this moment in history, when both the West and the communist world are vying for acceptance by the uncommitted Third World, it seems appropriate to examine carefully the important institutions of each side. National bibliography is such an institution. Its status in a particular nation affects the manner in which information is collected, organized, packaged, and disseminated in that country.

An attempt will be made here to do two things: 1) trace briefly the development of Soviet national bibliography from its beginnings under tsarism to the present time and 2) describe the current activities of the All-Union Book Chamber, the Soviet national bibliographic center. Because the Soviet publication program in national bibliography is fully explicated in Tanja Lorković's careful translation, there is no need to go over this ground in any detail, except to bring the information up to date. Instead, the historical, legal, organizational, archival, statistical, and bibliothecal aspects of Soviet national bibliography will be examined.

The growth and development of the Soviet national bibliographic system to date has been truly impressive. Now, with computerization, the possibilities for still more effective bibliographic controls look promising. Nations that have not yet developed a national bibliographic system may look to the Soviets for a model. The appeal of the Soviet system lies in its clean organizational lines and clearly defined functional goals. It is difficult to say whether the uncommitted nations of the world will adopt the mandated Soviet system or the loosely organized system of the United States, where so much depends upon voluntary cooperation.

The notion is being advanced in some quarters that a nation's national bibliographic center should be an integral part of its national library.* This argument is calculated to appeal to those nations that are in need of some sort of center for registering their publishing output but have no plans for its location. Indeed, it is interesting to note that the Library of Congress has of late made statements to the effect that it is both a national bibliographic center** and a national library, although officially it is neither. The Soviets have chosen to keep the national library, the Lenin State Library, and the national bibliographic center (the All-Union Book Chamber) separate.

While it is not the purpose of this introduction to argue the merits of either a combined or separate national bibliographic center and national library, it is hoped that what follows will contribute in some way to an understanding of the problems of national bibliographic control in the world today.

The translation, Part II of this book, came about when it was realized that little had been published in English on the organs of Soviet national bibliography. Detailed information regarding title changes, periodicity, content, scope, arrangement, bibliographic entry, indexes, and the like was unavailable unless one were to examine the bibliographic publications individually, which would be infeasible in most cases. The translation was undertaken in the belief that bibliographers, catalogers, librarians, scholars, and even students will find a use for it as a reference tool.

In translating the Russian *Guide to the Organs of National Bibliography* (as found in Part II of this book), one of the most awkward terminological problems encountered was the translation of the title *Letopis' periodicheskikh izdanii SSSR*. Should it be rendered *Annals of Serial Publications of the USSR* or *Annals of Periodical Publications of the USSR*? While the latter is a literal translation and seems the safer choice to make, the former is more appropriate since it conforms to current American practice, which considers the periodical to be a type of serial. The term serial implies openendedness and continuity but not necessarily regularity or periodicity. The term periodical seems unsuitable for the overall class of publications produced serially because so many titles, especially the monographic series, are published aperiodically.

As bibliographic control on the international level develops, terminological problems will occur with greater frequency. The different uses of the terms serial and periodical in the United States and the Soviet Union is a case in point.

---

*Dorothy Anderson, "The Role of the National Bibliographic Centre," *Library Trends* 25 (January 1977): 645-663.

***The Library of Congress as the National Bibliographic Center: Report of a Program Sponsored by the Association of Research Libraries, October 16, 1975* (Washington, DC: Association of Research Libraries, February 1976).

Aside from this, the only other terminological problem was the translation of the Russian expression "gosudarstvennaia bibliografiia." Here again, rather than taking the literal route and rendering it "state bibliography," the more widely recognized expression, "national bibliography," has been chosen. Indeed, there are indications that even in the Soviet Union, expressions of opinion favor "natsional'naia bibliografiia" over "gosudarstvennaia bibliografiia," although the latter is used almost exclusively today in Soviet publications.

ACKNOWLEDGEMENTS

Recognition must be extended to those who over the past couple of years have contributed in one way or another to this work. The first translation was ably prepared by Nancy Patterson as a student project at Kent State University Library School. This translation was of great help to Tanja Lorković in preparing a complete translation of *Guide to the Organs of National Bibliography in the USSR*. My deepest appreciation goes to Bohdan Wynar for his patience and encouragement and to Tanja Lorković, Head, Catalog Department, University of Iowa, for the great effort expended in translating an unusually detailed reference work full of the most recondite facts and figures. Also, special recognition is extended to Marilyn Kann, presently Slavic cataloger and bibliographer at the University of Virginia, for her efforts in compiling the glossary of terms and expressions appropriate to the field of national bibliography. For copies of Book Chamber catalog cards showing use of the ISBD punctuation, no small measure of debt is owed to Nathalie Delougaz, Chief, Shared Cataloging Division, and John D. Reynolds, Head, Slavic Languages Section, Shared Cataloging Division, of the Library of Congress. Considerable help in seeing the manuscript to conclusion was provided by Susan C. Holte of the editorial staff of Libraries Unlimited, Inc. Finally, I am grateful to my family for allowing me to spend so many of my free hours on this undertaking.

Thomas J. Whitby
University of Denver

TABLE OF CONTENTS

PART I

INTRODUCTION

BEFORE THE REVOLUTION

Before examining the growth and development of national bibliography under the Soviets, a brief account of current bibliography in Russia from its beginning under tsarism to its transfer in 1917 to the Soviet government is in order and should be of interest to the reader. This background is necessary for a proper understanding and appreciation of Soviet bibliography, which inherited from tsarism not only the idea of the compulsory registration of publications but also the principal organ of current bibliography, *Book Annals* (Knizhnaia letopis'). An adequate background demands that the numerous attempts, both private and governmental, to regularly list publications be examined; that the pervasive role of censorship be explained; that the organs of current bibliography, especially *Book Annals*, be described; and that the notable censors and bibliographers of prerevolutionary bibliography be introduced.[1]

The idea of registering current publications was actually borrowed from Ludwig Bakmeister, whose *Russische Bibliothek*,[2] the first bibliographic journal in Russia, recorded book production from 1772 to 1789. This journal was issued for the purpose of stimulating interest throughout Europe in Russian literature and the attainments of Russian scholarship. Publication was set up to coincide with the international book fair which took place in Leipzig twice a year. In its sixteen year existence, Bakmeister's journal listed 1,123 items, including books, periodicals, maps, and music. All entries were transliterated, and annotations were supplied in German. Patterned after the better bibliographic journals of the West, the *Russische Bibliothek*, with its cumulative entries, was a list of exceptionally high quality.

The first to reestablish current bibliography after Bakmeister was Vasilii Grigor'evich Anastasevich. In 1820, Anastasevich compiled a catalog entitled *Catalog of Russian Books for Reading from the Library of V. Plavil'shchikov, Systematically Arranged*.[3] Plavil'shchikov was a well-known Saint Petersburg bookdealer. In 1815, he had opened in his bookstore a library that became a gathering place for scholars, literary figures, and other notables. When the number of titles reached 7,000 in 1820, he commissioned Anastasevich to compile a catalog for the collection. For six years, 1821-1826, annual supplements to the catalog, listing newly published books in the Russian language, were issued. Altogether, 8,840 items, including maps, periodicals, and music, as well as books, were listed in the catalog and its supplements. These supplements are considered the main source of current bibliographic information for the period.

After Plavil'shchikov's death, the entire library was transferred by will to Alexander Smirdin, another well-known bookseller and publisher. In 1828, Smirdin published the *Catalog of Russian Books for Reading from the Library of Alexander Smirdin, Systematically Arranged,*[4] which contained all the publications inherited from Plavil'shchikov as well as his own materials. Supplements were added in 1829, 1832, and 1847. The compilation of this catalog has also been attributed to Anastasevich, although there is substantial disagreement on the matter.[5] Be that as it may, the catalogs of Plavil'shchikov and Smirdin constitute the best record of newly issued publications in the first quarter of the nineteenth century.

In the year 1825, P. I. Keppen, editor, publisher, and scholar of some note, presented information in his *Bibliograficheskie listy* about new publications issued in Russia. Considered the most reliable and complete current bibliography for the year, it listed about 600 works of all types. Its listing of books about Russia (Rossica) is especially noteworthy.

In the early nineteenth century, it was not unusual for journals such as the *Son of the Fatherland* (Syn otechestva) and the *Moscow Telegraph* (Moskovskii telegraf) to carry listings of new publications. This is well exemplified by V. D. Komovskii, a well-known writer and bibliographer, who listed publications under the title "List of All Books Published in Russia in 1829"[6] in the periodical *Moskovskii vestnik* for 1830. Even Alexander Pushkin, the great Russian poet, made an attempt at current bibliography. In 1836, Pushkin inserted a "New Books" section in his *Contemporary* (Sovremmenik), an important literary journal. Coverage was limited almost exclusively to publications issued in Saint Petersburg and Moscow. Pushkin attempted to cover new publications in all fields of knowledge, including science, technology, and medicine. He supplied annotations and reviews to many of the books listed, which made his list a unique combination of registry and critical bibliography. Current bibliography in Russia would undoubtedly have been raised to a high level of scholarship if Pushkin's untimely death in 1837 had not put an end to the registering of all newly published works in his journal.

ADVENT OF THE GOVERNMENT

The involvement of the Russian government with the problems of current bibliographic control can be explained with brief references to political events of that period. Any description of state bibliographic registration must be discussed concomitantly with the system of censorship which affected publishing activities at that time. There had been official censorship in Russia as early as 1803, when that function was delegated to the Ministry of Education. In addition, there soon developed the secret censorship of the Ministry of Police. However, owing to the liberal attitude of Tsar Alexander I, who ruled from 1801 to 1825, censorship in this early period cannot be characterized as particularly severe.

After 1825, censorship became a more serious matter. The confusion brought about by the Decembrist Revolt caused the authorities to pay close attention to political and social literature. A series of censorship regulations were promulgated; and an elaborate, albeit confusing, system of censorship was instituted.

Of particular interest to the censors was periodical literature. Admiral Shishkov, minister of education under Alexander I, was of the opinion that periodicals were "the chief source for the circulation of so-called public opinion among the best educated part of the nation."[7] Periodicals had, in the opinion of S. S. Uvarov, later minister of education under Nicholas I, "a vastly farther reaching circle of action than books," and "in them with greater frequency is noticed the breach of censorship regulations."[8]

In the early 1830s, the censors took action against several journals. The magazine *Teleskop* was banned in 1836 for including in its pages the "Philosophical Letters" of Peter Chaadaev, in which the writer stated that Russia was devoid of a cultural tradition and must look to the West for enlightenment. Chaadaev was pronounced insane and committed to an asylum.

The minister of education, S. S. Uvarov, was the originator of the phrase "Orthodoxy, Autocracy, and Nationalism," which referred to the principles (the foundation) on which the reign of Nicholas I stood. Anything in word or deed that contravened those three precepts was doomed to extinction. The censorship provided an excellent means for discouraging and thwarting the attempts of the most ardent of the tsarist critics.

The Censorship Law of 1837, which was calculated to guarantee the purity of the literary air, required that every magazine be read by two censors and that everything passed by them be examined by a third censor. Even this triple censorship, which lasted many years, was considered inadequate to cope with the real and imaginary foes who were polluting the mainstream of publication. The famed Third Section, established in the private chancery of the tsar, busied itself with censorship affairs. It seems there was even distrust of the official censors themselves, a fear that through some oversight a document might slip by that would prove obnoxious to the government.

The Censorship Law of 1837 provided a mechanism for the surveillance of the work of the censors. This was the establishment of a special index called the "Index of Newly Published Books,"[9] inserted in the *Journal of the Ministry of Public Education*,[10] to register all publications. The founder of this journal, S. S. Uvarov, had selected as editor K. S. Serbinovich, who had a long record of censorship activities. He had been censor of the Main Censorship Office (Glavnoe pravlenie tsensurii), 1826-1827; was connected with the Petersburg censorship committee, 1828-1830; and had directed ecclesiastical censorship since 1836. Serbinovich did brilliant work as editor of the *Journal of the Ministry of Public Education*; and when the journal's offices were given responsibility for registration of all newly published books, his organizational skills proved invaluable.

The circumstances surrounding the inception of the "Index of Newly Published Books" were peculiar in that the index was not announced beforehand and was not even listed in the table of contents of the first issue. Apparently, this section, which was set up for the sole purpose of aiding the government in censoring, was not considered an integral part of the journal by the general reader.

For two years, the "Index of Newly Published Books" continued as a part of the monthly *Journal of the Ministry of Public Education*, but with separate pagination; after 1839, it appeared as a special publication, *Supplements to the Journal of the Ministry of Public Education.*[11] Its material was arranged systematically, and the entries were rather detailed and precise. The journal received little attention as a bibliographic tool; without a doubt, the censorship function determined the content, periodicity, and organization of the "Index of Newly Published Books." The function of registration *per se* was not recognized. Registration continued uninterruptedly for eighteen and one-half years to the end of the regime of Nicholas I. During this time, 21,898 items were listed. Then, as abruptly and quietly as it had begun, it was terminated.

In the last years of Nicholas's reign, censorship became increasingly severe. In 1848, when countries in western Europe were being shaken by revolutions, the tsar became concerned about the ineffectiveness of the triple censorship system that he had set in motion in 1837. He therefore created the famed "Committee of April 2" for the surveillance of publishing and the work of the censors. Not an official agency, the Committee did its work in strictest secrecy. It met in secret chambers in the Imperial Public Library, where a copy of each new work deposited in the library was set aside for the Committee's perusal. An examination of lists of publications prepared for the Committee by the printers provided a check on the receipt of depository copies. In this manner, the censorship begun in 1837 was strengthened, and any loopholes that might allow a work to slip through the censor's net were closed.

Immediately following the death of Nicholas I in 1855, a new censor, A. V. Nikitenko, was appointed by the minister of education. In some twenty years' experience in censorship activities, Nikitenko had cultivated a reputation as a liberal censor. One of his first acts was to dismiss Serbinovich as editor of the *Journal of the Ministry of Public Education*. The question of disbanding the cumbersome censorship apparatus was raised, as it was thought that its usefulness was outlived. Naturally, as the censorship function tapered off, the need to continue state registration of publications declined. In 1855, the "Index of Newly Published Books" was dropped as part of the *Journal of the Ministry of Public Education*.

In its day, the "Index of Newly Published Books" went unnoticed. A mere list of current publications apparently did not appeal to scholarly bibliographers, whose main interest was in the field of retrospective bibliography. Be that as it may, the "Index of Newly Published Books" registered the items with exceptional completeness and accuracy; and today it constitutes the most valuable source of information on publications of the time.

RESUMPTION OF STATE BIBLIOGRAPHIC REGISTRATION

The abrupt termination of state bibliographic registration in 1855 soon made itself felt, for there was no existing source for information on newly published books. In reaction, several private attempts at current bibliography were made. In 1856, almost simultaneously two lists of publications for 1855 were published. The first was "Russian Bibliographic Index for 1855,"[12] compiled by the librarian, P. P. Lambin. It was based on books deposited at the Academy of Sciences and was inserted in the *Supplement to the "Proceedings of the Academy of Sciences."*[13] The second was "Bibliography for 1855,"[14] a supplement to the periodical *Russkaia beseda.* At this time, one of the most important personalities in Russian bibliographic history, V. I. Mezhov, undertook current bibliography, first in *Homeland Record*[15] for 1856-1857, and subsequently in the *Journal of the Ministry of the Interior*[16] for the period 1858-1859. The journal that finally emerged as leader in the field was *Book Herald.*[17] Under the guidance of V. I. Mezhov, who had discontinued his work for the Ministry of the Interior, this journal made a systematic registration of publications, based on the depository copies in the Imperial Public Library, from 1860 to 1867.

Although censorship in the era of reform after the death of Nicholas was not severe, there were attempts to develop a censorship system. A powerful struggle ensued between the Ministry of Education and the Ministry of the Interior as to whom should have control of the censorship department. The latter won out on the grounds that the Ministry of Education, in its task to further education, could not be a sufficiently strict judge of the press. The censorship department was transferred to the Ministry of the Interior in 1863. A new censorship code was promulgated in 1865 that removed certain publications, notably periodicals, from preliminary censorship. Unfortunately, shortly after this order went into effect, a new censorship crackdown disturbed the publishing world. The attempt in 1866 on the life of Tsar Alexander II caused a further intensification of press censorship, and a number of journals were permanently shut down.

In the early 1860s, *Book Herald*, a non-governmental publication, listed current publications and fulfilled the needs of the censorship department as regards surveillance of the press. After the termination of *Book Herald* in 1867, however, there was not a single journal that carried current listings of publications. For this reason, it was necessary that state bibliographic registration be resumed. Starting in January 1869, lists were inserted in the *Government Herald,*[18] the official newspaper of the Russian government.

In the daily *Government Herald*, a list of current publications was printed weekly. This was an unsatisfactory arrangement because of the scattering of entries in the numerous issues of the newspaper and because of the fact that *Government Herald*, a newspaper, was not specifically designed for this important function. Consequently, the Chief Administration on Press Affairs began to publish its official fortnightly organ, *Index on Matters of the Press.*[19] The first issue came out in September 1872; the magazine lasted through 1878.

The *Index on Matters of the Press* included a list of new books published in Russia; a list of foreign publications scrutinized by the censor and pronounced

either suitable or unfit for circulation in Russia; a list of dramatic works examined by the censor and deemed permissible for presentation in the theatre;
information on Russian periodicals, such as permits, terminations, etc.; information on the book trade; advertisements; etc. In other words, it had a broad
informational scope of which the list of newly published books was an integral
part. The censorship functions which this document served are readily apparent.

When the *Index on Matters of the Press* was, for some undetermined reason, discontinued in 1878, the *Government Herald* was relied upon to take
its place. Registration in this newspaper continued uninterruptedly until 1903.
A new publication of the Chief Administration on Press Affairs, the *List of
Publications Issued in Russia*, was started in 1886. The *List* usually contained
author, title, and language indexes, and its arrangement was alphabetical, with
each entry numbered.

Until 1903, this listing consisted of reprintings from the *Government
Herald.* Because the *List of Publications Issued in Russia*[20] was published less
frequently than the *Government Herald*, the two organs of current bibliography
were able to exist side by side for a time. After the cessation of the *Government Herald* as the organ of primary registration, its cumulation, *List of Books
Published in Russia*, was published on a monthly basis. The monthly issues
were usually bound together, supplied with annual indexes and used as annuals.

From 1903 on, the *List of Publications Issued in Russia* was the organ
of primary registration. It was published annually until 1904 and on a monthly
basis through 1907, encompassing 21½ years of publication.

REFORM OF STATE BIBLIOGRAPHIC REGISTRATION

There had been discontent in bibliographic circles for some time about
the state of current bibliography. One objection to the two existing organs of
national bibliography, *Government Herald* and the *List of Books Published in
Russia*, was that, because of the avowed censorship function which those publications served, scholarly and cultural requirements were not being met. Furthermore, it was thought that a strongly organized and centralized system of
bibliography was needed to guarantee completeness of current registration.
Various learned bodies, including the Academy of Sciences, the Society of
Library Science,[21] and the Society of Bookdealers,[22] were concerned about
the state of affairs and held joint conferences to discuss the situation.

This agitation for better bibliographic service culminated in a conference
held at the Academy of Sciences in Saint Petersburg on 18 April 1906.[23] It
was attended by the director of the Chief Administration on Press Affairs
and by representatives of the most important bibliographic organizations in
Russia. Proposals were adopted for the systematic collection, registration, and
distribution of publications in Russia. The principal address at the conference
was made by A. V. Bel'gardt, director of the Chief Administration of Press
Affairs, who suggested that a library be established which would concentrate
in one place all current publications and that a weekly bibliographic journal,
listing new publications, be issued from the library. Thus came into being the
bibliographic journal of *Book Annals*,[24] under the Chief Administration on

Press Affairs of the Ministry of the Interior. This journal, taken over in 1917 first by the Provisional Government and then by the Soviet government, exists to this day as *the journal* of primary registration for newly published books.

When *Book Annals* was first published (the first issue was dated 14 July 1907), its program was broad in scope. On a weekly basis, *Book Annals* contained 1) an alphabetical list of books printed in Russia both in Russian and in other languages, 2) a subject index, 3) a list of outstanding articles from selected Russian newspapers and magazines, 4) a list of reviews of newly published books, 5) sundry news concerning book publishing and the book trade, and 6) advertisements. On a quarterly basis, it contained 1) a quarterly index of authors, 2) a cumulative subject index for the quarter, 3) an index of translations from Russian into other languages, and 4) leading articles. Finally, on an annual basis, there were indexes for authors and subjects.

When *Book Annals* began, it was announced that the weekly registration of current publications would satisfy scholarly as well as practical ends. Soviet bibliographers, in retrospect, have rejected this statement, contending that *Book Annals*, despite its avowed purpose, continued primarily to serve censorship purposes. Numerous lines of evidence, which need not be examined in detail here, are cited by the Soviet authorities to prove this point;[25] relaxed censorship restrictions after 1906, increased activity by the revolutionary press, unpublished correspondence between the head of the censorship department and the tsar, the prevalent illegal confiscation of publications by the secret police, and the lack of official concern for registration of politically harmless literature.

Whatever the reasons were for starting a new journal of current bibliography, it is nonetheless a fact that *Book Annals* far surpassed its predecessors in quality as a scholarly bibliographic journal. A. D. Toropov, one of the founders of the Russian Bibliographic Society, was appointed as editor and immediately began to systematize state bibliographic registration. Entries in *Book Annals* were becoming more exact and contained all the essential bibliographic elements; errors in registration were much less frequent than before. Although it was never claimed that complete coverage was attained, considerable progress was made in that direction. The principal reason for incompleteness was the non-delivery of publications to the Chief Administration on Press Affairs. Many government agencies, both at the state and local levels, failed to deliver their documents; some private societies were also lax in this connection.

Book Annals continued to be published uninterruptedly on a weekly basis until the abdication of the tsar on 2 March (15, new calendar) 1917. Under the Provisional Government, a commission[26] was established 8 (21) March 1917 to liquidate the Chief Administration on Press Affairs. Of necessity, this commission concerned itself with the registration of publications and the publishing of *Book Annals*. A subcommission "found necessary the creation of a special state bibliographical institution with wide scientific and practical plans under the name of Book Chamber."[27] Thus, the Russian Book Chamber[28] was founded 16 (29) May 1917 in Petrograd. One of the outstanding bibliographers of the time, S. A. Vengerov, was named director. The Book Chamber was charged with supplying the state libraries with copies of all publications issued in Russia. In 1917, only four libraries were recognized as depository libraries: the Public Library in Petrograd, the Moscow Rumiantsev Museum, the Academy of Sciences Library, and the Aleksandrovskii University in Helsingfors.[29] Despite difficulties inherent in reorganization, *Book Annals* continued to be published with regularity.

An indication of the growth of *Book Annals* is given by the following figures taken from M. B. Sokurova:[30]

1907	9,607 items	1912	34,630 items
1908	23,852 items	1913	34,006 items
1909	26,638 items	1914	32,338 items
1910	29,057 items	1915	26,044 items
1911	32,361 items	1916	18,174 items
		1917	13,144 items

The October Revolution, 25 October (7 November) 1917, created entirely new conditions for current bibliography, resulting in fundamental changes in the existing system of bibliographical organization. In the next section, these conditions and changes will be examined.

SUMMARY

Early compilations by private individuals attested to the need for current bibliography for scholarly and cultural purposes. In the main, these efforts were short-lived. The entrance of the Russian government into the field of bibliography (in the *Journal of the Ministry of Public Education*) placed current bibliography on a sounder footing than before. However, owing to its identification with censorship, state bibliographic registration of current publishing production did not wholly fulfill the long-felt desire for a registry that would satisfy scholarly and cultural needs. The vacillating tempo of censorship activities after 1855 prevented the establishment of a sound system of current bibliography.

A system of comprehensive bibliographic coverage was finally undertaken in 1907, when the mechanism for collecting, registering, and disseminating publications was centralized at the Chief Administration on Press Affairs. Before the revolution, the final step toward developing a system of bibliographic listing for scholarly and cultural purposes, was the establishment (in 1917) of the Provisional Government's Russian Book Chamber.

Table 1 shows both the private and the governmental attempts at current bibliography from 1772 to 1917. The compiler's name is given in parenthesis after the name of each list. The table indicates that current bibliography in the early years was exclusively the province of the individual bibliographer. From 1837 on, current bibliography was dominated by the government, although, from time to time, gaps were filled by lists undertaken privately.

Table 1

Lists of Current Bibliography in Tsarist Russia

Private	Coverage	Governmental
Russische Bibliothek (Bakmeister)	1772-89	
Catalog of Russian Books... *Plavil'shchikov* (Anastasevich)		
Catalog of Russian Books... *Smirdin* (Anastasevich?)	1820-28	
Bibliographic Lists (Keppen)	1825	
List of All Books Published in Russia in 1829 (Komovskii)	1829	
"New Books" in the *Contemporary* (Pushkin)	1836	
	1837-55	"Index of Newly Published Books" in the *Journal of the Ministry of Public Education*
	1855	*Russian Bibliographic Index for 1855* (Lambin)
"Bibliography for 1855" in *Russkaia beseda* (Compiler unknown)	1855	
Homeland Record (Mezhov)	1856-57	
	1858-59	*Journal of the Ministry of the Interior* (Mezhov)
Book Herald (Mezhov)	1860-67	
	1869-1902	*Government Herald*
	1872-78	*Index on Matters of the Press*
	1886-1907	*List of Publications Issued in Russia*
	June 1907-17	*Book Annals*

FOOTNOTES

[1] Most of the material in this section is taken from the following sources:
N. V. Zdobnov, *Istoriia russkoi bibliografii do nachala XX veka*, Izd. 2 (Moskva:
Izd-vo Akademii nauk SSSR, 1954); N. V. Zdobnov, *Sinkhronisticheskie
tablitsy russkoi bibliografii, 1700-1928 so spiskom vazhneishikh bibliograficheskikh trudov.* (Moskva: Izd-vo Vsesoiuznoi knizhnoi palaty, 1962); and
M. V. Sokurova, *Obshchie bibliografii russkikh knig grazhdanskoi pechati,
1708-1955,* Izd. 2-e. (Leningrad: 1956).

[2] *Russische Bibliothek zur Kentniss des gegenwartigen Zustandes der
Literatur in Russland* (Spb.: Herausgegeben von Hartwich Ludwig Christian
Bacmeister, 1772-1789) Bd. 1-11.

[3] *Rospis' rossiiskim knigam dlia chteniia iz biblioteki V. Plavil'shchikova,
sistematicheskim poriadkom raspolozhennaia.* V 3-kh ch. (Spb.: 1820).

[4] *Rospis' rossiiskim knigam dlia chteniia iz biblioteki Aleksandra Smir-
dina, sistematicheskim poriadkom raspolozhennaia.* V 4-kh ch. (Spb.: 1828).

[5] M. A. Briskman and A. D. Eikhengol'ts, *Bibliografiia; obshchii kurs*
(Moskva: Izd-vo "Kniga," 1959), p. 109. A further account of Anastasevich's
bibliographic work is provided by Marianna Tax Choldin in "Three Early
Russian Bibliographers," *Library Quarterly* 14 (January 1974): 1-28.

[6] "Spisok vsekh knig, vyshedshikh v Rossii v 1829 godu."

[7] Zdobnov, *Istoriia russkoi bibliografii*, p. 218.

[8] Ibid.

[9] "Ukazatel' vnov' vykhodiashchikh knig."

[10] *Zhurnal Ministerstva narodnogo prosveshcheniia.*

[11] *Pribavleniia k Zhurnaly Ministerstva narodnogo prosveshcheniia.*

[12] "Russkii bibliograficheskii ukazatel' za 1855 god."

[13] *Pribavlenie k "Izvestiiam Akademii nauk."*

[14] "Bibliografiia za 1855 god."

[15] *Otechestvennye zapiski.*

[16] *Zhurnal Ministerstva vnutrennikh del.*

[17] *Knizhnyi vestnik.*

[18] *Pravitel'stvennyi vestnik.*

[19] *Ukazatel' po delam pechati.*

[20] *Spisok izdanii, vyshedshikh v Rossii.* Later, in 1903, the title was changed
to *Spisok knig, izdannykh v Rossii.*

[21] Obshchestvo bibliotekovedeniia.

[22] Obshchestvo knigoprodavets.

[23] Russkoe bibliograficheskoe obshchestvo, *Russkiia bibliograficheskie organizatsii: ocherki ikh vozniknoveniia i deiatel'nosti* (Petrograd: 1915).

[24] *Knizhnaia letopis'*.

[25] Details of the Soviet argument are presented in the following article: N. V. Zdobnov, "Gosudarstvennaia bibliograficheskaia registratsiia pri tsarisme," *Sovetskaia bibliografiia* 4 (1935): 90-96.

[26] Osobaia komissiia po likvidatsii Glavnogo upravleniia po delam pechati.

[27] A. G. Fomin, *S. A. Vengerov, kak organizator i pervyi direktor Rossiiskoi knizhnoi palaty (nyne institut knigovedeniia)*, quoted in Vlad. Bonch-Bruevich, "K istorii organizatsii Rossiiskoi tsentral'noi knizhnoi palaty v Moskve," *Sovetskaia bibliografiia* 1 (1940): 151.

[28] Rossiiskaia knizhnaia palata.

[29] M. A. Godkevich, "Sovetskoe zakonodatel'stvo ob obiazatel'nom ekzempliare," *Sovetskaia bibliografiia* 1 (1940): 79.

[30] Sokurova, *Obshchie bibliografii russkikh knig grazhdanskoi pechati, 1708-1955*, p. 181.

UNDER THE SOVIETS

When the Soviets assumed the reins of government in 1917, the position of state national bibliography was stronger than ever, despite the disrupting influence of the revolution. The newly established Russian Book Chamber, headed by S. A. Vengerov, was a decided improvement over its predecessor, the Chief Administration on Press Affairs. While that agency had concerned itself only partly with bibliographic matters, the Russian Book Chamber was created a full-fledged bibliographic organization.

Book Annals, the organ of primary national bibliography, had been established in 1907 and was now ten years old. Its reputation as a reliable catalog of current publications was widespread, and it was, at least in purpose and scope, the type of list that bibliographers, librarians, and scholars had been struggling to create during the course of the nineteenth century. The national catalog, originally designed as a censorship tool, had been transformed into a listing of publications to meet bibliographic, scholarly, and cultural needs. Here, then, was the heritage of Soviet national bibliography: a national bibliographic center, an organ of primary national bibliography, and a bibliographic intent to list publications to serve a variety of needs.

THE RUSSIAN BOOK CHAMBER

The first period of national bibliography under the Soviet regime centered on the Russian Book Chamber at Petrograd and the struggle to have it moved to Moscow. Conditions during this period of civil war, famine, and general disorganization were not favorable to the smooth functioning of the Book Chamber. In spite of a decree of the People's Commissariat of Education, dated 24 February 1918, which confirmed the obligation of printing houses throughout the country to deliver eight copies of each publication to the Book Chamber, there was difficulty ensuring the delivery of these publications. In Petrograd, publications were sent by the printing houses directly to the Book Chamber; in Moscow, through the Moscow branch of the Book Chamber; and in other populous places, through the local soviets. This system had many inherent weaknesses, which were aggravated by the conditions of the country. In 1918 and 1919, as the central government grew stronger, the center of national bibliography became more and more isolated from the mainstream of activity in Moscow; and the receipt of publications from the printing establishments diminished. E. I. Shamurin, describing the prevailing conditions, wrote:

> After the victory of the Great October Revolution, the Russian Book Chamber did not direct its efforts toward deciding on the basic objectives set before it by the new state regime: securing the maximum completeness in the collection and registration of the obligatory copy of Soviet printed materials. Continuing to shirk the execution of objectives not of primary importance and not of immediate concern to national bibliography, the Russian Book Chamber was not even able to cope with its very basic objective—the regular and timely publication of lists of new publications in *Book Annals*. Delivery of the obligatory copies in this period was not secured, which showed up most negatively in the completeness of registration. According to data of the Petrograd State Public Library, which was confirmed by inspection of *Book Annals* for that period, approximately one-fourth of all books issued by the press in those years was received at the Russian Book Chamber. Decidedly incomplete was the receipt of the obligatory copy from the Ukrainian SSR and from the Transcaucasian Federation, where at that time no book chambers existed.[1]

S. A. Vengerov, director of the Book Chamber, strove to have a law passed which would ensure the delivery of publications to the Book Chamber. The seriousness of the situation was expressed by the director in one of his letters:

> Please, hasten the publication of the decree. Remember, that a book not delivered to the Book Chamber does not reach either the Public Library or the Rumiantsev Museum or the Academy of Sciences, i.e., it is lost to history. And the very memory of the book will disappear if it is not registered in *Book Annals*, by which all historians, bibliographers, and research workers are guided.[2]

There was general agreement with Vengerov that immediate action was needed to improve the situation. The question arose as to the location of the

Book Chamber, whether it should be in Petrograd or Moscow.[3] Vengerov insisted that it remain in Petrograd; other prominent bibliographers, notably B. S. Bodnarskii, chairman of the Russian Bibliographical Society, argued that it should be moved to Moscow, the seat of government. Bodnarskii's report on the Petrograd *Book Annals* was devastating to the interests of the Petrograd bibliographers. It presented facts and figures, indicating that *Book Annals* was registering only a part of current publishing and that, from a professional standpoint, it was not a first-rate catalog.[4]

LENIN DECREE OF 1920

This situation reached a climax early in 1920, and V. I. Lenin was called upon to give it his attention. After a review of the state of national bibliography as a whole, Lenin requested the drafting of a decree by the Small Sovnarkom. The text of the decree was presented to Lenin and signed 30 June 1920. Entitled "On the Transfer of Bibliographic Matters in the RSFSR[5] to the People's Commissariat of Education," it contained only five points:

1. Bibliographic matters in the RSFSR are transferred to the control of the People's Commissariat of Education.

2. It is the obligation of the People's Commissariat of Education to be responsible for registering the entire printed production of the RSFSR and for publishing lists of these publications.

3. The People's Commissariat of Education shall further the progress of bibliography to which end it shall establish new book chambers, take over the control of already existing book chambers and their agencies, open bibliographic institutes and courses, organize libraries devoted to bibliography, publish books and journals on questions of bibliography, regulate and coordinate the activity of all bibliographic institutions and societies.

4. The People's Commissariat of Education shall issue compulsory regulations about the free supply of newly issued publications to state and other libraries, and shall specify to what kinds of libraries the free obligatory copies may be supplied.

5. In carrying out the present decree, the People's Commissariat of Education shall issue compulsory regulations, and those guilty of violating them will be subject to penalty according to court sentence.[6]

On the basis of this decree, Narkompros[7] formed the Russian Central Book Chamber[8] in Moscow on 3 August 1920, and B. S. Bodnarskii, critic of the Russian Book Chamber, became the first director. The Russian Book Chamber in Petrograd was abolished. The newly formed Russian Central

Book Chamber was attached to the State Publishing House (Gosizdat), which was under the control of Narkompros. Here it remained until 1925.

The Lenin decree had immense significance for the development of Soviet bibliography. With the creation of the Russian Central Book Chamber, Soviet national bibliography was given a solid organizational footing. To ensure that the decree was carried out, a government department was put in control of the program and made responsible for its operation. The decree formed the basis of all future development of Soviet national bibliography with respect to the issuance of laws and regulations governing the collection, registration, and distribution of publications; the establishment of a series of organs of primary national bibliography in the republics of the USSR; and the development and coordination of bibliographic activities in general.

When the Book Chamber was located in Petrograd, the system of acquiring publications for registration and distribution had deteriorated to the point where only a small portion of the annual published production was handled each year. Consequently, *Book Annals* was incomplete and issued irregularly. In the first years of the existence of the Book Chamber, the matter of ensuring completeness in the collection and registration of publications and of the timely issuance of *Book Annals* devolved upon the director, who was powerless to enforce delivery from printing plants across the great length and breadth of the country.

To improve this situation, the Narkompros issued over a period of years a whole series of enactments covering the obligatory supply of publications to the Book Chamber and their allocation to certain libraries. This method of collecting and distributing publications in accordance with the law is known as the system of the obligatory copy, or legal deposit. The enactments defined the types of publications that were to be supplied and stipulated the quantities of each type required; they described the scope of the obligatory copy in terms of geographical coverage; and they designated which libraries were to receive copies of publications for deposit. In due course, these enactments served as models for Republic legislation.

Until 1928, the various enactments were issued by the government of the RSFSR through Narkompros. Receipt of publications from outside the RSFSR was controlled by the Book Chamber on the basis of contractual agreements with institutions in the union republics. In 1928, an all-union system of supply was established; and a tightly organized system of control over the supply of publications to the Book Chamber soon developed. Today, the dream of the Petrograd bibliographers is a reality; all publications issued within the borders of the USSR, with only certain designated exceptions, are delivered to the Book Chamber for listing in the national catalogs and are subsequently distributed to depository libraries.[9]

The sole organ of primary national bibliography of the Russian Book Chamber in Petrograd was *Book Annals*. Its purpose was to list the current production of books and other types of publications issued in the various languages within the borders of Russia. Various factors precluded completeness in the listing of all published materials. Although publications of various types came within the scope of this printed catalog, only a small portion of the pamphlets, periodicals, maps, leaflets, etc., were actually listed. In accordance with the Lenin decree of 1920, the Russian Central Book Chamber was made responsible for registering the "entire printed production of the RSFSR and for publishing lists of these publications." In time, as the enactments of the government came to embrace practically every major type of publication, the capacity of *Book Annals* to list all materials became sorely strained. *Book Annals* is, as its name suggests, primarily a vehicle for listing books. Other types of publications could be listed only as supplementary material; and registration, as a result, was apt to be incomplete.

The task of registering the entire printed production of the RSFSR, as required by the Lenin decree, imposed upon Soviet bibliographers the problem of determining the characteristics of each kind of publication. The various types were defined in a series of enactments calling for the delivery of obligatory copies to the Book Chamber. Because the growth of Soviet publishing made it impossible to list all types of publications in one catalog, a series of catalogs, or "annals," were developed to list the contents of periodicals and newspapers, maps, pictorial works, music, etc. (*Book Annals* is now confined to listing books and pamphlets.)

Today, the system of organs of national bibliography in the Soviet Union consists of the following: two weeklies—*Book Annals* (published since 1907) and *Annals of Journal Articles* (since 1926); one monthly—*Annals of Newspaper Articles* (since 1936); three quarterlies—*Music Annals* (since 1931), *Annals of Reviews* (since 1934); and three annuals—*Cartographic Annals* (since 1931), *Annals of Serial Publications of the USSR* (since 1933), and *Bibliography of Soviet Bibliography* (since 1941). This impressive array of national catalogs comprises a rather complete listing of current publishing in the Soviet Union. Only patents, standards, and technical catalogs, normally handled by other agencies, are excluded from these annals. Full descriptions of these national catalogs and other publications of the Book Chamber are given in the translation following Part I.

During 1923 and 1924, the Book Chamber was striving for completeness in the delivery of the obligatory copies within the RSFSR. Other problems pertaining to the content of *Book Annals*, such as the arrangement and description of entries, were also being given primary consideration. As stated in the Lenin decree of 1920, the responsibility of Narkompros did not extend beyond the limits of the RSFSR. Obviously, if an all-union system of national bibliography were to be erected in the Soviet Union, the position of the Book Chamber vis-à-vis corresponding organizations in the union republics would have to be strengthened. As an indication of the status of republic bibliography in 1924, only one catalog of current bibliography was in existence—*Annals of Ukrainian Publishing*[10] of the Ukrainian Book Chamber. At a conference of the directors of the book chambers of the RSFSR, Ukrainian SSR, and Belorussian SSR in October 1924, it was recognized that each republic should have its own catalog of current bibliography.

In august 1924, the Narkompros declared the Book Chamber the bibliographic center of the RSFSR and established a learned Council (Uchenyi sovet) under the director of the Russian Central Book Chamber. This Council was to be composed of the directors of the largest libraries and bibliographic organizations, who were to act as aides to the director of the Book Chamber in coordinating bibliographic work.

The strengthened position of the Book Chamber resulted in the convocation of the First All-Russian Bibliographic Congress in 1924, under the joint auspices of the Russian Central Book Chamber, the Russian Bibliographical Society, and the Leningrad Institute of Library Science. There were numerous requests to raise the Book Chamber from an institution of limited geographical scope to an all-union bibliographic center. The bibliographic work of the Book Chamber was subjected to considerable criticism, especially with reference to the quality of *Book Annals*, where the influence of the Brussels International Institute of Bibliography affected the form and content of the entries. The following recommendations (which, in time, materialized in concrete form) were made: compilation of an index of periodical articles, compilation of a repertory of the Soviet book, creation of a bibliographic publishing house, publication of a bibliographic journal, and the coordination of bibliographic work with other organizations.

The First All-Russian Bibliographical Congress recognized that, in spite of the inadequacies of its bibliographic work, the Book Chamber held a central position in the bibliographic affairs of the country. The Congress passed resolutions that were to determine the course of the Book Chamber for many years to come. Some of the immediate steps taken to carry out the resolutions of the Congress were the registration of provincial government publications; greater utilization of the entries in *Book Annals* by libraries in the compilation of their catalogs; adoption of a classification scheme for *Book Annals*; organization of a bibliographic information center to serve organizations and research workers; and publication of *Journal Annals* (later, *Annals of Journal Articles*) starting 1 January 1926.

The *Book Annual of the USSR*, a secondary bibliography cumulated from the weekly *Book Annals*, was started in 1927. Although it was issued rather irregularly at first, it has proved to be a first-rate reference work. In 1926, a subject classification for *Book Annals* was introduced, repudiating both the alphabetical and functional arrangements of entries formerly in *Book Annals*. In comparing this system (which bears a striking resemblance to the first summary of the Dewey Decimal Classification) with later modified editions, one can see the extent to which the Soviets have departed from the influence of Western bibliographic classification.[11] Soviet bibliographers claim that it is a scheme "based on the principles of a Marxist-Leninist classification science."

On 1 October 1925, the Russian Central Book Chamber was divorced from the State Publishing House and made an independent research institution. It was placed on the state budget and renamed the State Central Book Chamber of the RSFSR. In order to tie it more closely to research libraries and organizations, the Book Chamber was transferred to the Chief Administration on Scientific Institutions (Glavnauka),[12] which was controlled by Narkompros.

Separated from Gosizdat, the Book Chamber had difficulty in finding a publisher and printer for *Book Annals*, which experts from Gosizdat had stated was a poor financial risk. Although they had had no experience in this area, the directors of the Book Chamber decided to do their own publishing. They found a partner, the printing house of the Military Academy of the RKKA,[13] that was willing to undertake the weekly printing of about 1,000 copies of *Book Annals*. The arrangement proved to be sound: the catalogs, *Book Annals* and *Journal Annals*, were issued on a regular schedule, and, as a consequence, readership expanded.

The Second All-Russian Bibliographical Congress was in session from 25 November to 1 December 1926. Whereas the earlier congress had been organized by members of three bibliographic organizations, the second congress was arranged by a committee consisting of representatives from several organizations of independent purposes: the State Central Book Chamber, the Bibliographic Section of Glavpolitprosvet,[14] the Political Administration of RKKA, the Central Bureau on Regional Study, the All-Union Lenin Library in Moscow, the State Public Library in Leningrad, the Library of the Communist Academy, and others.

The atmosphere of the Second Congress was much different from that of the First Congress, with representatives from the various bodies presenting fresh viewpoints on the problems of bibliography. In recounting the work of the Second Congress, Shamurin says, "The essential and dominating atmosphere of the Second Congress was the struggle for political self-determination of Soviet bibliography," and "For the first time at full meaning was put the question of the political role of Soviet bibliography."[15] The following is a more complete description by Shamurin of the atmosphere of the Second Congress.

> The Second Congress plainly showed that bibliography is not an apolitical matter, not a quiet corner where one may screen himself off from life, but rather one of the active and fighting parts of socialist construction. The Congress showed also that bibliography is an arena and a weapon of class struggle, that in it too is carried on the struggle of the two worlds, of two world viewpoints—the bourgeois and the proletarian viewpoints, as in all other branches of science, literature, and art. It showed further that the construction of theory and methodology in bibliography hinges primarily on a clear perception by Soviet bibliographers of their place in this grandiose struggle, in their class self-determination, in their mastering the techniques of Marxist dialectics.[16]

The Second Congress did not consume all of its time discussing the political role of the Book Chamber. The same bibliographic problems that were reviewed at the First Congress came up for further attention: strengthening coordination between the State Central Book Chamber and the book chambers of the union republics; compilation of a general bibliography (repertory) of the Soviet book; organization of a publishing house; establishment of the

Book Chamber as the national center of documentation; and the elaboration of a Soviet system of classification appropriate to the organs of national bibliography, *Book Annals* and *Journal Annals*. Particular attention was given to the question of bibliographic work on national literatures. The Second Congress concluded that Soviet bibliography should rid itself of bourgeois theories of bibliography and that it should now make its own independent way.

THE YEARS OF EXPANSION

In the period following the Second All-Russian Bibliographical Congress, the activities of the Book Chamber expanded repidly. New organs of current bibliography were launched; the classification of publications was given close attention; the work of the Central Book Chamber and the republic book chambers was effectively coordinated; a reorganization of the Book Chamber on an all-union basis was completed; and special projects, such as centralized cataloging and the compilation of a repertory of the Russian book, were begun.

There had been previous discussion on the publication of printed cards in prerevolutionary Russia. The question was again raised after the October Revolution, and in October 1925, Glavpolitprosvet of the RSFSR began printing cards for mass libraries. In December 1926, at the Second Conference of Research Libraries of the RSFSR, the Book Chamber announced its project to publish printed cards for research libraries, beginning in 1927. This is the origin of centralized cataloging in Soviet Russia.[17]

An interesting aspect of Soviet centralized cataloging is that the bibliographic entries in *Book Annals* were closely patterned after those that appeared on the printed cards. Some libraries, in compiling their catalogs, utilized the entries in *Book Annals*. When the Book Chamber decided to publish printed cards, it simply took cognizance of the practice. Since the entries in *Book Annals* were made according to cataloging rules, it was a simple step to print them on cards.

In time, responsibility was delegated to the republic book chambers to publish printed cards for all books published within their respective republics. The Central Book Chamber in Moscow printed cards for publications issued in the RSFSR and in republics not served by local book chambers. This arrangement, attributable as much to language differences as to administrative demands, put the republic book chambers in a better position than the Moscow center to handle non-Russian Soviet publications. The printed cards published by the republic book chambers were composed according to the same cataloging rules that applied to the printed cards issued in Moscow. The significance of centralized cataloging, performed at both the central and republic book chambers, is that library card catalogs of high quality, compiled according to uniform rules, were established by the research libraries of the Soviet Union.

Closely related to the question of centralized cataloging was the long-hoped-for project of compiling a general bibliography of both prerevolutionary and Soviet publications. Compilation of a card repertory of the Soviet book began in 1927 on the basis of printed cards published in accordance with the centralized cataloging of books; cards for books published before 1927 were based on clippings from *Book Annals*. The following catalogs were originated: alphabetical and systematic card catalogs of the Soviet book (the latter arranged according to the Universal Decimal Classification); alphabetical and systematic catalogs of periodical and newspaper articles; and catalogs of maps, music publications, and reviews. Before World War II, many catalogs and card bibliographies were compiled. On 23 July 1941, a German bombing raid destroyed the building of the Book Chamber, resulting in the loss of the systematic catalog of the Soviet book and some four million cards. Fortunately, the alphabetic catalogs of the Soviet book were salvaged.

After the war, work was resumed on the compilation of a general bibliography of Soviet publications in the form of a union catalog covering the period 1707-1957. Participants in this undertaking were the Book Chamber and the three largest libraries in the Soviet Union: the Lenin State Public Library, the Saltykov-Shchedrin State Public Library, and the Library of the Academy of Sciences.

As indicated above, the publication program of the Book Chamber expanded rapidly following the Second Congress. In 1929, the journal *Bibliography* was started. Currently entitled *Soviet Bibliography* (Sovetskaia bibliografiia), it is the only journal in the Soviet Union totally devoted to problems of the theory and practice of bibliography. A journal of the highest quality, it is today the principal means of keeping abreast of bibliographic developments in the Soviet Union.

By 1937, six additional organs of national bibliography, listing music publications, maps, graphics, reviews, newspapers, and dissertations, had emerged. The system of organs of primary national bibliography was now complete. Other publications issued from the Book Chamber in the early thirties include a directory of periodical publications,[18] an index to series listed in *Book Annals,*[19] and a number of books on the theory and practice of bibliography.

An important organizational change took place on 27 November 1935, when the Presidium of the Central Executive Committee of the USSR reorganized the State central Book Chamber of the RSFSR into the All-Union Book Chamber and placed it within the jurisdiction of the Committee on the Management of Scientific and Educational Institutions.[20] On 1 January 1936, *Book Annals* and the other central organs of national bibliography published by the Book Chamber became all-union organs of national bibliography. Here, finally, was the legal recognition of the all-union scope of the Book Chamber. The existing agreements between the central Book Chamber in Moscow and the republic book chambers were abrogated, and the groundwork was laid for a new all-union coordinated network of book chambers.

A new set of regulations governing the Book Chamber was announced by the Kremlin on 27 July 1936.[21] Eight tasks were listed under general regulations:

1. Bibliographic registration and processing of all printed matter issued in the USSR

2. Organization of comprehensive bibliographic information for libraries and the general public on literature issued in the USSR

3. Centralized cataloging

4. Overall guidance of the work of the book chambers of the union republics and the autonomous republics of the RSFSR, and also the fulfillment of the functions of the Book Chamber of the RSFSR

5. Training and retraining of bibliographic cadres

6. Elaboration of bibliographic methods and methodological questions

7. Popularization of bibliographic and book knowledge

8. Service as a bibliographic reference source for government and party organs, institutions and organizations of the USSR

A further detailing of these bibliographic, administrative, and organizational tasks is provided in the statute. Especially important among the specific tasks was the Book Chamber's obligation to 1) control the delivery of the obligatory copies by the printers, 2) distribute the depository copies to designated libraries, and 3) provide uniform methods of bibliographic description for the entire system of organs of national bibliography in the USSR. The director was put in charge of all activities of the Book Chamber; he was to represent the Chamber in its relations with other institutions and conclude contracts and agreements necessary for accomplishing the objectives of the Chamber. This fundamental document outlined remarkably well the role the Book Chamber was to play in the ensuing years.

Another organizational change occurred in 1938, when the Book Chamber was placed within the jurisdiction of Glavlit,[22] the notorious Soviet censorship agency and one of the more important offices of the People's Commissariat of Education. Generally speaking, the Book Chamber was not directly affected by censorship activities since materials were censored prior to publication; the Book Chamber was only concerned with the output of the publishing industry. This approach to censorship was in marked contrast to that of the tsarist government, in which censors intervened only after publication, in many cases, too late to be effective.

REPUBLIC CENTERS OF NATIONAL BIBLIOGRAPHY

The creation of book chambers in all of the Soviet republics and three of the autonomous republics of the RSFSR has been of great significance in the development of Soviet national bibliography. Today, the All-Union Book Chamber in Moscow is at the apex of a network of seventeen republic book chambers. Each republic book chamber is responsible for the current registration of publications in the respective republics and autonomous republics, and each has its own set of organs of national bibliography. While some book chambers have highly developed publication programs (such as the Ukrainian Book Chamber), others have rather weak programs. All are obliged, however, to work closely with the Book Chamber in Moscow.

Coordination of the work of these widely scattered bibliographic centers is achieved primarily through meetings of the directors. To date, nineteen directors' meetings have been held, the first, in 1924 in Moscow; the most recent, in Moscow in July 1974.[23] Out of these meetings have come proposals and suggestions for the improvement and extension of the system of national bibliography at all levels.

Each republic book chamber has goals and objectives patterned after those of the Moscow Book Chamber: registration of all publications issued within the republic, publication of a national bibliography, maintenance of publication archives, deposit of publications in the principal libraries of the republic, centralized cataloging, distribution of catalog cards to local libraries, and the collection of statistical data on publishing.

A strengthening of these goals was achieved in 1971 when the All-Union Book Chamber prepared and had approved by the Committee on Publishing of the USSR Council of Ministers a statute which defined the role of the republic book chambers in rather concrete terms. A republic book chamber was defined as a "republic research center of national bibliography, publishing statistics, centralized cataloging, and a branch center of scientific and technical information in the areas of printing, publishing, book trade, and national bibliography."[24]

While the parent body, the All-Union Book Chamber, produces lists of everything published in the USSR (including the output of each republic and autonomous republic), the republic book chamber limits itself to republic publishing, except for desirable materials concerning the republic which have been published elsewhere within the Soviet Union. In other words, a work by a Ukrainian author or about the Ukraine published in Moscow should find its way into the appropriate Ukrainian organ of national bibliography.

The language problems that had existed for many years in publication and bibliographic description of the republic annals were overcome in the following manner. The All-Union Book Chamber uses the Russian language throughout its annals for entries of works published in the native languages of the republics. That is to say, a Georgian work listed in the annals of the Georgian republic would be listed in *Knizhnaia letopis'* in Russian, but with an indication of the original language. Works listed in the republic annals in the native languages include translations of the titles in Russian.

Until book chambers were established at the republic level, the coverage of the all-union organs of national bibliography was never really complete, despite legal requirements to the contrary. Obviously, it was difficult to ensure that works published at say, Khabarovsk, the Soviet Far East, would reach the bibliographic center in Moscow. In due course, the plan to have a book chamber in each union republic materialized (see table 2). The earliest republic book chamber was established in the Ukraine in 1922; the latest, in Moldavia

Table 2
List of Republic Book Chambers by Year of Founding

Book Chambers	1920	1930	1940	1950	1960	1970
Ukrainian SSR	1922					
Belorussian SSR	1922					
Armenian SSR	1922					
Georgian SSR	1924					
Azerbaidzhan SSR	1925					
Uzbek SSR	1926					
Turkmen SSR	1926					
Tatar ASSR	1926					
Bashkir ASSR	1929					
Chuvash ASSR		1931				
Tadzhik SSR		1937				
Kazakh SSR		1937				
Kirgiz SSR		1939				
Latvian SSR			1941			
Estonian SSR			1941			
Lithuanian SSR			1945			
Moldavian SSR				1957		

Compiled by the author from: Vsesoiuznaia knizhnaia palata. *Sorok let sovetskoi gosudarstvennoi bibliografii (1920-1960)* (Moskva: 1960).

in 1957. The book chambers of the Tatar ASSR, Bashkir ASSR, and Chuvash ASSR, all located within the RSFSR, were established in the period from 1926 to 1931. No serious attempt has been made to establish book chambers in other ASSRs, where publications are either deposited in local libraries or sent to the All-Union Book Chamber.

As described in the accompanying translation, the republic libraries of the ASSRs publish organs of national bibliography. A recent paper identifies an *Annals of Publishing* (Letopis' pechati) in sixteen ASSRs, including the three ASSRs which have full-fledged book chambers.[25] They are the Buriat, Dagestan, Kabardino-Balkarsk, Karelian, Komi, Mari, Mordovian, North Ossetian, Udmurt, Chechen-Ingush, Yakut, Kalmyk, Tuva, and, of course, the Tatar, Bashkir, and Chuvash ASSRs. The authors of the paper suggest that each state republic library set up a special section to handle the national bibliography.

Interesting data have recently been compiled on the origin and development of national bibliography in each autonomous republic of the RSFSR.[26] It is on the basis of such information, mainly publishing data, that decisions are made to establish organs of national bibliography at the local level. In fact, it was suggested as far back as 1949, at the Ninth Conference of Book Chamber Directors, that book chambers be set up in each autonomous republic. This suggestion seems not to have been taken seriously, for the state republic libraries still have the responsibility for national bibliography in thirteen out of the total of sixteen autonomous republics. Of course, establishing book chambers more widely and locally, especially throughout the vast territory of the RSFSR, would probably be a surer way of guaranteeing the registration of all printed matter and, at the same time, considering the multinational character of the USSR, of providing improved national bibliography locally.

As the translation in Part II reveals, the most complete set of republic organs of national bibliography exists in the Ukrainian SSR. It has separate annals for books, music literature, pictorial art works, reviews, and articles in periodicals and newspapers. In other republics, many of these types of publications are combined in only one or two annals. In Turkmen SSR, for example, there is only one organ of national bibliography, the *Publishing Annals of the Turkmen SSR*.

Such a broad approach to national bibliography within a multinational state, as applied by the Soviets, has not been attempted by any other nation. It is a highly organized, coordinated, and decentralized system, with national bibliography being not only an all-union matter but also a concern of each constituent republic and autonomous republic. In effect, each republic can lay claim to its own national bibliography. It is the totality of these local national bibliographies, in addition to the all-union national bibliography, which makes up the Soviet national bibliography.

FOOTNOTES

[1] E. I. Shamurin, "30 let sovetskoi gosudarstvennoi bibliografii," *Sovetskaia bibliografiia* 4 (1947): 6.

[2] Vlad. Bonch-Bruevich, "K istorii organizatsii Rossiiskoi tsentral'noi knizhnoi palaty v Moskve," *Sovetskaia bibliografiia* 1 (1940): 152.

[3] The capital was moved from Petrograd to Moscow in April 1918.

[4] B. S. Bodnarskii, "Petrogradskaia *Knizhnaia letopis'*," *Sovetskaia bibliografiia* 1 (1940): 153-161.

[5] Shortened name for Rossiiskaia Sovetskaia Federativnaia Sotsialisticheskaia Respublika (Russian Soviet Federated Socialist Republic), the name of the Soviet government from 1918 to 1922, when the USSR was formed. The RSFSR exists today as one of the constituent republics of the USSR.

[6] *Izvestiia VTsIK*, 9 July 1920, No. 149.

[7] Abbreviated form of Narodnyi komissariat prosveshcheniia (People's Commissariat of Education).

[8] Rossiiskaia tsentral'naia knizhnaia palata.

[9] Details about the Soviet legal deposit system in its early years may be found in Thomas J. Whitby, "Development of the System of Legal Deposit in the U.S.S.R.," *College and Research Libraries* 15 (October 1954): 398-406. The system is also dealt with comprehensively in IU. V. Grigor'ev, *Sistema knigosnabzheniia sovetskikh bibliotek.* (Moskva: Gos. izd-vo kul' turno-prosvetitel'noi literatury, 1956), pp. 22-33.

[10] *Litopys Ukrains'koho druku.*

[11] For a fuller description and analysis of the Book Chamber classification, see Thomas J. Whitby, "Evolution and Evaluation of a Soviet Classification," *Library Quarterly* 25 (April 1956): 118-127.

[12] Glavnoe upravlenie nauchnymi uchrezhdeniiami.

[13] Raboche-Krest'ianskaia krasnaia armiia (Workers' and Peasants' Red Army).

[14] Glavnyi politiko-prosvetitel'nyi komitet (Chief Committee of Political Education).

[15] E. I. Shamurin, "Gosudarstvennaia tsentral'naia knizhnaia palata za 15 let," *Sovetskaia bibliografiia* 4 (1935): 22.

[16] Ibid., p. 24.

[17] An interesting and detailed account of centralized cataloging in the USSR is to be found in Eleanor Buist, "Soviet Centralized Cataloging: A View from Abroad," *Library Trends* 16 (July 1967): 127-142.

[18] *Spisok periodicheskikh izdanii RSFSR v 1933 g.* Today this work is entitled *Annals of Serial Publications of the USSR* (Letopis' periodicheskikh izdanii SSSR).

[19] *Ukazatel' serii vypuski kotorykh zaregistrirovany v "Knizhnoi letopisi" za 1933 god.*

[20] Komitet po zavedyvaniiu uchenymi i uchebnymi uchrezhdeniiami.

[21] *Polozhenie o Vsesoiuznoi knizhnoi palate.* A translation of this regulation appeared in Paul Horecky, *Libraries and Bibliographic Centers in the Soviet Union*, Slavic and East European Series, Vol. 16 (Bloomington, IN, 1959), p. 167.

[22] Glavnoe upravlenie po delam literatury i izdatel'stvo.

[23] A listing of all directors' conferences to date is given in Appendix IV.

[24] A. P. Alekperov, "Novoe 'Tipovoe polozhenie o gosudarstvennoi knizhnoi palate soiuznoi respubliki,' " *Sovetskaia bibliografiia* 5 (1971): 78-81.

[25] I. I. Mikhlina and I. B. Chisheiko, "O sootnoshenii tekushchikh posobii gosudarstvennoi i kraevedcheskoi bibliografii v avtonomnykh respublikakh," *Sovetskaia bibliografiia* 4 (1974): 25-32.

[26] T. G. Dunaeva, "Vozniknovenie i razvitie gosudarstvennoi bibliografii v avtonomnykh respublik RSFSR," *Sovetskaia bibliografiia* 5 (1972): 13-29.

SOVIET NATIONAL BIBLIOGRAPHY TODAY

In this introduction to Soviet national bibliography, it is not possible to provide a complete history, or even a detailed examination of current activities, of the All-Union Book Chamber. That sort of undertaking, it seems, should be left to Soviet scholars, who have direct access to many primary sources not available outside the USSR. From time to time, however, the Soviets publish a collection of papers treating fairly comprehensively and historically the work of the Book Chamber. Such a collection, *Forty Years of Soviet National Bibliography (1920-1960)*,[1] was published in 1960. From it, one can derive a reasonably good picture of the salient activities of the Book Chamber in a historical perspective. For current information, careful attention to articles in the Book Chamber journal, *Sovetskaia bibliografiia*, is rewarding. Apparently, the Book Chamber still has no official history; and, if one is to understand Soviet national bibliographic developments, it is necessary to piece together the story of this unique institution from a great variety of sources.

FUNCTIONS OF THE ALL-UNION BOOK CHAMBER

In order to grasp fully the range of Book Chamber activities today, it is most expedient to start with the 1965 *Statute on the All-Union Book Chamber*, which superseded the 1936 statute discussed earlier. The functions of the Book Chamber,[2] somewhat altered after thirty years, are stated as follows:

1. Research in national bibliography, centralized cataloging, publishing statistics, and general book study

2. National bibliographic registration of Soviet publications through periodical organs of national bibliography, the so-called annals (letopisi), and cumulative bibliographic indexes

3. Centralized statistical accounting for publications issued in the USSR, the publication of statistical yearbooks and other statistical works about Soviet publishing

4. Centralized cataloging of Soviet publications and issuance of printed cards

5. Organization of a system of catalogs, showing in various ways the printed production of the USSR

6. Reference and bibliographic service to government and party organs, scientific institutions, public organizations, and publishers

7. Maintenance of the state archives of Soviet publishing

8. Receipt of the free control copies of publications and authority to insure full delivery of the stated number of copies by printing establishments to the All-Union Book Chamber and the distribution of the control copies to libraries

9. Preparation of scientific and technical information for the publishing field and its supply from a central point to publishers; printers; book trade organizations; scientific research, design, and construction organizations; and printing machinery construction plants

The basic function, of course, is bibliographic registration in the organs of national bibliography, which is made possible by the system of legal deposit. From these are derived the other important functions of research, statistics, cataloging, reference, publishing, archival deposit, and library collection building. Although these tasks have not changed appreciably since 1965, a new emphasis has been given them by the thrust toward automation of the bibliographic, cataloging, publishing, and statistical functions as a feature of the national system of scientific and technical information.

The reader's attention is directed to figure 1, which is a model of the interrelationships among the All-Union Book Chamber, the republic book chambers, printing plants, publishers, and libraries. This model is based on the author's knowledge of the systematic flow of publications from printer to book chamber to library. It is an open system, characterized by a steadily increasing input of publications and by an expanding variety of output products, such as catalog cards, bibliographies, statistical compilations, and various other automated products. This model gives an overview of Book Chamber activities not easily obtained through reading the literature and should be of help in understanding the discussion of particular activities and developments.

**Figure 1
System Flow Chart**

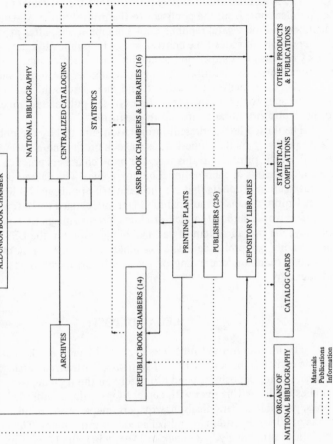

ALL-UNION BOOK CHAMBER

NATIONAL BIBLIOGRAPHY

CENTRALIZED CATALOGING

STATISTICS

ARCHIVES

REPUBLIC BOOK CHAMBERS (14)

ASSR BOOK CHAMBERS & LIBRARIES (16)

PRINTING PLANTS

PUBLISHERS (236)

DEPOSITORY LIBRARIES

ORGANS OF NATIONAL BIBLIOGRAPHY

CATALOG CARDS

STATISTICAL COMPILATIONS

OTHER PRODUCTS & PUBLICATIONS

———— Materials
-·-·-·- Publications
········· Information

The solid lines in the flow chart represent the movement of materials, i.e., publications, from the publisher to the printer to the All-Union Book Chamber and the several republic book chambers, and, after processing, to the depository libraries. One control copy of a publication, retained by the Book Chamber, is stamped and numbered for identification, counted for statistical purposes, described bibliographically for the annals and the printed cards, classified, analyzed by subject, and then sent to the Archives for storage. In accordance with the law, other copies of the publication are distributed to the depository libraries around the country.

The dotted lines represent information supplied by the publisher to the book chambers that functions as a check on the actual receipt of publications from the printers. In this way, the book chambers practically guarantee the completeness of their national bibliographies. The dashed lines indicate the publication products that are the hallmark of national bibliography in the Soviet Union: organs of national bibliography; catalog cards for libraries; statistical works; and automated products, such as magnetic tapes. Depicted in this way, the overall system of national bibliography in the USSR today is more readily comprehended. The examination of particular activities should provide a fuller understanding of the highly organized Soviet national bibliography.

LEGAL DEPOSIT

The most important functions of the All-Union Book Chamber—bibliographic registration, compilation of statistics, centralized cataloging, archival storage, library deposit—depend ultimately on the legal deposit system, which supplies the Book Chamber with copies of everything published in the USSR: books, pamphlets, periodicals, newspapers, maps, music publications, pictorial works of all kinds, and many miscellaneous printed items. The most recent legislation, surprisingly, goes back to 1948, when the USSR Council of Ministers issued a decree concerning the supply of major libraries with the free and priced types of depository copy.

Except for IU. V. Grigor'ev's 1956 book on book procurement practices of Soviet libraries, the literature has been silent (aside from occasional references) on the matter of legal deposit. In trying to account for this, one is prone to speculate that perhaps the details of legal deposit cannot be disseminated because of the "Secrets Law of 1956." This interpretation seems extreme, but how can one otherwise account for the curtain of silence surrounding this important question in the Soviet library and bibliographic literature? The latest statement on the legal deposit system appears under the heading "obligatory copy" in the 1976 dictionary published under the editorship of the late O. S. Chubar'ian. A portion of the entry is worth quoting because it gives the most up-to-date, however incomplete, statement available about legal deposit.

In the USSR there are three types of obligatory copy: free, departmental, and priced. The *free copy* comprises the complete set of domestic publications for the entire country (all-union), for individual republics (republican), or for region (local), sent gratis to bibliographic institutions and large libraries. The largest libraries receive the free copies through the All-Union Book Chamber. The first, most complete set received by the Book Chamber is stored in the archives of the Soviet press. All state republic libraries and the largest special libraries of the union and autonomous republics receive the free republic obligatory copy. Regional and territorial libraries receive the free local copy. Synonym: Control copy. The *departmental obligatory copy* is a set of publications issued by agencies of a particular department and sent to interested organizations and institutions of a given department. The *priced obligatory copy* is a set of publications issued in the USSR and received by the large libraries of the country through the Central Collector of Research Libraries.[3]

This entry does not, unfortunately, give the number of copies of each type of publication sent by the printers to the Book Chamber as free obligatory copies, nor does it provide us with a list of the all-union depository libraries entitled to receive the obligatory copies. The most recent listing of depository libraries available is taken from a private communication, dated 9 May 1958, from the director of the All-Union Book Chamber to the author. It includes 31 libraries that receive all publications, twelve libraries and organizations that receive only those publications which correspond to their acquisition profiles, and 34 libraries and organizations that take the remainder of the depository copies sent to the Book Chamber. Also listed are major state, academy, university, special, party, and government libraries, as well as certain specialized organizations.

Certainly, the Soviet legal deposit system, both from conceptual and practical standpoints, is an impressive, if not unique, foundation for one of the world's most remarkable national bibliographies.

ORGANS OF NATIONAL BIBLIOGRAPHY

Since the publication of the 1967 handbook that is included here in translation, several changes have taken place in the bibliographic organs of the All-Union Book Chamber. Except for these and the annual publishing details on each title, however, the information in the handbook is essentially up to date.

One of the all-union annals did undergo a title change. In 1976, *Letopis' izobrazitel'nogo iskusstvo* (Annals of Pictorial Art) became *Letopis' izoizdanii* (Annals of Pictorial Art Publications).

Perhaps the most dramatic change has occurred in *Book Annals*. In addition to the usual basic issue and supplementary issue that comprise the standard weekly and monthly issues of *Book Annals*, it has been announced in the latest Mezhdunarodnaia Kniga export catalog that, starting in 1979, *Book Annals* will also be issued in 25 subject series for both the basic and supplementary issues. These series will not be issued weekly but will come out monthly, quarterly, and at other frequencies. Furthermore, 24 separate subject series of *Annals of Journal Articles* will be issued monthly, in addition to the parent annals. This new publication venture is evidently an attempt to reach many libraries which, because of their more limited scope, wish to receive only portions of *Book Annals*. It should be noted that all the series are devoted to scientific and technical subjects, while the social sciences and humanities are not represented at all. This emphasis seems to reflect the Soviet attitude toward scholarship and research at the present time.

The first volume of the important retrospective compilation *Gazety SSSR, 1917-1960* was published in 1970. It is a comprehensive listing of the newspapers of Moscow, Leningrad, and the capitals of the union republics. A second volume, covering local, regional, territorial, district, and topical newspapers, was published in 1976.

In Kazakhstan, Armenia, and Uzbekistan, several useful retrospective bibliographies and indexes have been published in recent years. These are listed under the editor's notes in the appropriate sections of the translation.

It should be pointed out that, while the organs of national bibliography are at the heart of the publication programs of the All-Union Book Chamber and its sister republic book chambers, other types of publications are also published. These deal with various aspects of bibliography, bibliology, and the publishing and book trade and include retrospective bibliographies, catalog cards, treatises, journals, statistical works, and so forth. Unfortunately, the scope of this introduction to Soviet national bibliography precludes discussion of all types of publications issued by the book chambers.

STATISTICS

The All-Union Book Chamber is as much a center for the compilation of statistics as it is a bibliographic center. It derives its authority to perform this statistical function from the 1965 statute. The State Committee on Publishing, Printing, and the Book Trade of the USSR Council of Ministers[4] oversees this operation. Since the control copy of all publications must, by law, be sent by the printers, the Book Chamber is able to collect exact and complete data on the extent of publishing in the USSR. These statistics are systematically analyzed by computer and published in annual compilations for the benefit of interested parties, such as statisticians, economists, publishers, book trade personnel, teachers, librarians, agitators, and propagandists. These statistical annuals have been published regularly since 1955.

In the recent compilation *Publishing USSR in 1976* (Pechat' SSSR v 1976 godu), detailed statistics are given for books and pamphlets, dissertations, calendars, pictorial works, music publications, graphic arts works, maps, periodicals, continuations, agitators' notebooks, bulletins, and newspapers.

The statistics in each category of publication are presented in tables by publisher, language, availability, subject field, type of literature, and political administrative divisions of the country. The data are given in terms of number of items published, number of copies, number of printer's sheets,[5] average press run, and cost of the entire run in thousands of rubles.

In 1976, 84,304 books and pamphlets were published; and the total press run came to 1,744,515,000 copies. The average run for a particular book or pamphlet was, therefore, 20,690 copies; and the average size of a single book or pamphlet was 10.5 printer's sheets. If a printer's sheet is taken at sixteen pages each, then the average size of a Soviet monograph in 1976 was 168 pages, a statistic, incidentally, not given in the Book Chamber's annual compilation. Totals of all types of publications received by the Book Chamber in 1976 under legal deposit are given in table 3.

Table 3

Publishing in 1976 by Type of Material

Type of Material	Number	Number of Copies
Books	52,915	1,222,680,000
Pamphlets	31,389	521,835,000
Sheet and Other Printed Products Not Included in the Basic Types of Publications	245,437	1,496,151,000
Author Abstracts of Dissertations	29,586	6,134,000
Daily Calendars	13	39,455,000
Pictorial Art Publications	12,709	2,690,629,000
Music Publications	1,714	21,235,000
Cartographic Publications	470	48,843,000
Journals	1,350	2,320,189,000
Agitators' Notebooks	41	17,218,000
Collections	245	10,727,000
Bulletins	3,223	720,628,000
Newspapers	7,844	38,457,593,000
Serialized Novel	1	38,323,000

Compiled by the author from: Vsesoiuznaia knizhnaia palata. *Pechat' SSSR v 1976 godu; statisticheskii sbornik* (Moskva:"Statistika," 1977), pp. 7-13.

The third and largest item in the table is an interesting statistic because it represents nonperiodical types of publications which the Book Chamber receives automatically under legal deposit. These publications, although counted, do not receive individual treatment. Instead, they receive group processing, a kind of simplified method for handling large quantities of miscellaneous items effectively.[6]

Since 1956, publishing statistics have been reported by the Book Chamber to UNESCO for incorporation in its statistical yearbooks, including, for reported translations, the *Index translationum*. In order to make meaningful comparisons of one country's publishing statistics with another's, it is necessary to define precisely the terms and expressions used in the presentation of data. What is a book? A pamphlet? A periodical? Without such definitions, a comparison of statistics is meaningless. In presenting Soviet publishing statistics, the Book Chamber, in accordance with UNESCO's 1964 definitional requirements, presents precise definitions of the various terms. Until 1964, the Book Chamber did not distinguish in its statistical tables between books and pamphlets; consequently, Soviet book production statistics in the past have appeared to be inflated. The 1976 figure for books and pamphlets, 84,304, actually represents 52,915 books and 31,389 pamphlets. A book is defined as a nonperiodical publication over 48 pages in length, while a pamphlet (brochure) is defined as a publication over four pages, but no more than 48 pages, in length.

A further qualification of Soviet book statistics is needed because the printing unit on which counting is based is not title but the individual volume, issue, or part of a work. A multivolume work, therefore, counts as more than one unit.

Today, the range and detail of Soviet publishing statistics is very impressive. Considering that statistics gathering, along with national bibliography and centralized cataloging, is considered one of the three main functions of the Book Chamber, it is not surprising that so much has been achieved.

ARCHIVES

One of the largest collections of publications in the Soviet Union is the Research Archives of the All-Union Book Chamber (NAVKP).[7] In coverage, its size can be compared to the collections at the Lenin State Library in Moscow and the Saltykov-Shchedrin State Public Library in Leningrad. Its size can be attributed to the fact that one copy of each publication sent to the Book Chamber from the printers is deposited in it for indefinite storage. Presumably, the Archives affords a nearly complete record of Soviet publishing; only the years 1917-1920 are incomplete.

Each type of publication is sent to the Archives; this includes books and pamphlets, issues of periodicals and newspapers, maps, music publications, pictorial art works, and even minor leaflet-like publications. These are stored by category in suitable boxes with covers and placed upright on metal shelving. Temperature and humidity controls are provided, as well as fire protection. Each item bears a registration number by which it is arranged. This number also appears on the printed catalog cards prepared by the Book Chamber. At the present time, there are about 53 million items safeguarded in the Archives.[8]

The concept of an archives for all materials published within a particular country may be unique with the Soviets. Most countries consider the national library or other large libraries adequate for the purpose of collection preservation. The Soviets, however, have made the special archives a feature of their national bibliography. As recently as 1967, a statute was issued specifying the functions of a typical state archives.[9] This particular statute dealt with the publication archives in the republic book chambers. Three main archival functions are imposed upon all republic book chambers:

1. Perpetual storage and preservation of publications placed in the collection

2. Completeness in collection acquisition, and the identification and eradication of gaps

3. Utilization of the collection by personnel of the various departments of the republic book chamber so they may work and answer questions more effectively

According to this statute, archives may acquire publications from the unused stocks of libraries and even purchase needed materials. In all archives, the deposit copies are to be stored first by type of publication and then by year. Photocopying (but not borrowing) is allowed.

Judging from comments in the literature, the condition of the archives in different republics is very uneven in terms of storage facilities available, coverage of publications, and even completeness of the collections. It is believed that the 1967 statute, patterned as it is on the activities of the Research Archives in Moscow, provides a firm basis for the uniform development of archives throughout the USSR.

CENTRALIZED CATALOGING: DESCRIPTIVE

Fragmentation of effort is the only way to describe the state of centralized cataloging in the USSR. This is due to the fact that responsibility for cataloging has been divided to such an extent that different libraries and organizations have their own special provinces of work. As national bibliographic center (together with its republican counterparts), the All-Union Book Chamber seems the logical choice for overall centralized cataloging; but it shares responsibility with the Lenin State Library for cataloging current publishing. This sharing of responsibility can be compared to the division of labor that exists in cataloging for research libraries and cataloging for mass, i.e., public, libraries. This arrangement is not to be discounted, for the Book Chamber, basically research library oriented, is less attuned to the requirements of mass libraries than is the Lenin State Library. Cataloging in the fourteen republics outside the RSFSR, however, is carried on principally by the republic book chambers, often for both research and mass libraries. For some years, publishers have attempted to provide cataloging and printed cards for books; but this experiment has gradually tapered off until only a few places, such as the Ukrainian SSR and the Turkmen SSR, continue the practice.[10]

The Library of the USSR Academy of Sciences catalogs its own publications, providing printed cards to many libraries within its network of departments, institutes, laboratories, museums, observatories, and field stations. The All-Union Institute of Scientific and Technical Information (VINITI) and the State Public Scientific and Technical Library (GPNTB) provide extensive cataloging of scientific and technical materials, while the All-Union State Library of Foreign Literature catalogs foreign materials in the social sciences and the humanities. Cataloging of older materials (those published prior to 1927, before the Book Chamber began to issue catalog cards) has been the province of the Saltykov-Shchedrin State Public Library in Leningrad. Rather than an overall system of centralized cataloging, we have a decentralized system whereby individual organizations perform cataloging for either a special category of materials or a particular type of library.

Since centralized cataloging is performed by a number of libraries and organizations, each having its own defined area of specialization, whether it be Soviet publications, foreign publications, scientific and technical materials, or retrospective materials, it is not unusual to find in the catalog of a particular library catalog cards from various sources. It should be added that many catalogs also contain numerous manuscript cards prepared for materials for which no cards were available at the time of cataloging.

With so many organizations providing cataloging copy, one would expect a chaotic situation in library catalogs. Surprisingly, this is not the case, probably because of the application throughout the libraries of the Soviet Union of the *Uniform Rules of Description of Publications for Library Catalogs*, a seven part set of rule books (the second edition published between 1959 and 1970).[11] These rules are the result of many years' work by the Interagency Cataloging Commission, which, with the cooperation of the largest libraries and many specialized agencies, has been elaborating the descriptive cataloging rules since 1949. All book chambers, the Lenin State Library, the Saltykov-Shchedrin State Public Library, and other large libraries and organizations, supposedly follow these instructions, which cover the description of books, serials, maps, music publications, graphic materials, technical publications (patents, standards, etc.), sound recordings, and audiovisual materials.

Due to the widespread introduction of the International Standard Bibliographic Description (ISBD) throughout the world, both the Anglo-American and the Soviet cataloging rules of description are being revised. Part 6 of a new set of rules under the collective title, *Rules of Bibliographic Description of Publications*, has already been published.[12] Issued by the Interagency Cataloging Commission at the Lenin Library, Part 6 is devoted to a variety of technical publications, including standards, patents, engineering drawings, industrial catalogs, price lists, technical reports, and translations.

ps://

Eventually, all parts of the descriptive cataloging rules will be brought into conformity with the ISBD documents as they become available. That the highly technical Part 6, to which the ISBD punctuation conventions have been adapted, has been issued first attests to the Soviets' concern about the bibliographic control of types of material that perhaps do not receive the attention they should in other countries.

Catalog cards for monographs received by libraries from the Book Chamber have, since 1974, carried the punctuation marks adopted in the ISBD (M). Minor variations in the application of the ISBD in American and Soviet cataloging practice do exist; but, according to one recent report,[13] the Soviets are very close to fully applying the standard ISBD.

The catalog cards shown below (reduced slightly) produced by the Book Chamber in 1978 clearly demonstrate to what extent Soviet cataloging practice, following the ISBD, differs from American methods:

Оганесян, Джемма Ивановна, Симонян, Перчануш Амаяковна.
Русская речь : Учебник для VII кл. арм. школы . — 5-е изд. — Ереван : Луйс, 1978. — 230 с.;, ил.; 22 см.
На пер. авт. не указаны:
В пер. : 25 к. 45.000 экз.

I. Загл. II. Соавт. — — 1. Русский язык — Учебники и пособия для нерусских школ.

808.2 (075.3-9.198.1)

№9247 43.6.2
65 №449 [78-15133] в тп
Вс.кн.пал. 13.03.78 О-361

O702 / 336060178

Русский язык : Учебник для 4-го кл. школ с укр. яз. обучения / [Г. М. Иваницкая, Н. А. Пашковская, Н. В. Сурова, Г. П. Цыганенко]. — 9-е изд. — Киев : Рад. школа, 1978 . — 160 с., ил.; 21 см.
В пер. : 20 к. 300.000 экз.

I. Иваницкая, Галина Марковна и др. — — 1. Русский язык — Учебники и пособия для нерусских школ.

808.2 (075.3-8.3)

№12952 43.6.2
65 №617 [78-23412] в тп
Вс.кн.пал. 10.04.78 Р894

Р 60601-101/М210(04)-78 23-78

The first card illustrates that in Soviet cataloging practice 1) joint authors are placed together in inverted form in the main entry; 2) author statements are not always included; 3) the collation is placed in the body of the entry; and 4) in the tracings, the added entries are placed ahead of the subject headings. The second card shows that an author statement is included when the authors' names do not appear on the title page. It is also notable that, for title entries, normal paragraph indentions are preferred to hanging indentions. Apart from these differences between Soviet and American cataloging practices, it is apparent that the details recorded on the Book Chamber cards are in close agreement with the provisions of the ISBD.

CENTRALIZED CATALOGING: SUBJECT

It is interesting to note that less attention has been given to subject cataloging than to descriptive cataloging in Soviet library literature. Although the situation is rapidly changing, few articles dealing with subject cataloging have appeared in the literature. Subject headings, however, have appeared on Book Chamber cards for many years; and subject cataloging practice appears to be analogous to that in the United States. The reluctance to promote the alphabetical subject catalog (like the avoidance of alphabetical indexes in books and alphabetically arranged periodical indexes) reflects the Soviet preference for systematically arranged catalogs, indexes, and tables of contents.

The reader should be aware that the dictionary catalog does not exist as such in Soviet libraries, and the lack of separate subject catalogs in most libraries is not surprising. The Soviets, much in line with general European practice, have always stressed the systematic, or classed, catalog, which is generally accepted as the principal public catalog in Soviet libraries.

A recent study was made, comparing the subject headings assigned by the Book Chamber to scientific and technical materials with those assigned by technical libraries in different industries to the same materials. It was concluded that three measures should be taken in order to bring about an improved and uniform system of centralized subject cataloging:[14] 1) to discourage individual libraries from doing their own subject cataloging, the issuance of printed cards from the Book Chamber should be speeded up so that cards and documents arrive at libraries and information services together; 2) the types of documents suitable for subject cataloging should be expanded to include articles from specialized journals; and 3) the Book Chamber should publish a list of its subject headings and periodically supplement it with lists of new, revised, and cancelled headings.

It is apparent that the practice of subject cataloging in the Soviet Union lags far behind that in the United States. If the Soviets are to ever reach parity with American practice, a much greater commitment must be made to the subject catalog and, at the very least, the publication of a standard list of subject headings. Perhaps the accelerating interest in library automation and the very real concern with computerized information retrieval will bring about the needed change in direction.

BIBLIOGRAPHIC CLASSIFICATION

A revised and expanded classification of knowledge for bibliographic purposes was published by the Book Chamber in 1971.[15] Like its predecessor, which was published in 1965, it is intended for use in arranging entries in *Book Annals*, the *Annals of Journal Articles*, and other organs of national bibliography. While both editions have 31 classes, the latest edition introduces class 14, "Cybernetics. Semiotics. Informatics," and rearranges some of the other classes. The detailed classification is hierarchical, uses a pure numerical notation including decimals, and is provided with a detailed relative index. This is, of course, a bibliographic classification for use in the national bibliography and is not intended as a library classification. However, classification numbers derived from it and assigned to publications cataloged by the Book Chamber appear on the printed catalog cards along with decimal classification numbers.

It is interesting to note that the Book Chamber does not assign numbers from the *Library and Bibliographic Classification*,[16] the monumental multi-volume classification of knowledge developed in the sixties by the Lenin State Library, the Saltykov-Shchedrin State Public Library, the Library of the USSR Academy of Sciences, and the All-Union Book Chamber. Developed for use by research libraries, the BBK, as it is commonly called, consists of 21 main classes and, like the Book Chamber bibliographic classification, has a Marxist orientation. It is likely that before long, the BBK will be applied by the Book Chamber in its centralized cataloging and classification operation.

The current configuration of the Book Chamber classification may be compared with the 1965 classification in the accompanying translation.

1. Marxism-Leninism

2. Social Sciences

3. Philosophy. Sociology. Psychology

4. Economics. Economic Sciences

5. History. Historical Sciences

6. International Communist Movement. Communist and Workers Party

7. International Relations. Internal and External State Politics

8. International Trade-union Movement

9. International Youth Movement

10. State and Law. Juridical Sciences

11. Military Sciences. Military Affairs

12. Statistics. Demography

13. Science. Science Study

14. Cybernetics. Semiotics. Informatics (List continues on page 54)

15. Natural Sciences

16. Technology. Industry

17. Agriculture and Forestry. Agricultural and Forestry Sciences

18. Transportation

19. Communication

20. Procurement. Commerce. Public Catering

21. Communal Affairs. Community Services

22. Public Health. Medical Sciences

23. Physical Culture. Sports

24. Culture. Education

25. Philology

26. Belles-lettres. Folklore

27. Children's Literature. Folklore for Children

28. Arts. Art Study

29. Religion. Atheism

30. Publishing. Bibliology

31. General Reference Works. Encyclopedias. Calendars. Collected Works

Ever since the adoption in 1926 of a subject classification for the arrangement of entries in *Book Annals*, there has been constant modification of either the number or the arrangement of main classes. Although the present outline of 31 classes has obtained since 1946, there is still a great deal of tinkering with the sequential arrangement of classes.

What the Soviets have achieved, however, is a dynamic classification based on Marxist theory. Success in the use of the scheme may depend to a degree on one's knowledge of the underlying philosophy. The uninitiated, impressed more by the practicality of a scheme than by its philosophical foundations, are likely to become frustrated in attempting, say, a retrospective search of the literature.

Some years ago, this author wrote, "That certain utilitarian features, such as permanency and stability, have been neglected is a serious shortcoming that could be remedied by closer attention to an objective approach to the fields of knowledge and less emphasis on the demands of communist dogma. It is highly unlikely, however, in view of the dominance of Marxism-Leninism in Soviet classification, that a new and different approach to the organization of knowledge is possible."[17] Since that statement was made, nothing has occurred that would cause the author to substantially alter his opinion.

STANDARDIZATION

The fiftieth anniversary of the standards movement in the USSR was in 1975. In most countries, standardization has been a characteristic of advanced technological development; but standardization in bibliography, library science, and information science is a fairly recent phenomenon. According to a recent study,[18] the Soviets have now published fourteen state standards (thirteen of which have direct application in bibliography) in a series entitled "System of Informational and Bibliographic Documentation." All of these standards have been published since 1969. The range of their coverage is provided in the following listing:

GOST 7.1-69	*Description of Publications for Bibliographic and Informational Publications*
GOST 7.2-69	*Description of Periodical Publications for Catalogs*
GOST 7.3-69	*Description of Books for Catalogs*
GOST 7.4-69	*Imprint Data in Publications*
GOST 7.5-69	*Formatting of Articles for Journals*
GOST 7.6-69	*Bibliographic Strip*
GOST 7.8-70	*Periodical Title Abbreviations*
GOST 7.9-70	*Abstracts and Annotations*
GOST 7.10-70	*Table of Contents of Journals and Continuations*
GOST 7.11-70	*Abbreviations of Words and Word Combinations in Cataloging and Bibliographic Description*
GOST 7.12-70	*Abbreviations of Russian Words and Word Combinations in Cataloging and Bibliographic Description*
GOST 7.12-70	*Rules for the Description of Special Types of Technical Documentation for Catalogs*
GOST 7.13-70	*Thesaurus. General Statement. Form of Presentation*

Another Soviet standard (not in the series) is GOST 16448-70, *Bibliography, Terminology, and Definitions,* which has provoked wide-ranging discussions in the literature about various aspects of introducing standardized terminology into practice.

The theory behind standardization in bibliography is that standards are essential in the exchange of bibliographic information among libraries and other organizations. Standards may be established for a broad spectrum of topics, including terminology, abbreviations, bibliographic description, formatting of papers, transliteration, etc. They should, if developed cooperatively among nations through such organizations as the International Organization for Standardization (ISO) and the International Federation of Library Associations (IFLA), facilitate the international exchange of information, especially in automated information systems. The All-Union Book Chamber has already adopted the ISBD (M) and is participating in the development of national bibliographic standards such as those listed in the preceding paragraph. The Book Chamber is expected to play a major role in such international programs as Universal Bibliographic Control, of which standardization is a basic feature.

AUTOMATION

It has been pointed out that the All-Union Book Chamber lags behind other Soviet organizations in the development of an automated information system.[19] The Lenin State Library, the State Public Scientific and Technical Library, and the All-Union Institute of Scientific and Technical Information all have advanced programs of automation. The reasons for the Book Chamber's lack of development in automation are not difficult to find: 1) it lists and analyzes only Soviet publications, leaving the exploitation of foreign literature to others; 2) the existing system of national bibliography has been remarkably successful in its use of traditional methods; and 3) it lacks competition in its own field of bibliographic specialization. It may also be that Book Chamber personnel, satisfied with the status quo, have been reluctant to change from traditional, manual methods to modern, computerized procedures. Should the Book Chamber be successful in catching up with other information agencies, it may very well become the most important bibliographic agency in the Soviet Union.

Over the past 25 years, the worldwide competition for scientific discoveries and technological innovations has focused attention on the All-Union Institute of Scientific and Technical Information (VINITI), which, with its stable of 77 abstract journals, covers on a current basis the world's scientific and technical literature. The Book Chamber, because of its concentration on current bibliographic information about Soviet publications (including the extensive literature in science and technology), is gaining increased attention; and it is thought that the Book Chamber should be automated to the same extent as VINITI.

The drive to develop an automated system for national bibliography seems to have gained momentum as a result of the special concern in the Soviet Union today for the promotion of scientific and technical information. In 1966, the USSR Council of Ministers called for a unified national system of scientific and technical information; and the All-Union Book Chamber was recognized as a component of that system. In support of that position, a Central Bureau of Scientific and Technical Information on the Press (TSBNTI) was established in the Book Chamber in 1967 to provide technical information to organizations in the printing, publishing, and book trade fields.[20] Similar offices were set up in the republic book chambers.

A further step was taken when the State Committee on Science and Technology of the USSR Council of Ministers involved the Book Chamber and its republic counterparts in the plan for the "creation of a single system of scientific and technical information in the country based on the use of machine methods in the searching, processing, reproduction, retrieval, and transmission of information materials."[21] Subsequently, special concern for the widespread dissemination and application of scientific and technical information in society was expressed—first, in the 1974 enactment of the Central Committee of the Communist Party, "On Increasing the Role of Libraries in the Communist Education of the Workers and in Scientific and Technical Progress"; and later, in the statement approved at the Twenty-fifth Congress of the Party on "Basic Directions for the Development of the National Economy, 1976-1980."

In 1972, the Book Chamber undertook a systematic study of the flow of the control copy of publications through the stages of registration and bibliographic processing. Two years later a system design plan for an automated system was drawn up. It covered goals, tasks, time constraints, manpower requirements and training suggestions, etc. The system that was finally adopted (rather hastily, it is admitted) is called ASOI—Bibliography, or Automated System for Processing, Storing, and Retrieving Information—Bibliography. This automated system for national bibliography is referred to in the literature as a subsystem of the National System of Scientific and Technical Information (GSNTI).

Examination of ASOI—Bibliography reveals that it is composed of the following seven functional subsystems:[22]

1. Receipt, processing, and machine input of information

2. Archival preservation of information

3. Computerized production of informational publications

4. Retrospective information searching

5. Processing and retrieval of statistical data

6. Control and administration of the system

7. Transmission of data over long distance communication channels

As designed, the system will be used to: 1) prepare such publications as catalog cards, the organs of national bibliography, indexes, annuals, and statistical compilations; 2) provide bibliographic reference services; and 3) exchange information in machine-readable form with other information-oriented organizations, such as the republic book chambers.

Realizing the difficulties of trying to implement the entire program at one time, the architects of the plan have divided the undertaking into two phases. In the first, the objective is "to work out an automated system for processing, storing, and retrieving bibliographic and statistical information on books and pamphlets."[23] Phase two, to be carried out within the 1976-1980 time frame, i.e., within the tenth five-year plan, envisions automatic preparation and issuance of information about periodicals and continuations, the creation of computerized catalogs of both current receipts and retrospective materials, and searching on the basis of machine-readable catalogs.

By introducing an automated information system into national bibliography, the All-Union Book Chamber expects to accomplish a great deal by way of attacking old, abiding problems and by finding solutions to the new challenges placed before it by the demands of modern science and technology. The literature suggests that the Book Chamber hopes to accomplish the following:

1. Elimination of duplication of effort on the part of the All-Union Book Chamber and the republic book chambers

2. Enhanced communication between all-union and republic book chambers

3. Reduction in time lag between the receipt of publications at the Book Chamber and the delivery of catalog cards, etc., to subscribers

4. Keyboarding bibliographic data only once into the computer for the production of catalog cards, entries in the weekly national bibliography, alphabetical indexes, etc.

5. Automated production of catalog cards, annals, annuals, indexes, etc.

6. Packaging of bibliographic and statistical data in machine-readable form

7. Delivery of scientific and technical information in useful forms to scientists, engineers, and technicians

8. On-line access to bibliographic and statistical data

9. Exchange of bibliographic data at both the national and the international levels using standard bibliographic description

The implementation of ASOI—Bibliography may well encourage the Soviets to try to overcome the United States' lead in the development of automation for library and bibliographic purposes.

FOOTNOTES

[1] Vsesoiuznaia knizhnaia palata, *Sorok let sovetskoi gosudarstvennoi bibliografii (1920-1960)* (Moskva: 1960), 269 p.

[2] E. O. Maio-Znak, "Vsesoiuznaia knizhnaia palata na sovremennom etape," *Sovetskaia bibliografiia* 4 (1974): 10-11.

[3] O. S. Chubar'ian, *Slovar bibliotechnykh terminov* (Moskva: "Kniga," 1976), pp. 101-102.

[4] Gosudarstvennyi komitet Soveta Ministrov SSSR po delam izdatel'stv, poligrafii i knizhnoi torgovli.

[5] A unit of measurement used in calculating printed production. It is equivalent to one side of a sheet of paper measuring 60 x 92 cm. Printed on both sides and folded, it becomes a signature, which forms one section of a book.

[6] A. I. Serebrennikov, "Zadachi gosudarstvennoi bibliografii i problema polnoty otbora izdanii," *Sovetskaia bibliografiia* 6 (1975): 15-16.

[7] Nauchnyi arkhiv Vsesoiuznoi knizhnoi palaty.

[8] IU. I. Fartunin, "60 let Vsesoiuznoi knizhnoi palate—tsentru gosudarstvennoi bibliografii," *Sovetskaia bibliografiia* 5 (1977): 6-13.

[9] "Tipovoe polozhenie ob Arkhive pechati respublikanskoi knizhnoi palaty," *Sovetskaia bibliografiia* 4 (1967): 20-22.

[10] V. V. Nemchenko, "Nekotorye voprosy gosudarstvennoi bibliografii i tsentralizovannoi katalogizatsii," *Sovetskaia bibliografiia* 5 (1975): 4.

[11] *Edinye pravila opisaniia proizvedenii pechati dlia bibliotechnykh katalogov,* Izd. 2. (Moskva: 1959-1970).

[12] *Pravila bibliograficheskogo opisaniia proizvedenii pechati. Ch. 6. Bibliograficheskie opisanie spetsial'nykh vidov normativno-tekhnicheskikh i tekhnicheskikh dokumentov i literatury* (Moskva: "Kniga," 1977). 156 p.

[13] Nathalie P. Delougaz, Susan K. Martin, and Robert Wedgeworth, "Libraries and Information Services in the U.S.S.R.," *Special Libraries* 68 (July/August 1977): 261.

[14] R. D. Potapova, "Issledovanie sovmestimosti tsentralizovannoi predmetizatsii s predmetizatsiei v otdel'nykh bibliotekh," *Sovetskaia bibliografiia* 5 (1975): 30.

[15] Vsesoiuznaia knizhnaia palata, *Klassifikatsiia literatury v organakh gosudarstvennoi bibliografii.* Metodicheskie materialy po gosudarstvennoi bibliografii, Vyp. 26. Izd. 5. (Moskva: Izd-vo "Kniga," 1971). 308 p.

[16] *Bibliotechno-bibliograficheskaia klassifikatsiia. Tablitsy dlia nauchnykh bibliotek* (Moskva: 1960-1968).

[17] Whitby, "Evolution and Evaluation of a Soviet Classification," p. 127.

[18] B. A. Semenovker, "Sovremennoe sostoianie standartizatsii v bibliografii," *Sovetskaia bibliografiia* 4 (1975): 12.

[19] S. S. Panterov, "O sozdanii avtomatizirovannoi sistemy podgotovki i vypuska izdanii gosudarstvennoi bibliografii vo Vsesoiuznoi knizhnoi palate," *Sovetskaia bibliografiia* 5 (1974): 6.

[20] "Novoe 'Tipovoe polozhenie o gosudarstvennoi knizhnoi palate soiuznoi respubliki,' " *Sovetskaia bibliografiia* 5 (1971): 79.

[21] Ibid., p. 80.

[22] N. N. Gruzinskaia and I. S. Teliatitskii, "O putiakh sovershenst-vovaniia gosudarstvennoi bibliografii na baze vnedreniia avtomatizirovannoi sistemy vo Vsesoiuznoi knizhnoi palate," *Sovetskaia bibliografiia* 4 (1976): 5.

[23] Ibid.

CONCLUDING REMARKS

Current national bibliography in Russia before the revolution was the province of both the individual bibliographer and the tsarist government. Although privately undertaken bibliographies were generally serious attempts to list the total publishing output for cultural purposes, their existence was precarious; and they were, in the main, short-lived. Government bibliographies, on the other hand, were compiled and published in accordance with the demands of censorship. Their scope, therefore, was less universal than that of the private undertakings. They had the advantage, however, of support from the government, which assured their position and endowed them with longer life. It is worth noting that when the interest of the government in current bibliography waned, as it did in the periods 1856-1857 and 1860-1867, individual bibliographers did not hesitate to launch their own listings to fill the gaps. As a result of these complementary efforts, the record of publishing production in tsarist Russia is almost uninterrupted for the period 1836-1917. Current bibliography prior to 1836 is not nearly so continuous, and the record contains several large gaps.

The most significant event in current bibliography in prerevolutionary Russia was the establishment in 1907 of the weekly catalog *Book Annals*, which listed all new publications on a current basis. Also of far-reaching importance was the founding of the Russian Book Chamber in 1917 under the Provisional Government.

The new regime inherited the Book Chamber and *Book Annals* from its predecessors. Its role since then has been to extend the influence of these legacies throughout the land. This has been accomplished in a very complete and thoroughgoing manner, utilizing the machinery of government to achieve its purpose.

The essential goals of the Book Chamber have been the achievement of a complete and current national bibliography, centralized cataloging, statistical accounting of all printed matter, and the establishment of a system of depository libraries throughout the country. These goals were not attained overnight; rather, it has been a gradual accretion over a period of many years. Even today, the goals (especially centralized cataloging) are not fully realized. The successes so far achieved have been the result of the independent approach of the Soviets to the organization of national bibliography. Believing that the voluntary delivery of publications to a national center for registration would be ineffective, the Soviet government initiated laws which made it mandatory for all printing and publishing establishments to submit copies of publications issued by them to a national center. These laws were effective only in the RSFSR. Extension of this principle to other parts of the union was attempted by means of contracts, but this proved ineffectual. Finally, a system of legislation for the USSR as a whole was established. This is the legal deposit system, or "system of the obligatory copy," that exists at the present time.

Legislation determines what is needed: it provides, on the one hand, for the collection of all published materials and, on the other hand, for the final disposition of the collected materials to the national depository centers and archives. It establishes a steady flow of material from the points of origin, the printing houses, to the ultimate destinations, the various libraries and archives that have been selected as recipients of the depository, or obligatory, copy.

After collection, the publications are recorded in the organs of national bibliography, a system whose content is determined by the form of the publications listed. All types of printed matter are registered in separate catalogs, which are issued periodically on a current basis. The materials, for the most part, are arranged within an officially adopted classification scheme and are described in accordance with standard rules of bibliographic entry.

The seventeen republic book chambers are patterned after the All-Union Book Chamber in Moscow. Together, they form a highly effective network of bibliographic control over all materials published throughout the Union. Now, with the introduction of computerization, refinements in bibliographic techniques, communications, and publication are bound to occur at an accelerating pace.

The process of collection, registration, and distribution of publications comprises the organization of national bibliography in the Soviet Union. The system of legislation welds the separate segments of this process into an integrated whole; and the All-Union Book Chamber, supported by the republic book chambers, provides the process with a pivotal center. In outline, this process forms a simple organizational pattern, but the sum of its parts forms a highly complex bibliographic system.

PART II

GUIDE TO THE ORGANS OF
NATIONAL BIBLIOGRAPHY IN THE USSR

ВСЕСОЮЗНАЯ КНИЖНАЯ ПАЛАТА

ГОСУДАРСТВЕННАЯ БИБЛИОГРАФИЯ СССР

Издание 2-е,
переработанное и дополненное

Справочник

Издательство „Книга"
Москва 1967

All-Union Book Chamber

GUIDE TO THE ORGANS OF NATIONAL BIBLIOGRAPHY IN THE USSR

Second Edition, Revised and Enlarged

"Kniga" Publishing House
Moscow   1967

Translation of

Gosudarstvennaia bibliografiia SSSR; spravochnik
Izd. 2, pererabotannoe i dopolnennoe
Izdatel'stvo "Kniga"
Moskva 1967

Translated by
Tanja Lorković

Edited by
Thomas J. Whitby

FROM THE AUTHORS

This guide contains information about the organs of national bibliography published by the All-Union Book Chamber (Vsesoiuznaia knizhnaia palata) and by the book chambers of the union and autonomous republics. It is the second, revised and enlarged edition of *Gosudarstvennaia registratsionno-uchetnaia bibliografiia v SSSR* (National Bibliography in the USSR), compiled by IU. I. Masanov and published in 1952. The present guide is updated by information gathered after the issuance of the first edition and expanded by means of a more detailed treatment of the publications of the Book Chamber.

Throughout the text, the publications of the All-Union Book Chamber are carefully distinguished from one another. All types of publications are represented in them; information about territorial, chronological, and linguistic peculiarities are provided; and the basic methods of description, the organization of the material, the structure of the publications, and the availability of indexes are described. *Book Annals*, as the basic publication in the system of organs of national bibliography, has received the most complete treatment.

There is less detailed information about publications of the republic book chambers. The principles of selecting material for inclusion and the techniques of description are not delineated since the methods of compiling the organs of national bibliography in all book chambers are basically identical. Pertinent publications of the state republic libraries of the autonomous republics in which there are no book chambers are reviewed briefly. The present status of the organs of national bibliography is described, and historical information about changes in methods of compiling each publication is given in brief.

In the section "Publications of the All-Union Book Chamber" (following the description of those annals which contain gaps or omissions in the registration of specific materials), additional information about other sources which record these materials is inserted. In the section "Publications of the Book Chambers of the Union and Autonomous Republics" (following the description of the annals), a list of basic general bibliographies of a retrospective nature is inserted, supplementing or expanding the material registered in the annals. Publications that have been issued by book chambers, libraries, and other republic institutions appear in the list.

This work has been compiled by senior bibliographers I. B. Gracheva and V. N. Frantskevich under the general editorship of A. I. Serebrennikov. Material for the section "Publications of the Book Chambers of the Union and Autonomous Republics" was prepared by G. P. Nagel'Arbatskaia in collaboration with L. M. Korchagina. During compilation, materials prepared by the editorial staff of the All-Union Book Chamber and by senior bibliographer L. A. Karakash, as well as comments of the book chambers of the union and autonomous republics, were frequently used.

INTRODUCTION

The steady growth of published literature in the nation is a clear indication of the blossoming of Soviet science and culture. In the past fifty years,* the number of books and pamphlets issued in the USSR has come to over two million titles. Currently, the annual press run of books significantly exceeds a billion copies; nearly eight thousand newspapers and more than four thousand periodicals and serials are published. Soviet publishing has become truly massive. Finding one's way in this huge number of books has become more difficult as the volume of published literature has increased. Consequently, the role of bibliography, dedicated as it is to serving the requirements of science and the national economy and to raising the cultural level of the people, has increased in importance.

In a general system for an information and bibliographic service, national bibliography has special significance. Because it regularly records and registers printed works, such as books, periodicals, newspapers, music, maps, etc., that have been issued in the USSR, the national bibliography is a reliable source of current information about Soviet literature. National bibliography also serves as the basis for other types of bibliography, for bibliographic reference work, and for the statistical analysis of printed production in the interest of planning and improving the publishing business.

In prerevolutionary Russia, national bibliographic registration was incapable of meeting either the needs of scientific work or the requirements of readers. It was, first of all, a means of press surveillance by the tsarist government. The Russian Book Chamber (Rossiiskaia knizhnaia palata), organized in Petrograd on 10 May 1917, was the first special agency designated to carry out the national bibliography. For various historical reasons, it did not become a genuine center of national bibliography.

---

*Editor's Note: that is, up to 1967.

After the Great October Socialist Revolution, national bibliographic registration in our country was put on a firm scientific footing, given new objectives, and provided with a wider range of activities. Lenin's decree of 30 June 1920 on the organization of bibliographic affairs spelled out the problems and forms of national bibliography and laid a solid foundation for the general development of bibliography and library work in the USSR. On the basis of this decree, the Russian Central Book Chamber (Rossiiskaia tsentral'naia knizhnaia palata) was established in Moscow.

In the development of the Lenin decree, republic book chambers were created on the basis of government enactments of the union and autonomous republics. By 1922, the organization of book chambers was begun in the Ukraine, Belorussia, Armenia, Georgia, and Azerbaidzhan. In the period 1926-1939, book chambers were organized in the Uzbek, Turkmen, Kazakh, Tadzhik, and Kirghiz Soviet Socialist Republics and also in the Tatar, Bashkir, and Chuvash Autonomous Soviet Socialist Republics. Book chambers were created in the Latvian and Estonian Soviet Socialist Republics in 1941; in the Lithuanian Soviet Socialist Republic in 1945, and in the Moldavian SSR in 1957. Since then, in those autonomous republics of the Russian Soviet Federated Socialist Republic where there are no book chambers, responsibility for the national bibliography has been given to the state republic libraries.

In 1936, by an enactment of the Central Executive Committee of the USSR, the Russian Central Book Chamber was reorganized on an all-union basis. This legally established its position as the center of national bibliography and publishing statistics in the Soviet Union.

In the established network of specialized bibliographic institutions, the All-Union Book Chamber (Vsesoiuznaia knizhnaia palata) carries out the overall bibliographic registration of publications. The registration of publications in the union and autonomous republics is carried out correspondingly by the book chambers of the union republics and the book chambers or state republic libraries of the autonomous republics.

The basis of the national bibliography, which provides for a complete record of publication in the USSR, is the free control (obligatory) copy of publications supplied by the state to the book chambers and the largest libraries of the country. All printing establishments of the country are obliged to send, free of charge, specified numbers of copies to the All-Union Book Chamber. Republic printing establishments must also supply copies to their book chambers. The bibliographic registration of publications is accomplished by a system of periodical bibliographic publications, or annals, which provides a complete representation of works being published in the country.

Although there is organizational and methodological unity in the system of organs of Soviet national bibliography, certain differences in organizational structure and bibliographic presentation of the material exist in the all-union and republic editions. In all the book chambers, publications are treated separately by type; but, depending on such conditions as the volume of material under consideration, the information about them is placed either in separate publications, i.e., annals, or in special sections of particular annals.

The all-union bibliographic registration of publications is carried out in Russian, regardless of the language of the text. Bibliographic registration in the union and autonomous republics is carried out in the language in which the work is published. This shows the division of labor between the All-Union Book Chamber and the republic book chambers. In the republic book chambers, the basic bibliographic information is given in translation in Russian so that the annals are more accessible to a wider circle of readers.

In the last decade, the majority of republic book chambers have been supplementing their organs of national bibliography with special sections devoted to works published outside their republics but which, from the standpoint of content, authorship, and language, are linked to them. The book chambers of the Ukrainian SSR and the Georgian SSR publish this information in separately issued indexes. In the annals of the book chambers of the Belorussian, Lithuanian, and Estonian republics, literature published in socialist countries is also found in these sections. However, the principles of selecting all types of materials, the methods of describing them, and the system of arranging them in the annals of the All-Union Book Chamber and the republic book chambers, are basically the same. Uniformity in the system is achieved through general instructions and methodological materials.

For purposes of agreement on general organizational and methodological questions, all-union conferences of the directors and other administrative personnel of the book chambers have been held since 1924. At the ninth conference of directors, convened by the All-Union Book Chamber in 1949, the *Regulation Concerning the System of Publications of the All-Union Book Chamber and Book Chambers of the Union and Autonomous Republics,* which has preserved its basic significance to the present time, was debated and adopted.

The All-Union Book Chamber has a highly diversified system of publications. Different types of printed works (books and pamphlets, periodicals and newspapers, music, pictorial art publications, geographic maps) are registered in regularly published organs of national bibliography such as *Book Annals, Annals of Serial Publications of the USSR, Music Annals, Annals of Pictorial Art Publications,* and *Cartographic Annals.*

Periodical and continuing publications are described analytically: articles, reviews, and other writings within publications, issued in Russian in the Soviet Union, are covered. These materials appear in *Annals of Journal Articles, Annals of Newspaper Articles,* and *Annals of Reviews.*

In addition, the All-Union Book Chamber issues annual bibliographic guides: *Book Annual of the USSR* and *Bibliography of Soviet Bibliography.* The *Book Annual of the USSR* cumulates the basic materials described in *Book Annals* for the year. The *Bibliography of Soviet Bibliography* gives information about bibliographies in the organs of national bibliography as well as bibliographies found in books and articles.

The principles and methods of literature selection and bibliographic description for the organs of national bibliography registering specific types of printed matter are different from those used for organs covering materials from periodical publications. For the annals registering separate types of publications (books and pamphlets, periodicals, music, etc.), the selection of material for listing is carried out within broad limits and with great thoroughness. The bibliographic description of these annals (apart from the elements stipulated by the general rules of description) includes supplementary information necessary for statistical records and the bibliographic reference work of the book chambers. Press run, size, price, manner of printing, etc., are indicated.

For the annals covering materials from periodicals, the choice of sources and the writings from them is done selectively. Special attention is paid to materials from scholarly periodicals and the most important general political newspapers. Bibliographic description in those annals in which periodical and continuing publications are described analytically is shorter and includes a minimum of information necessary for the purpose of bibliographic identification.

The arrangement of materials in the organs of national bibliography is done in accordance with the characteristics of the particular type of publication. Descriptions of books, journals, articles, and reviews (and, in part, pictorial art publications) are arranged by fields of knowledge corresponding to the system of classification developed specially for the organs of national bibliography. For music, maps, newspapers, and most pictorial art publications, special schemes corresponding to the nature of each type of publication are used.

The rules for selecting, describing, and classifying material for the annals and for compiling supplementary indexes have been published by the All-Union Book Chamber since 1947 in a series entitled *Metodicheskie materialy po gosudarstvennoi bibliograficheskoi registratsii* [Methodological Materials on National Bibliographic Registration]. Twenty-four issues have been published in this series, including the following operating instructions:

Instruktsiia po otboru materiala dlia registratsii v organakh gosudarstvennoi bibliografii [Instructions for the Selection of Materials for Registration in the Organs of National Bibliography] Moscow, 1958. 37 p.

Metodicheskie ukazaniia po bibliograficheskomu opisaniiu knig v "Knizhnoi letopisi" i na pechatnykh kartochkakh tsentralizovannoi katalogizatsii (Dopolneniia k "Edinym pravilam opisaniia proizvedenii pechati dlia bibliotechnykh katalogov") [Methodological Directions for the Bibliographic Description of Centrally Cataloged Books in "Book Annals" and on Printed Cards (Supplement to the Uniform Rules for the Description of Printed Works for Library Catalogs)] Moscow, 1961. 63 p.

Klassifikatsiia literatury v organkh gosudarstvennoi registratsionno-uchetnoi bibliografii [The Classification of Literature in the Organs of National Bibliography] 4th ed. rev. Moscow, 1965. 191 p.

Vspomogatel'nye ukazateli k organam gosudarstvennoi bibliografii.
Metodika sostavleniia [Auxiliary Indexes to the Organs of National
Bibliography. Methods of Compilation] Moscow, 1963. 32 p.

Instruktsiia po sostavleniiu "Letopisi muzykal'noi literatury"
[Instructions for Compiling the "Annals of Music Literature"] Moscow,
1964. 90 p.

Instruktsiia po sostavleniiu "Letopisi pechatnykh proizvedenii
izobrazitel'nogo iskusstva" [Instructions for Compiling the "Annals
of Pictorial Art Publications"] Moscow, 1966. 44 l.

Instruktsiia po bibliograficheskomu opisaniiu statei i retsenzii
[Instructions for the Bibliographic Description of Articles and Reviews]
2d ed. rev. and enl. Moscow, 1963. 78 p.

Instruktsiia po sostavleniiu ezhegodnika "Bibliografiia sovetskoi
bibliografii" [Instructions for Compiling the Annual "Bibliography of
Soviet Bibliography"] Moscow, 1963. 19 p.

In addition, the All-Union Book Chamber is guided by the following
methodological materials:

Edinye pravila opisaniia proizvedenii pechati dlia bibliotechnykh
katalogov. Ch. 1, Vyp. I. *Opisanie knig.* [Uniform Rules for the Description of Printed Works for Library Catalogs. Part 1, Issue I. The Description of Books] 2d. ed. rev. and enl. Moscow, Lenin State Library of
the USSR, 1959. 669 p.

Sokrashcheniia russkikh slov v bibliotechnom i bibliograficheskom
opisanii [Russian Abbreviations in Library and Bibliographic Descrip-
tion] Moscow, 1966. 32 p. (All-Union Book Chamber. Interagency
Cataloging Commission, Lenin State Library of the USSR)

Besides these, the All-Union Book Chamber uses a series of working instructions in compiling the organs of national bibliography.

The system of organs of national bibliography has evolved gradually.
The first and oldest publication is *Book Annals*, which originated in 1907.
In the prerevolutionary period and during the first years of Soviet power,
Book Annals was the only organ of bibliographic registration. Besides books,
it recorded other types of printed works: music, maps, periodicals, newspapers,
posters, leaflets, etc. In the period 1924-1925, the recording of nonbook
materials in *Book Annals* was gradually discontinued.

In the mid-twenties, new bibliographic publications began to appear:
The Annual of the State Central Book Chamber of the RSFSR and *Journal*
Annals. The thirties saw a further development and strengthening of national
bibliography. In 1931, *Cartographic Annals* appeared, as did *Music Annals*;
in 1933, *List of Serial Publications*; in 1934, *Pictorial Art Annals*; in 1935,
Annals of Reviews; and in 1936, *Newspaper Annals.* By 1936, the system of
organization of national bibliography that exists today was already basically

established; each type of printed work appeared in a corresponding standard annals. Sometime later, the annual *Bibliography of Soviet Bibliography* was published.

Meanwhile, between the discontinuance of the registration of nonbook materials in *Book Annals* and the beginning of the publication of standard annals, gaps appeared in the recording of music, maps, pictorial art publications, periodicals, and newspapers. During the Great Patriotic War, certain annals were not issued.

Gradually, the gaps in registration are being filled. As regards maps, they have been eliminated by the issuance of *Cartographic Annals* for the periods 1941-1950 and 1951-1953. The gap in the registration of periodicals (with the exception of newspapers) was eliminated by the issuance of the ten volume collective index *Periodical Press of the USSR, 1917-1949*. The first volume of the bibliographic reference *Newspapers of the USSR, 1917-1960* is about to be issued, and subsequent volumes are being readied for printing.*

During the Great Patriotic War, when individual annals were temporarily discontinued, *Book Annals* filled the gaps in the current registration of music, posters, and other publications. The republic book chambers carried out the formidable task of eliminating gaps in the publication record for those periods when their organs of national bibliography either had not been issued or were published intermittently. Retrospective indexes, both general and specialized, were compiled. The majority of these indexes recorded works published during the Soviet era, but several book chambers also compiled retrospective bibliographies covering the prerevolutionary years.

The organs of national bibliography are being steadily improved in accordance with actual requirements. As the system of bibliographic information develops, their profiles are being defined more precisely in terms of completeness and bibliographic methods. At the present time, when informational and bibliographic services are becoming highly specialized, national bibliography takes on particular significance. Its national character, universality, systematization, and completeness make it a reliable basis for all bibliographic work in the USSR and an immediate source of useful information about our own literature in all fields of knowledge.

Book chamber publications are used for various purposes in the work of libraries and scientific institutions. With the organs of national bibliography, many activities are possible: providing readers with information about new literature; the acquisition of library materials; the compilation of both general and special recommended aids and indexes; the selection of literature in certain branches of knowledge or for definite categories of readers; bibliographic reference work; the organization of exhibits; etc.

By using the publications of the book chambers, one can determine systematically what printed works (books, periodicals, music, etc.) are being

---

*The first volume of *Gazety SSSR 1917-1960* was published in Moscow in 1970 by the publishing house "Kniga." Vol. 2 was published in 1976.

published in the USSR as a whole as well as in individual republics and what types of literature (social and political, historical, artistic, technical, etc.) are being released as individual works or being published in periodicals and newspapers. Scanning the systematic divisions of any particular field of knowledge or topic in the current issues of the annals, one can obtain a rather complete overview of the books, newspaper and periodical articles, book reviews, etc., being issued in that field.

In reference and bibliographic work, the organs of national bibliography are used for finding the most diversified facts about publications. What books, journal and newspaper articles, or reviews have been written by a certain author? Where was a certain book published and by which publisher? What literature is there on a particular question in a particular language? Where is to be found a specific review or article that the reader wants? What reviews are there on a particular work of fiction or on a specific scientific book, play, film scenario, etc.? What books were issued in a certain series? What music scores were published for individual types of music and for individual performances? What posters or other visual aids are there on a specific topic? All this information the librarian and reader can obtain by using the appropriate publications of the book chambers.

The supplementary indexes are important in using the publications of the book chambers. Through them, the contents of the organs of national bibliography are opened up. For example, the author indexes are helpful in searching for information about the works of individual authors, composers, and artists. The series index provides information about books being issued in a particular publisher's series. Facilitating the selection of literature being published in the languages of the peoples of the USSR and in foreign languages is a list of these languages in each issue of *Book Annals*. A subject index aids in the location of literature on a specific, usually narrow, question. The geographic index facilitates the selection of literature having a regional basis.

The organs of national bibliography help libraries to render assistance to readers in all those cases where the library catalogs cannot. Thus, for example, a library that does not have a catalog of reviews can provide critical reviews with the *Annals of Reviews* of the All-Union Book Chamber or with the appropriate annals of the republic book chambers. For informational, reference, and bibliographic work in the libraries of scientific, cultural, and educational institutions and organizations, the publications of the book chambers are indispensable sources of information about Soviet publishing.

PUBLICATIONS OF THE
ALL-UNION BOOK CHAMBER

BOOK ANNALS
(Knizhnaia letopis')

Published since 1907,[1] *Book Annals* comes out in two parts: a basic part and a supplement,[2] distinguished by content and frequency. The basic part, which is published weekly, comprehensively records books and pamphlets intended principally for wide distribution: scholarly monographs, popular brochures, practical manuals, handbooks, reference works, textbooks, fictional works, dictionaries, and encyclopedias.[3] It includes a few types of works, otherwise listed in corresponding organs of national bibliography, which have, as well as their own characteristics, the features of a book, such as serial publications of the type "transactions" [i.e., "trudy"][4]; music publications in which the literary text predominates over the musical; bound albums of printed pictorial works; and atlases and albums of geographic maps.

Each year, materials from the basic issues, with the exception of "transactions" without distinctive titles, are brought together in the *Book Annual of the USSR*.[5] The supplement, which is issued monthly, records selected material which is not intended for wide distribution: official, instructional, normative, program-methodological, and informational type publications. Usually, it does not include publications limited in scope and reader interest, ephemeral materials, very short publications of up to four pages inclusive, publications with printings up to 100 copies, and publications run off on duplicating machines. Books for the blind and dissertation abstracts are recorded in special sections.

Book Annals has changed with the passage of time in terms of the types of material it records and the territorial and language criteria used in selecting materials. Since 1934, works published in the territory of the USSR have been recorded regardless of the language of publication.

In the prerevolutionary period, 1907-1917, publications issued in Russia in the Russian language or other languages were recorded. In the period 1917-1924, the publications which came out mainly in the territory of the RSFSR were recorded. During this same period, especially until 1922, books and pamphlets published in the Ukraine, Northern Caucasus, Transcaucasia, Central Asia, Siberia, and Belorussia were recorded, but with large gaps. In the years 1925-1927, only publications issued in the RSFSR were recorded. In 1928-1933, works published in other republics in Russian and West European languages were added.

These changes did not affect the basic purpose of *Book Annals*: the listing of widely published books. *Book Annals* has recorded this production very fully except during the first post-revolutionary years, the period of civil war, and the period of the Great Patriotic War, when the required deposit copies were not sent to the book chambers.[6] The changes mainly concern two categories of printed works: 1) publications of the nonbook type, such as journals, newspapers, music, cartographic publications, and printed pictorial works, which were recorded off and on in *Book Annals* until 1946; and 2) publications not intended for mass distribution, which in different years were variously recorded in *Book Annals* with respect to fullness and form. They were either listed with the general book production or placed in a special supplement.

From 1907 to 1917, *Book Annals* listed various types of printed works: books, pamphlets, maps, music, leaflets, and also government documents. In addition, Issue No. 2 for 1907 included information about suppressed publications. From 1908 on, it listed periodical publications; from 1908 to 1913, selected lists of articles from certain periodical publications; in 1908 and 1909, it included the section "Rossica"; and in the period 1914-1916, the section "Alphabetical Lists of Works Examined by Foreign Censorship." Not recorded fully in prerevolutionary *Book Annals* are publications which were not subjected to the censor's surveillance: official, governmental, district council (zemstvo) materials, and a few so-called "suspected" publications.

Besides books and pamphlets, *Book Annals* recorded during the years 1917-1925 other types of publications which were received as part of the required depository copy: journals and newspapers, music, posters, leaflets, and so forth. In 1924 and 1925, it gradually curtailed the listing of these publications but temporarily restored them during the years 1939-1945. *Book Annals* has always included publications having book-like qualities, such as albums and atlases, continuing publications of the "transactions" type, and so forth. In the years 1929-1953, only those "transactions" which appeared as monographs or monographic collections were recorded. In 1945, lists of leaflets from the Great Patriotic War were included in separate numbers of *Book Annals*.

Types of Printed Works Recorded in Book Annals

Years	Books and Pamphlets	Geographic Maps	Music	Printed Pictorial Works	Periodicals and Newspapers	Articles	Reviews
1907	+	+	+	+	–	–	–
1908-1913	+	+	+	+	+	+	–
1914-1916	+	+	+	+	+	–	–
1917-1918	+	+	+	+	+	–	–
1919	+	–	+	+	+	–	–
1920-1921	+	+	+	+	+	–	–
1922	+	–	+	+	+	–	–
1923	+	+	+	+	–	–	–
1924-1925	+	+	–	+	+	–	–
1926-1938	+	–	–	–	–	–	–
1939-1940	+	+	+	+	+	–	+
1941	+	+	+	+	+	–	–
1942	+	–	+	+	+	–	–
1943-1944	+	–	+	+	+	–	+
1945	+	–	+	+	–	–	+
1946-1967	+	–	–	–	–	–	–

The plus symbol signifies the recording of the given type of printed work in *Book Annals*.

The rules for selecting publications not intended for mass distribution were revised a number of times. In Soviet times, *Book Annals* recorded official, government, program-methodological, and informational publications up to 1923 without any special restrictions; and the quantity of these recorded publications was determined by the obligatory copies received. In 1923 (with Issue No. 3) and 1924, official and government documents of local significance, slogans, proclamations, announcements, and so forth were excluded.

After 1925, the listing of official and government publications was expanded anew. They were recorded rather fully from 1938 through May 1941 when a supplement to *Book Annals* was being published. In 1941, publication of the supplement was interrupted. Items normally recorded in it were then recorded with limitations in the regular issues of *Book Annals* (with No. 28); only significant material intended for mass distribution was listed.

Since 1961, *Book Annals* has again been issued in two parts, but the supplementary issue still records only important items intended for mass distribution. More recently, the selection of publications in this category has become more precise and has been limited by the development of the system of subject and specialized bibliographies.

In 1963-1965, special types of technical literature and documentation listed in *Book Annals* selectively (technical catalogs containing descriptions of various machines, instruments, and materials; standards, technical requirements and similar publications; standard building designs) were gradually excluded. They were being extensively covered in special bibliographic publications, such as the biweekly *New Industrial Catalogs,*[7] the annual *Index of State Standards,*[8] and the annual *Index of Machine Building Norms.*[9]

The number of program-methodological materials recorded has also been curtailed. Since 1966, all publications of this type intended for educational institutions have been excluded.

Because so many official and scientific items are being run off on duplicating machines, the number of these publications recorded has increased since 1959.

Bibliographic Description

Books are entered in *Book Annals* in Russian regardless of the language in which they are printed. Until 1938, some of the non-Russian books were entered in the language of the original. Bibliographic description consists of author's name, title, subtitle, place of publication, publisher (up to 1951, the printing house was also indicated), year of publication, pagination, illustrations, size, number of copies printed, and price. At head of title data, i.e., information about the institution in whose name the book is being published, series title and also the names of persons who took a creative part in composing the book are included. The language of publication is indicated for those books not printed in Russian. Titles which do not reveal the theme of the book are briefly explained through the subtitle or notes. The contents of some types of collections are shown. In certain years during the prewar period, the contents of collections were given in full. Since 1923, corporate authors have been given for official publications and the presence of bibliographies noted. At the end of the entry, the decimal classification number is given. First editions are indicated by the letter "p."

Since 1964, abstracts of dissertations have been described more briefly. Information about size, number of copies printed, presence of a bibliography, and so forth is omitted. The same is true for books for the blind. Since 1966, the abbreviation "op" has been used to indicate books printed by duplicating machines.

Examples of Entries*

Tsetkin, K. Vospominaniia o Lenine. M., Politizdat, 1966.
40 s. 20 cm. 100,000 ekz. 7 k.   3K26 (003)

Slavianskoe vozrozhdenie. Sbornik statei i materialov. [Red. kollegiia: S. A. Nikitin (otv. red.) i dr.]. M., "Nauka", 1966. 250 s. s ill. 22 cm. (AN SSSR. In-t slavianovedeniia). 1500 ekz. 1 r. 10 k. V per. - Chast' teksta na bolg., serb. i frants. iaz.

Shkvarkin, V. Komedii. [Vstupit. stat'ia I. Shtoka. Primech. L. Nimvitskoi]. M., "Iskusstvo", 1966. 374 s.; 14 l. ill. 17 cm. 5000 ekz. 1 r. 4 k. V per.

Soderzh.: Chuzhoi rebenok. – Vesennii smotr. – Strashnyi sud. – Prostaia devushka. – Prints Napoleon.   891.71-2

Arrangement of Material

Bibliographic entries are arranged in *Book Annals* in systematic fashion according to the scheme *Classification of Literature in the Organs of National Bibliography*.[10] Special sections of the *Supplementary Issue* record abstracts of dissertations and books for the blind.

Basic Divisions of the Classification Scheme

I.   Marxism-Leninism

II.   Communist Party of the Soviet Union

III. All-Union Lenin Young Communist League. Soviet Youth

IV.   Social Sciences

V.   Philosophy. Socio-Political Doctrines

*Translations of entries appear in Appendix III.

VI.	History
VII.	Economics. History of Economic Studies
VIII.	International Relations. Political and Economic Conditions in Foreign Countries
IX.	Building Communism in the USSR
X.	Planning. Statistics. Accounting. Organization and Management of Production
XI.	Finance
XII.	Labor in the USSR
XIII.	State and Law
XIV.	Military Science. Military Affairs
XV.	Natural Sciences. Mathematics
XVI.	Technology. Industry
XVII.	Agriculture
XVIII.	Transportation. Transportation Engineering
XIX.	Communication
XX.	Commerce. Procurement. Public Catering
XXI.	Communal Affairs. Community Services
XXII.	Public Health. Medical Sciences
XXIII.	Physical Culture. Sports
XXIV.	Culture. Education. Science
XXV.	Philology. Linguistics
XXVI.	Literary History and Criticism. Belles-lettres. Folklore
XXVII.	Children's Literature
XXVIII.	Arts
XXIX.	Atheism. Science and Religion. Religion
XXX.	Publishing. Bibliology. Library Science. Bibliography
XXXI.	General Reference Works. Encyclopedias. Calendars. Collected Works

In accordance with methodological instructions on classification, the basic divisions are constantly being developed and made more specific as the need arises. For example, new concepts growing out of developments in science and technology, such as bionics, technical aesthetics, space medicine, etc., are systematically being added to the scheme.

Over the years, the arrangement of material in the annals has changed. In *Book Annals* for 1917, just as in prerevolutionary years, entries were placed in a single alphabet by authors' surnames and the first words of titles. In the period 1918-1925, entries were arranged by type of publication: books and pamphlets, leaflets, posters, proclamations, music, and so on. In 1925, the section "Books and Pamphlets" had nine subsections arranged according to purpose. Since 1926, entries have been arranged by subject on the basis of the decimal classification system. The scheme has changed in the course of time and has lost its decimal base. During the war years, the classification system began with the section "The Great Patriotic War of the Soviet People." Since 1947, the basic arrangement has been relatively stable.

In certain years, the systematic arrangement of literature was sometimes combined with groupings by type of publication or by publications of certain territories or languages. These groupings were published either within single issues of *Book Annals* or in special and supplementary issues.

During the years 1928-1933, there were two special supplements to *Book Annals: Cumulative List of Non-Periodical Publications Issued in the Union Republics (except the RSFSR) in Russian and West European Languages*[11] and the *Special Issue,*[12] which recorded books in Turkish, Mongolian, Finno-Ugrian, and other languages of the peoples of the RSFSR besides Russian.

In 1934, *Book Annals* was issued as a separate composed of three sections: A. The Russian Book; B. The Book in the RSFSR in Other Languages; and C. The Book in the USSR (except RSFSR). From 1938 through May 1941, *Book Annals* was issued in two parts: a basic and a supplement. This division has also been true since 1961. In the 1938-1941 period, materials in the supplement were grouped by publisher or type of publication (catalogs of journals and newspapers, screen plays of films, etc.) within systematic divisions.

Since 1961, the classified arrangement of material in the basic issue and the supplement has remained unchanged. Since Issue No. 12 of *Book Annals* for 1935, special sections of the *Supplement* have listed books and pamphlets received two or more years late. Books received during the current year but published in a previous year are listed in the usual way.

Indexes and Other Aids

A separate quarterly publication, *Book Annals. Auxiliary Indexes,*[13] is issued for the basic issue and the supplement. It contains name, geographic, and subject indexes.

The name index lists the persons who took part in the composition of a book: authors, commentators, editors, translators, illustrators, authors of introductory articles and forewords, and other such persons mentioned in the bibliographic entries. Besides these, it includes the persons to whom books are dedicated.

The geographic index includes the names of physiographic, administrative territorial, economic, geological, and historical geographic entities which have been dealt with in the works listed. The administrative territorial headings are broken down by topical subheadings which basically correspond to the first divisions of the classification system used in the organs of national bibliography.

The subject index reflects the contents of publications recorded in *Book Annals* with the exception of collections of diverse content, secondary school textbooks, methodological handbooks for correspondence courses, and fiction.

The annual *Index of Series Publications*[14] serves as an auxiliary index to *Book Annals* and can also be used as an independent bibliographic guide because it contains basic information about books in publishers' monographic series.

In every issue of *Book Annals*, there is a "List of Languages (except Russian) in Which Books Have Been Published."

Every year the first issue of the annals contains the full text of the classification system and a foreword, "From the Editor," briefly describing the arrangement and purpose of the annals. The system of auxiliary indexes has varied over the years, depending on the content and arrangement of the annals.

Basic Auxiliary Indexes

Types of Indexes	Years
Name	1907-1917, 1924-1934, 1938-1967
Geographic	1938 (I semiannual), 1940, 1941 (Jan-May), 1952-1967
Subject	1907-1917, 1926-1928, 1930, 1940, 1941 (Jan-May), 1956 (II semi-annual)-1967
Classified	1908-1915, 1924, 1925, 1933, 1934
Corporate Author	1924, 1925, 1938-1941 (Jan-May), 1950
Series	1933-1941 (Jan-May), 1946-1967
List of Languages (except Russian) in Which Books Have Been Published	1934-1940, 1947-1967

Changes in content, frequency, and form of the basic indexes and the appearance of incidental auxiliary indexes are shown in the following chronological schedule.

Chronological Schedule of Auxiliary Indexes[15]

Years	Types of Indexes; Frequency or Form of Publication
1907-1916	In each number: Author index. Subject index. Quarterly or semiannual (bound with separate numbers of *Book Annals*): Author index. Subject Index. Annual indexes: Author index (for 1908-1909). Classified index (for 1908-1915). Index to *Annals of Periodical Press for 1908* (indexes of authors and subject to the division "List of articles . . ." bound with the Classified Index 1908). Cumulative annual index to Alphabetical List of Banned Publications . . . for 1914 (bound with No. 11 for 1915); for 1915 (bound with No. 50 for 1915); for 1916 (bound with No. 1 for 1917).
1917	To numbers 1-5 (bound with No. 7): Author index. Subject index. In numbers 6-50: Author index. Subject index. *Index to Book Annals for 1917.* [Author index. Subject index]. Petrograd, 1919. 160 p.
1918-1923	No indexes.
1924	In each number: Alphabetical index (I. Authors, editors, translators. II. Corporate authors. III. Authors of bookcovers and illustrations). Classified index (by the decimal classification system). Index of publications issued in the union and autonomous republics.
1925	In numbers 1-18: Alphabetical index (I. Authors, editors, translators. From No. 8 on, only authors. II. Corporate authors. III. Authors of bookcovers and illustrations). Classified index (by the decimal classification system).
1926	In each number: Author index. In almost every number: Subject index to the classified sections.

Years	Types of Indexes; Frequency or Form of Publication
1927	In each number: Author index. In a few numbers: Subject index to the classified sections.
	Alphabetical index [authors and titles] *for 1927.* M., 1928. 258 p.
1928	In numbers 1-5: Author index. In some numbers: Subject index to the classified sections.
	Alphabetical index of authors for the first half of the year 1928.
	Alphabetical index [author and title] *for 1928.*[16] M., 1929. 300 p.
1929	To every four numbers: Alphabetical index of authors and titles.
	Alphabetical index [author and title] *for 1929.*[16] M., 1931. 382 p.
1930	To every six numbers: Alphabetical index of authors and titles. In some numbers: subject index to the classified sections.
	Alphabetical index [author and title] *for 1930.*[16] M., 1935. 456 p.
1931	To every six numbers: Alphabetical index of authors and titles.
	Alphabetical index [author and title] *for 1931.*[16] M., 1936.
1932	To numbers 1-10 and 11-15 two separate issues: Alphabetical index of authors and titles.
1933	*Alphabetical index* [author and title] *for 1933.*[17] M., 1935. 527, IX p.
	Classified index for 1933.[17] M., 1935. XIV, 476 p.
	Index of series, issues of which are recorded in Book Annals for 1933. M., 1934. 126 p. (Published in No. 60. It came out also as a separate offprint).
1934	*Alphabetical index* [author and title] *for 1934.* M., [1935].
	Classified index for 1934. M., [1935].

(Table continues on page 86)

Years	Types of Indexes; Frequency or Form of Publication
1935-1937	*Index of series, issues of which are recorded in Book Annals for 1934.* M., 1935. 187 p. (Published in No. 60a. It came out also as a separate offprint). *Index of series, issues of which are recorded in Book Annals . . .* *for 1935.* M., 1936. 163 p. (Published in No. 60a). *for 1936.* M., 1937. 196 p. (Published in No. 60a). *for 1937.* M., 1938. 164 p.
1938	In numbers 1-30: Auxiliary indexes. (A. Legislative and directive materials of Soviet, Party, and Trade union organs of the USSR and the union republics with commentaries on them. B. Educational, program-methodological, and scientific-reference literature. C. Children's literature. D. Literature for the blind. E. Chronological index of historical, biographical, and memoir literature. F. Topographic index. G. List of languages (besides Russian) in which books are printed). In numbers 31-60a: List of languages (besides Russian) in which books are printed. To numbers 1-10, 11-20, 21-30, 31-45 (bound with Nos. 15, 36, 42, 56), to numbers 46-60a (they came out in a separate issue): Auxiliary indexes (1. Index of authors, editors, translators, illustrators and personalia. 2. Index of corporate authors. 3. Index of publishers' series).
1939	Quarterly: Auxiliary indexes (1. Name index. 2. Index of organizations, institutions, and enterprises. 3. Index of series. 4. Index of languages).
1940	Monthly: Auxiliary indexes. (1. Name index. 2. Index of corporate authors. 3. Subject index. 4. Geographical index. 5. Index of series. 6. Index of languages).
1941	Monthly (Jan-May): Auxiliary indexes. (1. Name index. 2. Index of corporate authors. 3. Subject index. 4. Geographical index.

(Table continues on page 87)

Years	Types of Indexes; Frequency or Form of Publication
	5. Index of series). Monthly and semiannually (June, July-Dec): Name index.
1942-1943	Quarterly: Name index.
1944	Monthly: Name index.
1945	Quarterly: Name index.
1946-1951	Quarterly: Name index (In 1950, the quarterly issues included also an Index of corporate authors). Index of series, issues of which are recorded in *Book Annals* for . . . year.
1952-1955	Quarterly: Auxiliary indexes (Name index. Geographical index). Index of series, issues of which are recorded in *Book Annals* for . . . year.
1956-1967	Quarterly: Auxiliary indexes (Name index. Subject index.[18] Geographical index). Index of series, issues of which are recorded in *Book Annals* for . . . year.[19]

List of Numbers Issued
Book Annals, 1907-1967

Years	Issues per Year	Number of Issues per Year
1907	1-24	24
1908-1910	1-50	50
1911	1-51	51
1912-1916	1-50	50
1917	1-50	40
1918	1/4-46/50	13
1919	1-52	31
1920[20]	1/32; 33 (1)-47/48 (15/16)	16
1921	1-24	24
1922	1-21/24	21
1923-1924	1-24	24
1925	1-23/24	23
1926	1-52	52
1927	1-51; 52I; 52II	53
1928	1-52	52
1929	1-51; 52a; 52b	53
1930	1-72	72
1931	1-72; 72a; 72b	74
1932-1933[21]	1-60	60
1934[21]	1-60; 60a	61
1935-1936[21]	1-60; [60a]	61
1937-1939	1-60; 60a	61
1940	1/2-56; 56a	56
1941	1/2-47/50	37
1942-1943	1-24	24
1944	1-51/52	49
1945	1/2-52	47
1946	1-52	52
1947-1948	1-48	48
1949-1967	1-52	52

The discrepancy between the issue numbers and the total number of issues in certain years is caused by combining some numbers and by the occasional publication of additional issues.

Special and Supplementary Issues

Knizhnaia letopis'. Svodnyi spisok neperiodicheskikh izdanii, vykhodiashchikh v predelakh soiuznykh respublik (krome RSFSR) na russkom i zapadnoevropeiskikh iazykakh [Book Annals. Cumulative List of Nonperiodical Publications Issued in the Union Republics (except the RSFSR) in Russian and West European Languages] [22] 1928-1933. This is a supplement to *Book Annals*.

1928	Nos. 1/2, 3, 4		1931	Nos. 1, 2, 3, 4
1929	Nos. 1, 2, 3, 4		1932	Nos. 1, 2, 3/4
1930	Nos. 1/2, 3, 4		1933	Nos. 1/2 - 11/12

Entries for books published in West European languages are given in the language of the original.

The annual auxiliary indexes to *Book Annals* also cover materials of the *Cumulative List*.

Knizhnaia letopis'. Spetsial'nyi vypusk [Book Annals. Special Issue] 1928-1933. Includes books in the languages of the peoples of the RSFSR except Russian. [23]

1928	Nos. 1, 2, 3, 4		1931	No. 1/4
1929	Nos. 1, 2, 3/4		1932	No. 1/4
1930	No. 1/4		1933	Nos. 1/2, 3, 4

In the issues for 1928 and 1929, entries for books are given in the original. Issue No. 4 for 1928 has a special list in Russian of books published in the Buryat-Mongolian, Georgian, Chinese, Korean, and Japanese languages. In issue No. 2, there is a list of books in the Buryat-Mongolian, Chinese, and Korean languages. In the issues for 1930-1933, all entries for books are in Russian.

The annual auxiliary indexes to *Book Annals* for 1933 also cover material from the *Special Issue*.

Knizhnaia letopis'. Dopolnitel'nyi vypusk [Book Annals. Supplementary Issue] 1938-May 1941, 1961-1967.

1938	Nos. 1[24]-12		1941	Nos. 1-5 (Jan-May)
1939	Nos. 1-4		1961-1967	Nos. 1-12 (each year)
1940	Nos. 1-4			

In the 1938 issue, every number contains auxiliary indexes similar to those of the basic issue. In the 1941 issue, every number has name indexes. In the issues for the years 1961-1967, the *Supplementary Issue* has its own separately published auxiliary indexes similar to those of the basic issue.

Ukazatel' knig, ne uchtennykh v "Knizhnoi letopisi" za 1941-1944 gg. [Index of Books Not Recorded in *Book Annals* for 1941-1944].

Issue No. 1. M., 1945. 88 p.
Issue No. 2. M., 1947. 44 p.
Each issue has a name index.

Footnotes

[1] In the prerevolutionary period, *Book Annals* was published by the Chief Administration for Publishing (Glavnoe upravlenie po delam pechati). The first number was issued in Petersburg on 14 July (old style) 1907.

[2] Since 1956, the AUBC has also kept a special record of publications not entered in either part of *Book Annals*.

[3] These types of publications are usually assumed to be publications of wide distribution, regardless of the quantities in which they are printed.

[4] In 1961, the supplement (Nos. 1-5) recorded "transactions" which did not have distinctive titles; subsequently, the basic part (No. 20 on) recorded these publications.

[5] *Ezhegodnik knigi SSSR.*

[6] Gaps in the listing of books have been filled by supplementary records both in the current issues of *Book Annals* and in separately issued publications.

[7] *Novye promyshlennye katalogi.*

[8] *Ukazatel' gosudarstvennykh standartov.*

[9] *Ukazatel' normalei mashinostroeniia.*

[10] *Klassifikatsiia literatury v organakh gosudarstvennoi registratsionno-uchetnoi bibliografii.*

[11] *Svodnyi spisok neperiodicheskikh izdanii, vykhodiashchikh v predelakh soiuznykh respublik (krome RSFSR) na russkom i zapadno-evropeiskikh iazykakh.*

[12] *Spetsial'nyi vypusk.*

[13] *Knizhnaia letopis'. Vspomogatel'nye ukazateli.*

[14] *Ukazatel' seriinykh izdanii.*

[15] The "List of Languages (except Russian) in Which Books Have Been Published," which appears in each number of the annals for 1934-1938 and 1947-1967 (in 1939-1940—in separately published issues of auxiliary indexes), is not noted here.

In the lists of auxiliary indexes and lists of issued numbers, the names of the indexes and sections of the annals are given according to the primary source.

[16] Besides materials of the basic issue of *Book Annals*, the index covers materials of the "Cumulative list of nonperiodical publications . . ."

[17] Besides materials of the basic issue of *Book Annals*, the index covers materials of the "Cumulative list . . ." and the "Special Issue."

[18] Subject index comes out beginning with the third quarter of 1956.

[19] Since 1961, it has come out under the title *Ukazatel' seriinykh izdanii* [Index of series publications]. It is published separately for the basic and supplementary issues of *Book Annals*.

[20] After the abolition of the Chief Administration for Publishing in 1917, *Book Annals*, up to the combined issue 1/32 for 1920, was published by the Russian Book Chamber in Petrograd; from No. 33 (1), 1920 on, by the Russian Central Book Chamber in Moscow.

[21] No. 60 for 1933 and Nos. 60a for 1934-1936 include only an annual index of series.

[22] In the *Cumulative List* for 1928, only publications in Russian are listed.

[23] Books are recorded in the languages of the peoples of the RSFSR related to Turkish, Mongolian, Finno-Ugrian, and other groups of languages. Books in Slavic and West European languages published in the RSFSR are listed in the basic issue of *Book Annals*.

[24] Published under the designation *Special Issue*.

■ ■ ■

BOOK ANNUAL OF THE USSR
(Ezhegodnik knigi SSSR)

The *Book Annual of the USSR*, which has been devoted to books and pamphlets since 1925, has been published since 1927.[1] It records those publications intended primarily for wide distribution: scholarly monographs, popular pamphlets, practical handbooks, manuals and reference books, textbooks, belles-lettres, dictionaries, and encyclopedias, which have been listed in the basic issue of *Book Annals* during the corresponding year. Of the continuing publications of the "transactions" type, only those which have distinctive titles are included.

The *Book Annual of the USSR* is issued in two volumes. The first contains works on politics, education and pedagogy, fiction, and children's literature. In addition, physical culture and sports, language, art, publishing, library science and bibliography, and general reference are covered. The second volume contains works on the natural sciences, technology, industry, agriculture, transportation, communication, trade, community affairs, and medicine.

Until 1943, the annual was published in one volume. Annuals for 1943 and 1944 consisted of three issues arranged by subject; for the period 1945-1956, of two semiannual issues; and for the period 1957-1965, of two volumes, also arranged by subject. The annual covers the majority of materials recorded by *Book Annals* for any particular year.

The territorial criteria for selection, as well as the types of literature covered by the annual, have changed in the course of time. In the annuals for 1925-1929, all books in Russian were included, while in the years 1925-1927, only those books in Russian published in the RSFSR were covered. The annual for 1925 had, besides the list of books, a "Classified Index of Articles Found in the Most Important Journals of 1925" and also statistical material. Each of the annuals for 1925-1929 has a bibliographic survey of the literature on the book. Later, the limitations for inclusion of materials became less stringent, and almost all publications in *Book Annals* were listed in the annual for 1935. Subsequently, selection became stricter again; and, as a result, the number of included government, methodological, and informational publications declined.

Since 1951, government instructions, building designs, free instructional materials enclosed with machines and instruments for their maintenance and operation, booklets about industrial safety, booklets on sanitation, etc., have been omitted. Since 1954, government publications of provincial organizations have been eliminated. Subsequently, selection was directed at further limiting those ephemeral and narrowly distributed publications. Since 1961, the annual has encompassed books and pamphlets from the basic issue of *Book Annals.*

Bibliographic Description

The annual follows basically the same rules as *Book Annals* does, although the entries are slightly simplified and abbreviated. For example, the surnames of compilers and editors are not given if they are not on the title page or if the book is entered under the author. Illustrators are indicated only in entries of artistically illustrated publications and books for preschoolers. Bibliographies, size of publication, edition number, and so on are also not indicated.

A uniform entry is frequently used for related publications: new editions, translations into various languages of the same work, and several parts (volumes, issues) of the same work. The series entry is given under a single entry number.

Arrangement of Material

Material is arranged systematically according to the classification scheme used in the organs of national bibliography. For this purpose, there has been a more detailed expansion of the classification's subdivisions.

Indexes and Other Aids

Every volume or issue of the annual has the following indexes: name, title, and, since 1961, subject, as well as an index of books in languages of the peoples of the USSR except Russian and foreign languages, and, since 1965, an index of translations from foreign languages.

The name index includes persons mentioned in bibliographic entries: authors, compilers, editors, authors of introductory articles and notes, translators, etc., as well as persons to whose lives and activities works are dedicated.

The title index records only those books entered under title and books whose authors or compilers are not shown on the title page.

The index of books in the languages of the peoples of the USSR (except Russian) and in foreign languages includes names of authors, titles, and corporate authors, appearing in the entry heading. Entries are arranged alphabetically according to language.

The index of translations includes names of authors and titles in the entry headings. Entries are arranged alphabetically according to the names of countries.

The subject index reflects the contents of books in the annual except for multivolume collections, secondary school textbooks, and belles-lettres.

In 1925, the annual had only one auxiliary index—the subject index. Until 1957, the name and title indexes were combined into one alphabetical index.

Every volume of the annual has a preface, which briefly describes the publication. The table of contents in each volume shows the classification scheme and gives a full list of all headings or rubrics.

List of Issues Published

Ezhegodnik Gosudarstvennoi tsentral'noi knizhnoi palaty RSFSR [Annual of the State Central Book Chamber of the RSFSR] 1925-1929.

Issue 1. The Book in 1925. M., L., 1927. 696 p.
Issue 2. The Book in 1926. M., L., 1928. XL, 462, [2] p.
Issue 3. The Book in 1927. M., L., 1930. XLVIII, 672 p.
Issue 4. The Book in 1928. M., L., 1930. LVI, 700 p.
Issue 5. The Book in 1929. M., L., 1931. LVII, 796 p.

Ezhegodnik knigi SSSR [Book Annual of the USSR] 1935, 1941-1965.

1935	M., 1936. XXXVI, 1572 p.
1941	(II semiannual)[2] M., 1950. 478 p.
1942	M., 1950. 564 p.
1943	Issue 1. M., 1947. 144 p. Issue 2. M., 1947. 254 p. Issue 3. M., 1947. 108 p.
1944	Issue 1. M., 1946. 142 p. Issue 2. M., 1946. 282 p. Issue 3. M., 1946. 134 p.
1945	I semiannual. M., 1949. 367 p. II semiannual. M., 1951. 292 p.
1946	I semiannual. M., 1946. [Bound ed.: 1947]. 466 p. II semiannual. M., 1947. 561 p.
1947	I semiannual. M., 1947. [Bound ed.: 1948]. 516 p. II semiannual. M., 1948. 606 p.
1948	I semiannual. M., 1949. X p., 852 col. II semiannual. M., 1950. XI p., 1048 col.
1949	I semiannual. M., 1950. XI p., 1064 col. II semiannual. M., 1951. XI p., 1000 col.
1950	I semiannual. M., 1951. XI p., 1096 col. II semiannual. M., 1952. XI p., 1160 col.
1951	I semiannual. M., 1952. XI p., 992 col. II semiannual. M., 1953. XI p., 1088 col.

1952	I semiannual. M., 1953. XI, 549 p.
	II semiannual. M., 1954. XI, 546 p.
1953	I semiannual. M., 1954. XI, 522 p.
	II semiannual. M., 1954. XI, 468 p.
1954	I semiannual. M., 1955. XI, 481 p.
	II semiannual. M., 1955. XI, 499 p.
1955	I semiannual. M., 1956. XI, 565 p.
	II semiannual. M., 1956. XI, 557 p.
1956	I semiannual. M., 1956. [Bound ed.: 1957]. IX, 641 p.
	II semiannual. M., 1958. IX, 678 p.
1957	Vol. 1. M., 1958. V, 677 p.
	Vol. 2. M., 1959. VII, 634 p.
1958	Vol. 1. M., 1960. VII, 720 p.
	Vol. 2. M., 1960. VII, 646 p.
1959	Vol. 1. M., 1961. VII, 841 p.
	Vol. 2. M., 1961. VII, 765 p.
1960	Vol. 1. M., 1962. VII, 902 p.
	Vol. 2. M., 1962. VII, 839 p.
1961	Vol. 1. M., 1963. VII, 937 p.
	Vol. 2. M., 1963. VII, 1015 p.
1962	Vol. 1. M., 1963. [7], 952 p.
	Vol. 2. M., 1963. VII, 1047 p.
1963	Vol. 1. M., 1964. VII, 961 p.
	Vol. 2. M., 1964. VII, 1055 p.
1964	Vol. 1. M., 1965. VII, 938 p.
	Vol. 2. M., 1965. VII, 1038 p.
1965	Vol. 1. M., 1966. VIII, 885 p.
	Vol. 2. M., 1966. VIII, 950 p.

Information about books and pamphlets for the years when the annual was not published can be obtained by looking through the complete set of *Book Annals* to 1925 and for 1930-1934 and 1936-1941.

The *Bibliographical Annual*,[3] compiled under the editorship of I. V. Vladislavlev (for 1911, 1912, 1913, 1914, 1921-1922, 1922-1923, 1923-1924, 1924), chronologically precedes the *Book Annual of the USSR*. In addition to books, these annuals include periodical articles and reviews, with the exception of the annual for 1923-1924, which does not include entries for articles.

Footnotes

[1] For the years 1925-1929, it was published under the title *Ezhegodnik Gosudarstvennoi tsentral'noi knizhnoi palaty RSFSR* [Annual of the State Central Book Chamber of the RSFSR]. It was not issued for the years 1930-1934 or 1936-1941.

[2] First semiannual issue for 1941 was not published.

[3] *Bibliograficheskii ezhegodnik.*

■ ■ ■

ANNALS OF SERIAL PUBLICATIONS OF THE USSR
(Letopis' periodicheskikh izdanii SSSR)

Published since 1933, the *Annals of Serial Publications of the USSR* represents a system of separate and interrelated publications, each distinguished from the other by type of material and time period covered. Because most journals and newspapers are published without substantial changes over long periods of time, the full list of periodical and continuing publications is issued only once every five years.[1] Information concerning new journals and newspapers or those which changed their titles or ceased publication is published annually in a special issue. A separate annual issue gives information about serial publications of the "transactions" type.

The annual issues are published under a general title with distinguishing subtitles: *Annals of Serial Publications of the USSR. New, Renamed, and Ceased Journals and Newspapers;*[2] and *Annals of Serial Publications of the USSR. Transactions, Contributions, Collections, and Other Serials Publications.*[3] The quinquennial issue comes out under the same general title but does not have a subtitle.[4] The issues of the annals which differ in content and time period in which the materials were recorded also have other characteristics.

Annals of Serial Publications of the USSR. New, Renamed, and Ceased Journals and Newspapers comes out annually except for the years coinciding with the last year of the five-year cumulation, when all additions, changes, and deletions are recorded directly in the cumulation. As a rule, coverage begins on January 1 of the first year of the five-year period and ends on April 1[5] of the current year, i.e., the year of the publication of the annals. For example, an issue for the period 1 January 1950 through 1 April 1951 came out in 1951. Within the five-year period, each issue is a cumulation of the material for the previous year(s). That is, the issue published in 1952 cumulated material for the period 1 January 1950 through 1 April 1952.

Annals of Serial Publications of the USSR. Transactions, Contributions, Collections, and Other Serials comes out annually except for the year coinciding with the last year of the five-year cumulation, when all additions, changes, and deletions are recorded directly in the cumulation. It records those serials the numbers (volumes, issues, etc.) of which were received by the Book Chamber during the year.

The quinquennial issue of the annals records journals and newspapers which were published without change up to and during the registration period. It cumulates the materials of the annual issues and records the publications for the last year of the registration period of the quinquennial issue which are not covered by the annual issue.

With the publication of the quinquennial issue, the annual issues are superseded. Materials in the quinquennial issue together with the following annual issues give a complete record of all periodical and continuing publications in the USSR for the corresponding period. Basically, the same principles obtain in selecting various types of periodical and serial publications for inclusion in both the quinquennial and annual issues.

Journals and transactions [i.e., trudy] [6] are recorded in the annals comprehensively, while bulletins and informational publications are added selectively. Specialized departmental publications are not included.

All-union, republic, regional, territorial, city, interdistrict, and district newspapers are recorded comprehensively. Not recorded are the less important newspapers, such as those of enterprises, institutions and educational bodies, kolkhoz and sovkhoz newspapers, and temporary newspapers. The annals recorded such newspapers through 1936.

Until 1950, serials were recorded in one annual publication. [7]

The territorial and chronological criteria used for selecting materials have changed. The issue for 1933 records those publications which were being published in the RSFSR as of July 1 of that year. The issue for 1934 includes publications which came out in the USSR in the first half of the year; works which came out in the RSFSR in the second half of 1933 are listed in a supplement. In subsequent years, the annals recorded materials issued in the territory of the USSR.

In 1934-1937, the annual issues recorded material for the first half of the current year and the second half of the previous year. The issue for 1938 contains information for the first half of 1938 and, in a supplement, information for July-December 1937 and 1938. In 1939 and in the years 1946-1949, materials for the full calendar year were recorded. The issue for 1939 records journals issued in 1939 as well as those of the previous year which were issued or recorded late.

Bibliographic Description

The three editions of the annals conform basically to the same rules of bibliographic description. The bibliographic entries contain the following information about a publication: title; subtitle; first year of publication; frequency; place of publication; publisher; and "at head of title" information (the latter for journals and continuations); language in which the publication is printed, if not in Russian; years of publication; indication of the volumes, issues, or numbers (the latter for serial publications of the "transactions" type and newspapers); size and number of type pages (in the case of newspapers);[8] number of copies printed; price; and notes about changes in title, reorganization, and so forth which took place during the registration period. In the quinquennial issues, subtitles are usually omitted from the entries of city and regional newspapers.

Publications in the languages of the peoples of the USSR (except Russian) and in foreign languages are entered in the annals in Russian. Since the quinquennial issue for 1961-1965, the original title of the newspaper has been shown in parentheses after the translation into Russian. Titles of newspapers using non-Russian or non-Latin alphabets are given in Russian transcription.

Examples of Entries

District newspaper

Avangard. Izd. s l iiulia 1932 g. pgt. Klimovo. 3 raza v ned. 42 cm. 4 p. 2000 ekz. 2 k.

1961 No. 1 (2901) – 155 (3055)
1962 No. 1 (3056) – 50 (3105) (1 ianv. – 25 apr.)
1965 No. 1 (3106) – 116 (3221) (3 apr. – 30 dek.)

Pereryv v izd.: 26 apr. 1962 – 2 apr. 1965. Nazv.: po No. 50 (25 apr.) 1962 "Kolkhoznyi put' ".

Journal

Aziia i Afrika segodnia. Ezhemes. nauch. i obshchestv.-polit. zhurn. In-ta narodov Azii i In-ta Afriki Akad. nauk SSSR. Izd. s iiulia 1957. M., "Nauka". Reziume na angl. iaz.

1961-1965. TS. 30 k.
Nazv.: po No. 2 1961 "Sovremennyi Vostok".

Bulletin

Biulleten' TSentral'nogo nauchno-issledovatel'skogo instituta informatsii i tekhniko-ekonomicheskikh issledovanii chernoi metallurgii. Izd. s 1944. 2 raza v mes. M.

1961. 5000-5200 ekz.; 1962. 5000-5125 ekz.; 1963. 5000-5150 ekz.; 1964. 4300-5000 ekz.; 1965. 4050-4350 ekz. TS. 50 k.
Nazv.: po No. 9 1963 "Biulleten' TSentr. in-ta informatsii chernoi metallurgii". Izd-vo: po No. 7 1961 Metallurgizdat.

Serial Publication of the "Transactions" Type

Uchenye zapiski (Tuvin. nauch.-issled. in-t iazyka, literatury i istorii). Kyzyl.

Vyp. 9. 1961. 3000 ekz. 90 k.; vyp. 10. 1963. 1000 ekz. 90 k.; vyp. 11. 1964. 1500 ekz. 1 r.
Vyp. 1 — 1953; vyp. 8 — 1960.

Over the years, the form of the bibliographic description has changed. In 1933-1939, titles of publications were given in the language of the original. In 1933-1937 and 1946-1948, entries were put under corporate body. In 1933-1937, information was entered in abbreviated form using Roman numerals: I. year of publication; II. frequency; III. number of type pages; IV. size in centimeters; V. number of copies; VI. price.

Arrangement of Material. Auxiliary Apparatus

Within the three editions of the *Annals of Serial Publications of the USSR,* the structure, arrangement of material, and auxiliary indexes are different.

Annals of Serial Publications of the USSR (Complete Lists)

In 1933-1939 and 1946-1949, the list was published annually; since 1950, quinquennially. The quinquennial issue is published in two separately issued parts: *Journals, Transactions, Bulletins* and *Newspapers.*
Entries for journals, transactions, and bulletins are arranged systematically on the basis of the classification scheme used in the national bibliographies. Within the divisions of the scheme, material is grouped by type of publication: "Journals," "Transactions and Collections," "Bulletins and Informational Publications." It is then arranged alphabetically by title within these groupings, regardless of the language of text.
Newspaper entries are arranged according to the administrative territorial divisions of the USSR. All-union periodicals are cited in a special section at the beginning of the quinquennial edition.
Within the newspaper listing of any given republic, entries for those newspapers covering the entire republic are given first. Similarly, regional and territorial newspapers are first within their grouping, followed by city and district newspapers.
Entries for city and district newspapers are arranged alphabetically by the names of the cities and districts. Entries for newspapers serving districts whose boundaries do not coincide with administrative ones, such as newspapers of various railroads, river and steamship lines, and military districts, are listed in a special section.

The arrangement of material varies in the annual editions for 1933-1939 and 1946-1949 but has been stable since 1950. In the annuals for 1933-1934, arrangement is based on type of publication and language as follows: A. Journals in Russian; B. Transactions, Contributions, Collections, and Proceedings of Scientific Societies in Russian; C. Bulletins in Russian; D. Journals, Transactions, and Bulletins in Other Languages; E. Newspapers in Russian; F. Newspapers in Other Languages. Within these groupings, arrangement is alphabetical.

In 1935-1937, the arrangement of material is first by language and then by type of publication: A. Journals, Transactions, and Bulletins in Russian; B. Journals, Transactions, and Bulletins in Other Languages; C. Newspapers in Russian; D. Newspapers in Other Languages. Within these divisions, arrangement is alphabetical by title.

The annual for 1938 came out in two parts. In the first part, entitled *Journals*, material is arranged by language and then alphabetically by title; in the second part, *Newspapers*, material is arranged by area. Under the headings "District Newspapers" and "City Newspapers," entries are arranged alphabetically by title.

In Part I, *Journals*, of the annual for 1939, materials are arranged systematically: in each section, Russian journals are given first, followed by journals in other languages listed alphabetically by language. In Part II, *Newspapers*, material is arranged on an area basis: entries of city and district newspapers are given alphabetically by name of city or district within the regional heading; and entries for newspapers which serve districts whose boundaries do not coincide with the administrative ones, such as the newspapers of railroads, river and steamship lines, etc., are placed in a special section.

In the annals for 1946-1949, entries for journals, transactions, and bulletins are arranged in systematic order. Non-Russian publications are entered in Russian translation in each section in the general alphabet along with Russian publications. Entries for newspapers are arranged by area.

Each part of the *Annals of Serial Publications of the USSR* (Complete Lists) has its own set of indexes. Part I., *Journals, Transactions, Bulletins,* has the following indexes: Alphabetical Index of Journals; Alphabetical Index of Journals in the Languages of the Peoples of the USSR (except Russian) and in Foreign Languages; Index of Publishing Institutions and Organizations; List of Abbreviations or Acronyms of Publishing Organizations and their Full Names; Index of Journals by Place of Publication; List of Places of Publication of Journals by Republics; Journals of International Organizations.

Part II, *Newspapers,* has the following indexes: Classified Index of Newspapers on Special Topics and for Certain Groups of Readers; Alphabetical Index of Newspapers (in all Languages); Alphabetical Index of Newspapers in Languages of the Peoples of the USSR (except Russian) and in Foreign Languages; Index of Places of Publication.

Chronological List of Auxiliary Indexes
to Issues of the Complete Lists

Years	Types of Indexes
1933 (1st half-year)	Index of places of publication of journals and newspapers.
1933 (2nd half-year) 1934 (1st half-year)	Index of places of publication of journals and newspapers; Classified index of journals; Classified index of newspapers.
1934 (2nd half-year) 1935 (1st half-year) 1935 (2nd half-year) 1936 (1st half-year)	Index of places of publication of journals and newspapers; Classified index of journals and newspapers.
1936 (2nd half-year) 1937 (1st half-year)	Index of places of publication of journals and newspapers; Classified index of journals.
1937 (2nd half-year)- 1938 To Part I *Journals*	Index of places of publication of journals, transactions, bulletins (except of Moscow and of Leningrad); Index of corporate authors; Classified index of journals, transactions, bulletins.
To Part II *Newspapers*	Alphabetical index of newspapers in Russian; Alphabetical index of newspapers in other languages.
1939 To Part I *Journals*	Alphabetical index of journals in Russian; Alphabetical index of journals in other languages; Index of organizations, institutions, enterprises; Index of publishers; Index of places of publication (except Moscow and Leningrad); Index of editors.
To Part II *Newspapers*	Classified index of newspapers issued on special topics and for certain groups of readers; Alphabetical index of newspapers in Russian; Alphabetical index of newspapers in other languages.
1946, 1947, 1948, 1949 To Part I *Journals, Transactions and Bulletins*	Alphabetical index of journals in Russian; Alphabetical index of journals in languages of the peoples of the USSR (except Russian);

(Table continues on page 102)

Years	Types of Indexes
To Part II *Newspapers*	Alphabetical index of journals in foreign languages; Index of organizations, institutions and enterprises; Index of places of publication (except Moscow). Classified index of newspapers issued on special topics and for certain groups of readers; Alphabetical index of newspapers in Russian; Alphabetical index of newspapers in languages of the peoples of the USSR (except Russian); Alphabetical index of newspapers in foreign languages.
1950-1954 (quinquennial issue) To Part I *Journals, Transactions, and Bulletins*	Alphabetical index of publications in Russian; Alphabetical index of publications in other languages; Index of organizations and institutions; Index of places of publication.
To Part II *Newspapers*	Classified index of newspapers by special topic and for certain groups of readers; Alphabetical index of newspapers in Russian; Alphabetical index of newspapers in other languages.
1955-1960 (six year issue) To Part I *Journals, Transactions, and Bulletins*	Alphabetical index of journals; Alphabetical index of journals in languages of the peoples of the USSR (except Russian) and in foreign languages; Index of publishing institutions and organizations; List of acronyms of publishing organizations with their full names; Index of journals by place of publication; List of places of publication of journals by republic; journals of international organizations.
To Part II *Newspapers*	Classified index of newspapers in special fields and for certain groups of readers; Alphabetical index of newspapers (in all languages); Alphabetical index of newspapers in the languages of the peoples of the USSR (except Russian) and in foreign languages; Index of places of publication.

Annals of Serial Publications of the USSR. New, Renamed, and Ceased Journals and Newspapers

This annals has been issued since 1951. It covers publications since 1950. Each issue consists of two parts: *Journals* and *Newspapers*. Arrangement of material in both parts is alphabetical by title, although, in the part for newspapers covering material from 1 January 1961 to 1 April 1963, arrangement is by area.

Each part has a classified index, an alphabetical index for publications in the languages of the peoples of the USSR (except Russian), and an index of places of publication. In the part devoted to journals, there is also an index of publishing institutions and organizations. The issues covering 1 January 1950 to 1 April 1962 contain no alphabetical index of publications in the languages of the peoples of the USSR.

Annals of Serial Publications of the USSR. Transactions, Contributions, Collections, and Other Serials

This annals has been issued since 1952 and has recorded material since 1950. Material is arranged systematically and within each division by type of publication. For example, transactions and collections are given first, followed by bulletins and informational publications. The issue for 1950-1951 does not group by type of publication within the divisions. In the annals for 1953 and 1955-1958, there is a special section devoted to instructional, informational, and methodological materials.

This annals has the following indexes: an Alphabetical Index of Publications (in all languages), which had been until 1955 the Alphabetical Index of Publications in Russian; an Alphabetical Index of Publications in the Languages of the Peoples of the USSR (except Russian) and in Foreign Languages; an Index of Publishing Institutions and Organizations; an Index of Places of Publication (alphabetical); and, since 1961, a List of Places of Publication by Republic.

List of Numbers Issued

Spisok periodicheskikh izdanii RSFSR v 1933 g. (na1 iiulia). [List of Serial Publications of the RSFSR in 1933 (as of July 1)] M., 1933. 480 p.

Letopis' periodicheskikh izdanii SSSR [Annals of Serial Publications of the USSR] 1934-1937.

1934	M., 1934. 636 p.
1935	M., 1935. 1016 p.
1936	M., 1937. 302 p.
1937	M., 1939. 404 p.

Ezhegodnik periodicheskikh izdanii SSSR [Annual of Serial Publications of the USSR] 1938-1939.

> 1938
> > Part I M., 1939. 298 p.
> > Part II M., 1939. 312 p.
> 1939
> > Part I M., 1940. 288 col.
> > Part II M., 1940. 392 col.

Letopis' periodicheskikh izdanii SSSR [Annals of Serial Publications] 1946-1960.

> 1946 M., 1947. 616 col.
> 1947 M., 1948. 648 col.
> 1948 M., 1949. 726 col.
> 1949 M., 1950. 700 col.
> 1950-1954 M., 1955. 502 p.
> 1955-1960
> > Part I M., 1963. 1026 p.
> > Part II M., 1962. 873 p.

Letopis' periodicheskikh izdanii SSSR. Novye, pereimenovannye i prekrativ-shiesia zhurnaly i gazety [Annals of Serial Publications of the USSR. New, Renamed, and Ceased Journals and Newspapers] 1950-1965.

> From 1 January 1950 to 1 April 1951. M., 1951. 23 p.
> From 1 January 1950 to 1 April 1952. M., 1952. 33 p.
> From 1 January 1950 to 1 April 1953. M., 1953. 64 p.
> From 1 January 1950 to 1 April 1954. M., 1954. 96 p.
> From 1 January 1955 to 1 April 1956. M., 1956. 28 p.
> From 1 January 1955 to 1 April 1957. M., 1957. 96 p.
> From 1 January 1955 to 1 April 1958. M., 1958. 128 p.
> From 1 January 1955 to 1 April 1959. M., 1959. 164 p.
> From 1 April 1959 to 1 April 1960. M., 1960. 65 p.
> From 1 January 1961 to 1 April 1962. M., 1962. 33 p.
> From 1 January 1961 to 1 April 1963. M., 1963. 198 p.
> From 1 April 1963 to 1 April 1964. M., 1964. 51 p.
> From 1 April 1963 to 1 April 1965. M., 1965. 72 p.

Letopis' periodicheskikh izdanii SSSR. Trudy, uchenye zapiski, sborniki i drugie prodolzhaiushchiesia izdaniia [Annals of Serial Publications of the USSR. Transactions, Contributions, Collections, and Other Serials] 1950-1964.

> From 1 January 1950 to 31 December 1951. M., 1952. 172 col.
> From 1 January to 31 December 1952. M., 1953. 70 p.
> 1953 M., 1954. 77 p.
> 1955 M., 1956. 100 p.
> 1956 M., 1957. 128 p.

1957	M., 1958. 179 p.
1958	M., 1960. 220 p.
1959	annual was not published[9]
1961	M., 1963. 258 p.
1962	M., 1964. 270 p.
1963	M., 1964. 229 p.
1964	M., 1965. 220 p.

Information about journals and newspapers for 1908-1922 and 1924-1925 can be found in *Book Annals* for those years. In 1939-1944, information about new, renamed, and discontinued journals and newspapers was also published in *Book Annals.*

In 1926, every quarterly issue of *Journal Annals*[10] contained a special section entitled "List of Periodical Publications Issued in 1926 (Journals, Newspapers, Bulletins, and Publishers and Book Trade Catalogs)."

Information about journals, serial publications of the "transactions" type, and bulletins printed in the USSR up to 1950 can be found in the cumulative bibliographic index *Periodical Press of the USSR. 1917-1949,*[11] which was released by the Book Chamber publishing house in the years 1955-1963 in nine volumes (ten issues), each covering a subject area, and with a volume of cumulative indexes to the set.

The first volume consists of two issues and contains entries for journals, transactions, and bulletins concerned with social, political, and economic questions. Subsequent volumes are concerned with the natural sciences and mathematics; technology and industry; transportation, communications and municipal affairs; agriculture; cultural and educational activities; public health, medicine, physical culture, and sports; linguistics, literary history and criticism, belles-lettres, and art; and publishing, library, and bibliographic affairs.

Each bibliographic entry gives detailed information about the periodical. The arrangement is classified by subject. The following indexes are in each volume: Alphabetical Index of Journals; Index of Journals in the Languages of the Peoples of the USSR (except Russian); Index of Journals by Place of Publication; and Index of Publishing Institutions and Organizations. The final volume contains cumulative indexes for the entire set.

At the present time, the bibliographic reference guide *Newspapers of the USSR. 1917-1960*[12] is being compiled by the All-Union Book Chamber, the Lenin State Library of the USSR, and the Saltykov-Shchedrin State Public Library. The first volume, containing descriptions of newspapers published in Moscow, Leningrad, and the capitals of the union republics, is ready for publication. Work is proceeding on the preparation of other volumes which will contain entries for newspapers published in other cities and localities in the Soviet Union.[13]

The following indexes of a general nature precede the bibliographic work of the Book Chamber on Soviet periodical publications: N. M. Lisovskii, *Bibliografiia russkoi periodicheskoi pechati, 1703-1900 gg.* [A Bibliography of the Russian Periodical Press, 1703-1900] Petrograd, 1915; L. N. Beliaeva, M. K. Zinov'eva, and M. M. Nikiforov, *Bibliografiia periodicheskikh izdanii*

Rossii, 1901-1916 [Bibliography of Russian Periodicals, 1901-1916] Vol. 1-4. Leningrad, 1958-1961. (Saltykov-Shchedrin State Public Library). These works and those of the All-Union Book Chamber provide a total view of serials publishing in Russia and the Soviet Union from 1703 to the present time.

Footnotes

[1] *Annals of Serial Publications of the USSR. 1955-1960,* an an exception to the rule, recorded periodical and continuing publications for a six year period.

[2] Since 1967, the subtitle has been *Novye, pereimenovannye i prekrashchennye izdaniem zhurnaly i gazety.*

[3] This annual issue has the subtitle *Trudy, uchenye zapiski, sborniki i drugie prodolzhaiushchiesia izdaniia.*

[4] Editor's note: The issue for 1971-1975 shows a title change to *Letopis' periodicheskikh i prodolzhaiushchikhsia izdanii* [Annals of Periodical and Continuing Publications].

[5] The first of April is chosen as the final date of the period because the origin of new periodicals and newspapers and the discontinuance of others, as well as name changes, usually take place in the first quarter of the year.

[6] These publications have the characteristics of both journals and books (authors' monographs and collections of articles); therefore, they are recorded in both the *Annals of Serial Publications of the USSR* and *Book Annals.*

[7] In 1933, it was published under the title *Spisok periodicheskikh izdanii RSFSR v 1933 g. (na 1 iulia)* [A List of Serial Publications of the RSFSR in 1933 (as of July 1)] ; in 1939-1940 (for 1938-1939), under *Ezhegodnik periodicheskikh izdanii SSSR* [Annual of Serial Publications of the USSR]. During 1940-1945, the publication was not issued.

[8] In *Annals of Serial Publications of the USSR. 1955-1960* (Part II. Newspapers), the first and last numbers and dates of issuance of the newspapers are given.

[9] Information for this year can be found in the cumulation for 1955-1960.

[10] *Zhurnal'naia letopis'.*

[11] *Periodicheskaia pechat' SSSR. 1917-1949.*

[12] *Gazety SSSR. 1917-1960.*

[13] Editor's note: Two volumes have been published: *Gazety SSSR. 1917-1960.* Vol. 1. *Gazety Moskvy, Leningrada i stolits soiuznykh respublik* (Moskva: Kniga, 1970) and Vol. 2. *Kraevye, gubernskie, oblastnye, okruzhnye, uezdnye, raionnye, gorodskie, transportnye, voennye i drugie gazety* (Moskva: Kniga, 1976). The latter, 566 pages long, covers only letters A-I. Apparently, additional volumes are forthcoming.

■ ■ ■

MUSIC ANNALS
(Notnaia letopis')

Music Annals, a quarterly, has been published since 1931.[1] It records separately published musical works and stage music, collections of musical works and collections of folklore music, music literature for educational purposes, and music for the blind. It also lists books of music: musical compositions and dramatizations, musical plays, and other publications in which a literary text is combined with a musical one. Since 1939, it has also included musical works published in journals and newspapers. Since 1940, works in books have been listed.

Since 1954, each issue of the annals has contained entries for materials of the previous quarter. For example, Issue No. 1 includes materials received by the Book Chamber in October through December of the previous year.

Until 1934, *Music Annals* covered music published in the RSFSR. In the years 1932-1942 and 1945, literature about music was included, and in 1939-1940, the literary texts of songs. For the period 1941-1942, in addition to the above, photo-illustrations, concert programs, and librettos were included.

Bibliographic Description

Entries for music publications cite the surname of the composer who created or arranged the work, title of the work, subtitle, place of publication, publisher, year of publication, number of pages or leaves, size, number of copies printed, and price. If the title and subtitle do not adequately describe the theme and nature of the work, an annotation is supplied. Works in collections are analyzed. Entries are in Russian, but the original language of the text is indicated if it is not Russian.

Musical works are entered under the surname of the composer. Hymns, folk songs, revolutionary songs, and other works whose authors are not known and cannot be established are entered under title. The same treatment is given to musical compositions with four or more authors, as in readers and textbooks, and to collections of works of various composers in which the compiler shown on the title page does not appear to be, at the same time, the author of the arrangements of the works in the collection. The entries in the annals have not changed significantly in form and content over the years.

Examples of Entries

Grig, E. Dva simfonicheskikh tantsa. [Soch. 64, NoNo 2 i 3]. Instrumentovka dlia dukhovogo orkestra G. Sal'nikova. Partitura i golosa [25 orkestr. partii]. M., "Muzyka", 1966. 59 s. partit., 98 s. partii razd. pag. 22 cm. (Repertuar dukhovogo orkestra). 1,940 ekz. 1 r. 2 k. V papke.

Pesennik. Popul. pesni sovetskikh kompozitorov. [66 pesen. Khory, golos solo. Kiev, "Mistetstvo", 1966]. 261 s. 14 cm. 30,000 ekz. 1 r. V per. – V vyp. dan. sost.: N. M. Rybal'chenko. – Tekst paral. na ukr. i rus. iaz.

Arrangement of the Material

Music publications are first arranged by type of music: vocal, instrumental, vocal symphonic, and stage music. Within these categories, they are arranged by performance medium, such as chorus, orchestra, and so forth, and by genre of music, such as oratorio, opera, and so forth. Folklore music, collected works of composers, collections of works intended for various performance media, and instructional literature in music history and theory are put in separate sections.

Since 1946, entries of music for the blind and, since 1958, entries of music from books, magazines, periodical collections, and newspapers have been placed in a special section and arranged alphabetically with no indication of type and genre of music or performance medium. Since 1957, music for dances and plays, including descriptions of movement, have been set apart. Educational and instructional music literature is set apart within the sections of vocal and instrumental music.

Literature about music is found in every fourth number of the annals for 1932-1938; in a special part of each number for 1939-1941 and 1945; and in the final combined number for 1942.

Entries are arranged in classified order.

Basic Divisions of the Classification for Music
I.   Folklore music

II.   Vocal music
    A.   Choruses without instrumental accompaniment
    B.   Choruses with instrumental accompaniment
    C.   Vocal ensembles
    D.   Vocal solos

E. Collections of works for chorus, ensemble, and solo voice with and without accompaniment
F. Educational music literature for singing. Exercises in vocalization
G. Collections of works for children's singing. School choruses. Songs for children.

III. Instrumental music
A. Works for orchestra
B. Works for instrumental ensemble
C. Works for instrumental solos
D. Collections of works for various orchestras, instrumental ensembles, and solo instruments

IV. Mixed or combined collections of vocal and instrumental works

V. Vocal symphonic music. Stage music
A. Oratorio, symphony-cantata, and other vocal-symphonic works
B. Opera and musical drama
C. Operettas and musical comedy
D. Ballet and choreographic productions
E. Music for plays, films, and literary and radio programs
F. Children's operas, dramatizations and choreographic performances. Music for school performances and radio productions

VI. Collected works

VII. Educational music literature on music history and theory. Solfeggio and dictations. Musical works in musicological publications and methodological works

Indexes and Other Aids

In every quarterly issue of *Music Annals,* as a rule, the following indexes and bibliography are found: since 1938, a name index and list of publications used in compiling the annals and, since 1952, a title index of collections of music. The name index encompasses composers, editors, authors of musical arrangements and adaptations, compilers of musical collections, poets, and others, as well as persons to whom works are dedicated (personalia). The title index lists collections by various authors and folk songs, as well as different school and self-instruction manuals.

Since 1949, there have been annual cumulated indexes in every fourth issue. The fourth issue does not have its own indexes since this information is included in the annual cumulation. Since 1958, the annual "Index of Titles and First Words of Texts of Vocal Works" has been published as a separate edition. This index includes titles of vocal works in the languages of the peoples of the USSR and foreign languages, which are translated into Russian and arranged by language, and the first words of texts of vocal works in Russian. In 1955-1957, this index was published in No. 4 of the annals.

Since 1953, Issue No. 1 has presented the classification scheme of music publications and, since 1961, a foreword entitled "From the Editor."

The structure of the indexes has varied from time to time. In the years 1931-1937, there were no indexes. In some years, there were separate name indexes for various groups of persons, such as composers, performers, adapters, and so forth. In other years, all names were combined in a single alphabet.

Supplementary indexes were provided in certain years: in 1938, a "Thematic Index to the Section 'Songs of the Peoples of the USSR' " and an "Index of National Music and Songs of the Peoples of the USSR"; in 1939 and 1940, a "Thematic Index of Folk Songs, Songs of Soviet Composers and Poets and of Contemporary Foreign Songs" and an "Index of Musical Ensembles and Theaters" (entitled "Index of Ensembles" in 1940); and, in 1941, a "Thematic Index to Vocal Works, Literary Texts of Songs and Folk Songs." Issue No. 1 for 1941, published in 1943, contains the music classification for the *Annals of Music Literature of the Great Patriotic War.*

List of Numbers Issued

Notnaia letopis' [Music Annals] 1931-1938.

1931 Nos. 1/2, 3/4	The "Rules for Cataloging Musical Works", compiled by the Institute of Library Science of the Lenin Library, are found at the end of No. 1/2.
1932 Nos. 1, 2, 3/4	A List of Books and Articles about Music for 1932 is included in No. 3/4.
1933 Nos. 1/2, 3, 4	At the end of No. 4 is a List of Books and Articles about Music Listed in *Book Annals* and *Journal Annals* for 1933.
1934 Nos. 1/2, 3, 4	In No. 1/2, there is an appendix: Statistics of Music Production in the RSFSR for 1931-1933 (according to *Music Annals*) based on the divisions of the classification used in *Music Annals.* At the end of No. 4: List of Books and Articles about Music Listed in *Book Annals* and *Journal Annals* for 1934.
1935 Nos. 1, 2, 3, 4	At the end of No. 4: List of Books and Articles about Music Listed in *Book Annals* and *Journal Annals* for 1935 and a statistical table "Distribution of Music Production in the USSR for 1934-1935 by Performing Groups and Purpose."

1936 Nos. 1, 2, 3, 4	At the end of No. 4: List of Books and Articles about Music Listed in *Book Annals, Journal Annals,* and *Newspaper Annals* for 1936 and a statistical table "Distribution of Music Production in the USSR for 1936 by Performing Groups and Purpose."
1937 Nos. 1, 2, 3, 4	At the end of No. 4: Index of Books and Articles about Music LIsted in *Book Annals, Journal Annals,* and *Newspaper Annals* for 1937.
1938 Nos. 1, 2, 3, 4	At the end of No. 4: Index of Books and Articles about Music and Texts of Songs Listed in *Book Annals, Annals of Journal Articles,* and *Annals of Newspaper Articles* for 1938.

Bibliografiia muzykal'noi literatury [Bibliography of Music Literature] 1939-1940.

1939 Nos. 1, 2, 3, 4	Each number has two parts: 1. Literature about Music; and 2. Music and Literary Texts of Songs.
1940 Nos. 1, 2, 3, 4	Each number has two parts: 1. Literature about Music; and 2. Music and Literary Texts of Songs.

Letopis' muzykal'noi Literatury [Annals of Music Literature] 1941.

1941 Jan-June. M., 1951.	Publications issued in the second half of 1941 but not accounted for in *Annals of Music Literature of the Great Patriotic War of the Soviet People* (see below) are also listed.

Letopis' muzykal'noi literatury Velikoi Otechestvennoi voiny sovetskogo naroda [Annals of Music Literature of the Great Patriotic War of the Soviet People] 1941.

1941 No. 1 (July-Sept) No. 2 (Oct-Dec) M., 1943.	Each number has two parts: 1. Literature about Music; and 2. Music and Literary Texts of Songs.

Letopis' muzykal'noi literatury Velikoi Otechestvennoi voiny [Annals of Music Literature of the Great Patriotic War] 1942.

1942 No. 1/2 (Jan-Dec)	In No. 1/2: Music and Literary Music Materials.
No. 3/4 (Jan-Dec) M., 1945.	In No. 3/4: Materials from Journals and Newspapers about Music.

Letopis' muzykal'noi literatury [Annals of Music Literature] 1943-1966.

1943 No. 1/4 (Jan-Dec)
M., 1948. 28 p.

1944 No. 1/4 (Jan-Dec)
M., 1947. 48 p.

1945 Nos. 1, 2, 3/4   Each number has two parts: 1. Literature about Music; and 2. Music and Literary Texts of Songs.

1946-
1966 Nos. 1, 2, 3, 4
(each year).

Notnaia letopis' [Music Annals] 1967-

1967 Nos. 1, 2, 3, 4

Information about music published before 1923 can be found in *Book Annals.* Music was not recorded in the organs of national bibliography for the period 1924-1930. Music publications with predominantly literary texts, however, were always recorded in *Book Annals* as books and are therefore the exception.

Information on literature about music for the years when *Music Annals* was either incomplete or not published at all can be found in the section "Art" of *Book Annals, Annals of Journal Articles, Annals of Newspaper Articles,* and *Book Annual of the USSR* where such literature was recorded regularly. Reviews of music publications and works on questions in music have been included in *Annals of Reviews* since 1934.

Footnotes

[1] In 1931-1938, it was published under the title *Notnaia letopis',* which changed in 1939-1940 to *Bibliografiia muzykal'noi literatury* [Bibliography of Music Literature]. The January through June 1941 issues (not published until 1951) appeared under the name *Letopis' muzykal'noi literatury* [Annals of Music Literature] ; the July through December 1941 issues were published in 1943 under the title *Letopis' muzykal'noi literatury Velikoi Otechestvennoi voiny sovetskogo naroda* [Annals of Music Literature of the Great Patriotic War of the Soviet People] ; for the year 1942 (published in 1945), it was

called *Letopis' muzykal'noi literatury Velikoi Otechestvennoi voiny* [Annals of Music Literature of the Great Patriotic War]. For 1943-1966, it was *Letopis' muzykal'noi literatury*; and, since 1967, it has been called *Notnaia letopis'*.

■ ■ ■

ANNALS OF PICTORIAL ART PUBLICATIONS
(Letopis' pechatnykh proizvedenii izobrazitel'nogo iskusstva)

Published quarterly since 1934,[1] this annals records pictorial art works appearing in the Soviet Union, regardless of the method of reproduction: original prints (lithograph, engraving); reproductions of original pictorial works and photographs; and photographs printed on sensitized paper.

Only those prints, reproductions, and photographs which are published as separate leaves or in albums and have a certain number of copies per edition are recorded.

Various types of publications in which illustration plays an important part and in which there is no text, or the text only explains or supplements the illustrations, are included. These are such works as political posters; teaching methods posters, some containing tables, schemes, and diagrams; instructional posters on, for example, safety techniques; informational posters and ones aimed at publicity; posters for children; inexpensive popular prints; reproductions of paintings, drawings, engravings, and sculptures; plates, artistic postcards and photographic postcards; artistic albums and photo albums; and applied graphics, such as picture books for children, artistically decorated tabular calendars, and wall calendars.

Sheets and albums containing only pictures, such as reproductions and plates, are recorded comprehensively. Publications containing illustrations combined with literary text are recorded selectively, the predominance of illustrative matter over the text being the basic criterion of selection. Publications created by using stencils on fabric or film are not recorded, nor are publications issued without imprint date.

Over the years, the types of material covered, as well as the time spans of these materials, have varied. In 1934-1940, along with pictorial art works, publications about pictorial art, such as books, magazine articles, and eventually newspaper articles, were included. During 1939-1940, book illustrations were also recorded.

In the prewar period, the annual set of the annals covered materials received by the Book Chamber during the calendar year. The annals for 1941 listed only materials for the first half of the year, which is considered to be in the prewar period. Materials for the second half of 1941 were listed in the annals for 1942; materials for 1942, in the annals for 1943; while the annals for 1944 recorded materials for both 1943 (in No. 1/2) and 1944 (in No. 3/4).

From 1945 to 1953, the record covered materials of the current calendar year. Since 1954, each quarterly issue of the annals includes entries for publications of the preceding quarter. The first issue for the current year records materials received in the fourth quarter of the previous year.

Bibliographic Description

Entries for printed works of pictorial art consist of the name of the artist or photographer, author of the text, name of the work, place of publication, publisher, year of publication, size, number of copies printed, and price. Unclear titles are briefly explained. The subtitle records the location of place of exposition of the original work. For example, GTG stands for Gosudarstvennaia Tret'iakovskaia galereia. Finally, information about the method of reproduction—lithography, offset, facsimile or autotype—is given.

Entries for publications with non-Russian text are given in Russian with indication of the language of publication.

Posters, visual aids, popular prints, albums (except those of the works of one author), and applied graphics are entered under title. If there is no title, a part of the text best describing the theme or character of the publication is used. Portraits are entered under the surname of the person depicted. Reproductions and plates are entered under the surname of the artist.

The content of albums and serial sets of postcards and posters is, as a rule, revealed in detail in each entry.

In the entry for "Okna TASS"[2] in the annals for 1942 and 1943, the literary text of "Okna" is preserved in full.

Bibliographic description in the annals has not changed much during its years of publication.

Examples of Entries

Poster

Vyshe, dal'she, bystree. [Ko Dniu Vozdushnogo Flota SSSR]. Khudozh. V. Viktorov. M., "Sov. khudozhnik", 1965. 108x54 cm. 125,000 ekz. 10 k. – TSv. ofset.

Reproduction

Serov, V. Zarosshii prud. (GTG). M., "Pravda", 1965. 60x82 cm. 16,000 ekz. 30 k. – TSv. avtotipiia.

Plate

Zvontsov, V. M. V. Polovod'e. L., Kombinat grafich. rabot LOKhF RSFSR, 1966. 30x31 cm. 200 ekz. 3 r. – Ofort.

Portrait

Rustaveli Shota. Khudozh. E. Rakuzin. M., "Sov. khudozhnik", 1966.
60x47 cm. 10,000 ekz. 13 k. — Shtrikh. tsinkogr.

Album

Tantsuet Turkmenistan. Gos. ansambl' narodnogo tantsa Turkm. SSR.
[Fotoal'bom. Avt. teksta i foto S. Ataev. Stikhi P. Ionova]. Ashkhabad,
"Turkmenistan", 1965. 112 s. ill. i teksta. 22 cm. 2,000 ekz. 95 k. V per. —
Avtotipiia.

Arrangement of Material

Material in the annals is arranged by type of material: posters, portraits,
reproductions, etc. Within these divisions, the arrangement varies, depending
on the special nature of each type of material. In the largest division, "Posters,"
material is first arranged by special purpose or aim and then systematically.
The division "Portraits" includes publications without necessarily indicating
whether they are reproductions, plates, or photographs. Materials are grouped
by the activities of the persons depicted. The division "Postcards" has topical
subdivisions. In the division "Albums," a systematic arrangement is used. In
the divisions "Reproductions" and "Plates," entries are alphabetized by the
surnames of the artists.

The scheme of classification has changed, depending mainly on the
nature of the material recorded. By 1955, the first level of the classification
was basically stabilized.

Literature on art for 1934-1938 is found in every fourth number of the
annals, for 1939-1940, in a separate part of each number. Entries for the
literature on art are arranged systematically.

Basic Divisions of the Classification Scheme for
Pictorial Art Publications

I.   Posters
 A.   Political posters.[3] Satirical posters
 B.   Instructional and educational posters. Visual aids. Safety
       posters
 C.   Informational and publicity posters
 D.   Posters for children
 E.   Popular prints

II. Portraits

III. Reproductions

IV. Plates

V.   Postcards

VI.   Albums[3]

VII.   Applied graphics
Picture books for children
Artistically decorated calendars
Tabular calendars
Wall calendars

Indexes and Other Aids

Since 1934, the annals has had name indexes of artists and authors of texts and, since 1939, an index of persons to whom works are dedicated. The index of artists includes names of photographers also. In 1942-1945, the index of photographers was given separately.

As a rule, indexes appear in every issue of the annals. The annals for 1937, 1938, and 1940 have only annual indexes, which are found in the fourth number of each year. Since 1949, along with the three quarterly indexes, there has been an annual cumulated name index in the fourth number of each year.

In the first issue of the annals each year, the full text of the classification for pictorial art publications is given, as is a foreword, "From the Editor," which briefly describes the annals.

The system of indexes has not changed significantly over the years, but there have been years for which a few indexes are lacking.

In 1940, there was no index of artists; in 1937, 1938, and 1940, there were no indexes of authors of literary texts; and in the fourth number of 1936, there were no indexes.

Because book illustrations, literature about pictorial art, and other materials were listed in the annals, there were corresponding indexes. Thus, in every issue for 1939-1940, indexes of authors of books and articles, of persons to whom works are dedicated in the section "Literature of Pictorial Art," and of authors and titles of illustrated works for the section "Book Illustrations," were included. In Issue No. 4 of 1943, there was a cumulative index of numbers of "The Windows TASS" [Okna TASS] for 1941 and 1942; in 1944, there was an index of posters with texts in the languages of the Soviet peoples and in foreign languages; and in 1944-1945, there was an index of authors of musical texts and several other indexes.

List of Numbers Issued

Izo letopis' [Pictorial Annals] 1934-1938.

1934 Nos. 1, 2, 3, 4	At the end of No. 4: "List of Books and Articles of Pictorial Art Recorded in *Book Annals* and *Journal Annals* for 1934."
1935 Nos. 1, 2, 3, 4	At the end of No. 4: "List of Books and Articles of Pictorial Art Recorded in *Book Annals* and *Journal Annals* for 1935" and a statistical table, "Pictorial Art Production for 1934 and 1935."
1936- Nos. 1, 2, 3, 4 1938 (each year)	At the end of No. 4: "List of Books and Articles of Pictorial Art Recorded in *Book Annals, Journal Annals,* and *Newspaper Annals* for the Year. . . ."

Bibliografiia izobrazitel'nogo izkusstva [Bibliography of Pictorial Art] 1939-1940.

| 1939 Nos. 1, 2, 3, 4 | Each number has two parts: 1. Literature of Pictorial Art; and 2. Works of Pictorial Art. |
| 1940 Nos. 1, 2, 3, 4 | Each number has three parts: 1. Literature of Pictorial Art; 2. Works of Pictorial Art; and 3. Art Exhibitions Opened in the . . . Quarter of 1940. |

Letopis' izobrazitel'nogo iskusstva [Annals of Pictorial Art] 1941.

| 1941 No. 1/2 (Jan-June).
M., 1950. | Materials published in the first half of 1941 are listed in this issue. |

Letopis' izobrazitel'nogo iskusstva Velikoi Otechestvennoi voiny [Annals of Pictorial Art of the Great Patriotic War] 1942-1944.

| 1942 Nos. 1/3, 4 | In No. 1/3: materials published in second half of 1941. In No. 4: "Windows TASS" 1941. |
| 1943 Nos. 1, 2/3, 4 | In Nos. 1, 2/3: materials published in 1942 except those issued in 1941 but recorded in No. 1/3, 1942. In No. 4: "Windows TASS" 1942 and index of the "Windows TASS" issues for 1941 and 1942. |

1944 Nos. 1/2, 3/4   In No. 1/2: materials published in 1943
except for those from 1941 and 1942 but
not recorded earlier. In No. 3/4, which came
out in 1948 under the title *Annals of Pictorial Art*: materials published in 1944
including those from 1941-1943 not recorded
earlier.

Letopis' izobrazitel'nogo iskusstva [Annals of Pictorial Art] 1945-1966.

1945 Nos. 1, 2, 3/4

1946- Nos. 1, 2, 3, 4
1966 (each year)

Letopis' pechatnykh proizvedenii izobrazitel'nogo iskusstva[4] [Annals of
Pictorial Art Publications] 1967-

1967 Nos. 1, 2, 3, 4

Until 1925, pictorial art publications were listed in *Book Annals.* For
1926-1933, these types of publications were not recorded in the organs of
national bibliography except for albums which are always recorded in *Book
Annals* as books.

Catalogs of art exhibitions are recorded in *Book Annals*, but in certain
years they were also listed in *Annals of Pictorial Art.*

Information concerning literature about pictorial art is included in the
annals only for the period 1934-1940. This information is always recorded in
Book Annals, Annals of Journal Articles, Annals of Newspaper Articles, and
the *Book Annual of the USSR* in the division "Arts" under the headings
"Sculpture. Painting. Drawing," and "Applied Art."

Reviews of pictorial art publications and works of an artistic nature
have been found in *Annals of Reviews* since 1934.

Footnotes

[1] In 1934-1938, it was entitled *Izo letopis'* [Pictorial Art Annals] ; in
1939-1940, *Bibliografiia izobrazitel'nogo iskusstva* [Bibliography of Pictorial
Art] ; in 1941 (issue No. 1/2 published in 1950), *Letopis' izobrazitel'nogo
iskusstva* [Annals of Pictorial Art] ; in 1942-1944 (No. 1/2), *Letopis' izobrazitel'nogo iskusstva Velikoi Otechestvennoi voiny* [Annals of Pictorial Art of
the Great Patriotic War] ; in 1944 (No. 3/4 published in 1948) and 1945-
1966, *Letopis' izobrazitel'nogo iskusstva* [Annals of Pictorial Art] ; and since
1967, *Letopis' pechatnykh proizvedenii izobrazitel'nogo iskusstva.*

[2] Editor's note: Soviet political posters published during World War II.

[3] Material in these subdivisions is classified according to the basic divisions of the classification used in the organs of national bibliography.

[4] Editor's note: In 1976, title changed to *Letopis' izoizdanii.*

■ ■ ■

CARTOGRAPHIC ANNALS
(Kartograficheskaia letopis')

This annals has been published since 1931,[1] comes out annually, and lists geographic and historical maps, astronomical charts, and atlases published in the USSR.[2]

In the years 1934-1940, books and articles about geodesy, cartography, and geography were also included. In 1939, maps found in books were recorded; in 1940, maps found in books, periodicals, and collections. Maps were not recorded for the periods 1941-1945 and 1947-1953, but these gaps were eliminated in 1953 and 1954 with the publication of *Cartographic Annals* for 1941-1950 and 1951-1953.

Bibliographic Description

Entries disclose the contents of maps in full. Maps are entered under their titles. Up to 1941 and in 1946, the name of the territory depicted on the map was put in the heading of the entry. After the title, the subheading explaining the content, purpose, or form of the map, and information about persons or bodies responsible for making the map are given. The periodicity, place of publication, publisher, date of publication, number of sheets, number of copies printed, and price are also indicated. Cartographic features, such as scale and information about natural and social phenomena, are represented on the map by conventional signs.

Entries for atlases include an enumeration of the maps in the atlases. Entries for maps and atlases not in the Russian language are given in Russian with an indication of the language of the text.

Example of Entry

1 : 4.000.000

Evropa. Fiz. ucheb. karta. Dlia sred. shkoly. G-960. Sostavlena
Nauch.-red. kartosost. chast'iu GUGK v 1964 g. Red. Kursakova I. V. M.,
GUGK, 1965. 4 1. mnogokras. 23,000 ekz. 43 k.

[Scale: 40 km. to 1 cm. Hydrography: on the seas the winter boundaries
of ice floes, warm and cold currents; navigable and shallow sections of
rivers; navigable canals; lakes (freshwater, saltwater, dry). Relief: con-
tour lines, layered coloration, and indication of heights and depths.
Scale of heights: nine gradations; depths: four gradations. Swamps.
Salt marshes. Sands. Volcanoes. Glaciers and continental ice. Deposits
of useful minerals.
Population points with division of population into four categories, and
with capitals of countries and the union republics of the USSR. Means
of transportation: railroads with signs for railroad tunnels and ferries;
roads. Boundaries: national and those of the union republics of the
USSR.]

This type of entry has remained much the same over the years. Entries
for literature about geodesy, cartography, and geography recorded in the
annals in 1934-1940 follow the rules of bibliographic description for books
and articles.

Arrangement of Material

The annals has two sections: "Maps" and "Atlases."
In the section "Maps," material is arranged by territory as follows:
world maps, maps of parts of the world, and maps of individual countries,
with those of the USSR first.
Within each of these sections, maps are grouped by content: political,
political-administrative, economic, general geographic, and physical. A
subsequent grouping of maps is done according to scale.
Historical maps are placed at the end of the "Maps" division and are
arranged chronologically by period. Historical maps of the territories of
the USSR are an exception. They are arranged chronologically, immediately
following other maps of the USSR.
Atlases are grouped into general reference atlases and teaching atlases.
In *Cartographic Annals* for 1931-1938 and 1946, entries for maps
are arranged by area as follows: 1) world maps and atlases, 2) oceans and
seas, 3) USSR, 4) Europe, 5) Asia, 6) America, 7) Africa, 8) Australia,
and 9) Arctic and Antarctica.
Entries for books and articles on geodesy, cartography, and geography
in the annals for 1934-1938 are found at the back of Issue No. 3/4 arranged
systematically. Basic divisions in the annals for 1934-1937 are: 1) geodesy,

2) geography. In the annals for 1938, they are: 1) geodesy and aerial photography, 2) cartography, and 3) geography.

In the annals for 1939 and 1940, material is arranged in two sections: "Literature of Cartography" and "Maps." In the 1939 annals, the first part consists of the divisions "Geodesy and Aerial Photography," "Cartography," and "Bibliography and Reference Books." The second part is divided into the sections "Separate Publications," "Maps Found in Books," and "Atlases, Visual Aids, Textbooks Containing Maps." In the 1940 annals, Part I consists of two basic sections: "Geodesy" and "Cartography." Part II also has two sections: "General Geographic Maps" and "Special Maps."

Indexes

Cartographic Annals has the following indexes: since 1939, a name and geographic index;[3] and since 1956, an index of titles of tourist maps.

In the annals for 1939 and 1940, there is also an index of organizations, institutions, and enterprises that participated in making the maps. There is also a list of periodicals and newspapers used in compiling the annals. In the 1939 annals, there is also a title index of books and articles containing maps. In Issue No. 1 for 1940, there is an index of map nomenclature, and in Issue No. 4, an index of nomenclature used on sheet maps of the scale 1:1,000,000 and 1:500,000. In the annals for 1931-1938, there are no indexes.

List of Numbers Issued

Kartograficheskaia letopis' [Cartographic Annals] 1931-1938.

1931 Nos. 1/2, 3/4	
1932 Nos. 1/2, 3/4	
1933 Nos. 1/3, 4	
1934 Nos. 1/2, 3/4	At the end of No. 3/4: "List of Books and Articles on Geodesy, [Cartography], and Geography Recorded in *Book Annals* and *Journal Annals* for 1934."
1935 Nos. 1/2, 3/4	At the end of No. 3/4: "List of Books and Articles on Geodesy, [Cartography], and Geography."
1936 Nos. 1/2, 3/4	At the end of No. 3/4: "List of Books and Articles on Geodesy, [Cartography], and Geography Recorded in *Book Annals* and *Journal Annals* for 1936."
1937 Nos. 1, 2, 3, 4	At the end of No. 4: "List of Books and Articles on Geodesy, [Cartography], and Geography Recorded in *Book Annals* and *Journal Annals* for 1937."

1938 Nos. 1, 2, 3/4   At the end of No. 3/4: "List of Books and Articles on Geodesy, [Cartography], and Geography Recorded in *Book Annals, Journal Annals* and *Newspaper Annals* for 1938."

Bibliografiia kartograficheskoi literatury i kart [Bibliography of Cartographic Literature and Maps] 1939-1940.

1939 Nos. 1/2, 3/4   In each issue, there are two parts: 1) Litera-
1940 Nos. 1, 2, 3, 4   ture on Cartography; and 2) Maps.

Kartograficheskaia letopis' [Cartographic Annals] 1941-

1946 Nos. 1/2, 3/4
1941-1950 M., 1953. 215 p.
1951-1953 M., 1954. 165 p.
1954   M., 1955. 125 p.
1955   M., 1956. 148 p.
1956   M., 1958. 137 p.
1957   M., 1958. 113 p.
1958   M., 1959. 178 p.
1959   M., 1960. 161 p.
1960   M., 1961. 199 p.
1961   M., 1962. 177 p.
1962   M., 1963. 122 p.
1963   M., 1964. 182 p.
1964   M., 1965. 94 p.
1965   M., 1966. 92 p.
1966   M., 1967. 120 p.

Information about maps published up to 1931 may be found in *Book Annals* for the years 1917-1918, 1920-1921, 1923-1925, and also in *Book Annals* for the prerevolutionary period. Geographic maps published in 1919, 1922, and during 1926-1930 are not recorded in Book Chamber annals except for atlases which are always recorded as books. Information about literature on geodesy, cartography, and geography for the years when *Cartographic Annals* was not published or was incomplete can be found in *Book Annals, Annals of Journal Articles,* and the *Book Annual of the USSR.* Reviews of this literature and also of cartographic publications since 1934 are found in *Annals of Reviews.*

Footnotes

[1] In 1939-1940, it was published under the title *Bibliografiia kartograficheskoi literatury i kart* [Bibliography of Cartographic Literature and Maps].

[2] Atlases are also recorded in *Book Annals* as books.

[3] Since 1941, territorial names cited in the titles of basic and supplementary maps and maps found in atlases have been given in the geographic index. In the annual for 1946, there is no geographic index.

■ ■ ■

ANNALS OF JOURNAL ARTICLES
(Letopis' zhurnal'nykh statei)

This annals has been published since 1926.[1] It comes out weekly and covers articles, documents, and belletristic works found in journals, serials of the "transactions" type, and literary anthologies published in the USSR in Russian.

Scholarly periodicals are given the broadest coverage, while popular magazines are covered selectively. Such titles as *Rabotnitsa* (Working Woman), *Sel'skaia molodezh'* (Village Youth), and *Sovetskii ekran* (Soviet Screen), as well as satirical magazines and children's magazines, are excluded. Official bulletins and abstracting services are also omitted.

Papers from scholarly journals and transactions are covered rather completely, but materials from the popular, mass-produced magazines, only selectively. Sections in publications devoted to chronicling events (*Khronika*), exchanging experience (*Obmen opytom*), and providing technical news (*Novosti tekhniki*), as well as reprints from other periodicals and collections, are not generally covered, although some strictly informational type materials reaching article length and all scholarly reprints are included.

Also omitted are reviews of books and other works recorded in *Annals of Reviews.* Literary criticism, however, is included.

In content and coverage, the annals has undergone major change. The number of sources exploited has been growing steadily: 206 titles in 1926 grew to 2,000 in 1966.

Periodicals and serials issued within the RSFSR were covered by *Journal Annals* for the period 1926-1934. Since 1935, while publications of other union republics have been covered, the selection of RSFSR publications has been restricted.

In 1926, only the more important publications having a regular periodicity were covered. In subsequent years, the selection of scholarly periodicals was broadened. The number of sources increased because of the growing number of transactions (Trudy), proceedings (Izvestiia), contributions (Uchenye zapiski), and many irregular serials issued by scientific bodies. Furthermore, various nonperiodical collections were gradually included.

Because of the publication of the *Central Medical Abstracts Journal*[2] in the years 1928-1935, special medical journals were excluded, although lists of medical articles for 1927 are found in Issue No. 1 for 1928.

In the period 1929-1932, belles-lettres, i.e., poems, stories, etc., were not included. In 1934 and 1935, articles from *Pravda* and *Izvestiia* were included.

During the Great Patriotic War, because the receipt of periodical publications was interrupted, almost all periodicals and serials in Russian were covered by the annals. Many popular magazines and children's journals were included, and the coverage of nonperiodical collections was expanded.

In the postwar period, scholarly periodicals were once again given preference. Some popular magazines and all children's magazines were excluded, and, because of the increase in the number of periodical publications, nonperiodical collections were gradually dropped.

Gaps in the coverage of periodical articles which appeared in the war years were filled by the special *Index of Articles Not Recorded in 1941-1945*[3] (M., 1949. 84 p.).

Bibliographic Description

A typical bibliographic entry provides surname of the author of the article, title, subtitle, name of the journal or collection in which the article is found, year of publication, volume and issue number, and pagination. A short explanation for titles that are not sufficiently clear is provided. The entry is supplemented by other information and notes: surnames of translators and illustrators, presence of a bibliography or resumé, etc.

Minor selections of articles, notes, and scholarly communications centered around one theme are entered under a common title.

Examples of Entries

Umanskii, L. Kto mozhet stat' organizatorom. Ocherk psikhologii organizatorskoi deiatel'nosti. Molodoi kommunist, 1966, No. 9, s. 79-85. — Prodolzh. Nachalo: No. 8.

Rubinskii, IU. Latinskii kvartal. O polozhenii frants. studenchestva. Ocherk. Novoe vremia, 1966, No. 44, s. 29-32.

Rylov, IU. A. i Skuridin, G. A. K teorii ionizatsionnogo kalorimetra. IAdernaia fizika, t. 2, vyp. 4, 1965, s. 691-704. — Reziume na angl. iaz. — Bibliogr.: 9·nazv.

Iskander, Fazil'. Sozvezdie Kozlotura. Povest'. Novyi mir, 1966, No. 8, s. 3-75.

Changes in the rules of bibliographic description have applied mostly to information about source. During the years 1927-1937, a short, conventional form of entry for articles was used. This form gave information about the source in a simplified and schematic notation which had to be deciphered. For example, SO 2: 96-9 F' 27 meant *Statisticheskoe obozrenie*, No. 2, p. 96-99. February 1927. In 1938, a new style for the entry, which is in use today, was adopted.

Arrangement of Material

Material is arranged systematically according to the classification used in the organs of national bibliography.

For a time, every issue, beginning with No. 9 for 1934, contained a section entitled "Articles from the Newspapers *Pravda* and *Isvestiia*." Then, in 1935, articles from these newspapers were incorporated into the general list of articles.

Indexes and Other Aids

In each issue of the annals, there is a list of journals and serials from which the articles indexed in the issue are taken.

Since 1953, a separate publication entitled *Annals of Journal Articles. List of Journals and Collections from which Articles Recorded in . . . Are Taken*[4] has come out. In the years 1929-1938 and 1944-1952, these lists appeared as an appendix in the last issue of the annals for the year.

Another publication, *Annals of Journal Articles. Supplementary Indexes*,[5] comes out quarterly. It contains name and geographic indexes.

The name index includes names of authors of articles; authors, translators, and illustrators of artistic works; and names of persons to whom articles are dedicated. The geographic index includes names of physiographic, geological, administrative territorial, economic, and historical geographic entities. Within the heading "Administrative territorial," topical subheadings that correspond basically to the divisions of the classification used in the organs of national bibliography are provided.

Every first number of the annals contains the full text of the classification and a foreword, "From the Editor," briefly describing the annals.

There have been many changes in the system of indexes.

Chronological List of Auxiliary Indexes[6]

Years	Types of Indexes	Frequency
1926-1928	Subject	Quarterly
1929	Subject	Bimonthly
1930		
Jan-Feb	Subject	Every other month
March-Dec	No indexes	
1931-1937	No indexes	
1938	Name; corporate	Biweekly
1939		
1st half-year	Name; corporate	Weekly
2nd half-year	Name	Monthly
1940	Name; corporate; subject; geographic	Monthly
1941		
Jan-May	Name; corporate; subject; geographic	Monthly
June-Dec	Name	Every seventh month
1942-1943	Name	Quarterly
1944	Name	Monthly
1945-1948	Name	Quarterly
1949	Name	Quarterly and Annual Cumulation
1950-1955	Name; geographic	Quarterly and Annual Cumulation
1956-1967	Name; geographic	Quarterly

List of Numbers Issued

Zhurnal'naia letopis' [Journal Annals] 1926-1937

1926 Nos. 1-4	Each issue contains a List of Periodical Publications Issued in 1926.
1927- Nos. 1-4 1928 each year	In Issue No. 1 for 1928, there is a list of articles from medical journals for 1927.
1929 Nos. 1-6	

1930 Nos. 1/2-9/12	Five issues in all, with some combined.
1931 Nos. 1-18	Seventeen issues in all. No. 11/12 is a double issue.
1932- Nos. 1-24a 1933	Twenty-five issues each year.
1934 Nos. 1-24	Articles from *Pravda* and *Izvestiia* are listed in a special section beginning with Issue No. 9.
1935 Nos. 1-24	Articles from *Pravda* and *Izvestiia* are listed with other newspaper articles.
1936- Nos. 1-24 1937	Twenty-four issues each year.

Letopis' zhurnal'nykh statei [Annals of Journal Articles] 1938-

1938 Nos. 1-24	
1939 Nos. 1/3-60a	Fifty-nine issues in all.
1940 Nos. 1-56a	Fifty-seven issues in all.
1941 Nos. 1/2-45/50	Thirty-seven issues with a few double issues.
1942 Nos. 1-24	
1943 Nos. 1-23/24	Twenty-three issues in all.
1944 Nos. 1-51/52	Fifty-one issues in all.
1945- Nos. 1-52 1946	Fifty-two issues each year.
1947- Nos. 1-48 1948	Forty-eight issues each year.
1949- Nos. 1-52 1967	Fifty-two issues each year.

Supplementary Issues

Letopis' zhurnal'nykh statei. Ukazatel' statei, ne zaregistrirovannykh v 1941-1945 gg. [Annals of Journal Articles. Index of Articles Not Recorded in the Period 1941-1945] M., 1949. 84 p.

Letopis' zhurnal'nykh statei. Dopolnitel'nyi vypusk [Annals of Journal Articles. Supplementary Issue]

1949	M., 1950. 304 p.
1955	Nos. 1-4
1956	Nos. 1-4

Information about articles published before 1926 can be found in the *Annual of the State Central Book Chamber of the RSFSR*[7] for 1925, which contains a section entitled "Systematic Index of Articles in the Principal Journals for 1925." Information may also be found for earlier years in the *Bibliographic Annual,*[8] compiled under the editorship of I. V. Vladislavlev.

Footnotes

[1] During the years 1926-1937, it was published under the title *Zhurnal'-naia letopis'* [Journal Annals].

[2] *Tsentral'nyi referativnyi meditsinskii zhurnal.*

[3] *Ukazatel' statei, ne zaregistrirovannykh v 1941-1945 gg.*

[4] *Letopis' zhurnal'nykh statei. Spisok zhurnalov i sbornikov, stat'i iz kotorykh zaregistrirovany v . . . godu.*

[5] *Letopis' zhurnal'nykh statei. Vspomogatel'nye ukazateli.*

[6] From 1926 to February 1930 and from 1938 to the first half of 1939, indexes were found in each issue of the annals. Since the second half of 1939, the indexes have come out as separate publications.

[7] *Ezhegodnik Gosudarstvennoi tsentral'noi knizhnoi palaty RSFSR.*

[8] Editor's note: Eight annuals were published from 1912 to 1927 covering the period 1911 to 1924.

■ ■ ■

ANNALS OF NEWSPAPER ARTICLES
(Letopis' gazetnykh statei)

Published since 1936,[1] the *Annals of Newspaper Articles* comes out monthly and records, in Russian, articles, official documents, and belles-lettres published in the central and republic newspapers issued throughout the Soviet Union.

The annals uses a rather stable group of sources: the central newspapers devoted to general political and special topics; the general politically-oriented newspapers of the union republics; and the principal city newspapers of Moscow and Leningrad. About forty newspapers are covered.

Since 1966, the provincial editions of *Pravda, Krasnaia zvezda,* and *Sovetskaia Rossiia*; a provincial edition of *Sel'skaia zhizn'* with substituted zonal pages; and the rural edition of *Leningradskaia Pravda* have been included. A provincial edition of *Izvestiia* has been covered since June 1960.

In the prewar years, an attempt was made to place a larger number of newspapers under bibliographic control. Since 1939, territorial and regional newspapers and, since 1940, district and city newspapers have been covered to June 1941. In the postwar years, however, coverage of these newspapers was not resumed. Because of the war, there was a break in the coverage of republic newspapers from June 1941 through 1946.

The following materials are listed selectively in the annals: the most important which summarize information or which contain interesting factual material; official documents, such as texts and statements of decisions of the Central Committee of the Communist Party of the Soviet Union (TSK KPSS) and the Council of Ministers of the USSR, decrees, resolutions, international agreements, government notes; texts of reports, speeches, etc.; and literary works, such as stories, excerpts from novels, poems, songs, and satires. Reprints from periodicals are also listed.

Not listed are materials of only current importance: short news reports, correspondence and notes of a local nature, decrees and resolutions concerning personal awards, appointments, transfers, promotions, and poetic texts that accompany cartoons and satirical drawings. Also not listed are reviews of books and literary works published in periodicals which are already covered by the *Annals of Reviews*. But critical literary articles and surveys, reviews of performances, concerts, films, exhibitions, and other cultural and entertainment events are covered.

Material from *Pravda* and *Izvestiia* is covered fully, but material typical of other newspapers is used selectively. Official documents appearing in all newspapers are taken from *Pravda* and *Izvestiia* and, depending on the content of the document, sometimes from the corresponding specialized or republic newspaper.

For as long as the *Annals of Newspaper Annals* has been published, the principle of selective listing of material has remained unchanged except during the Great Patriotic War, when various material with wartime political significance was included.

The chronological coverage of the material listed has changed, however. Since the annals was put on a monthly basis in 1960, every issue has recorded material from newspapers of the previous month. In fact, No. 1 of the current year lists material from December of the previous year. In the annual set of the annals up to 1953, all issues of newspapers for the calendar year, from January 1 to December 31, were covered; in 1953, all issues from January 1 to December 26; and since 1954, all issues from the last number in December of the previous year.

Bibliographic Description

Each entry consists of those elements necessary for locating the article, document, or literary work cited: surname of author, title, name of newspaper, year and date of newspaper, and some supplementary information. Short annotations are given for items which do not show the theme and nature of

the material. Newspaper selections from important minor publications are
described under a general heading.

Examples of Entries

Sluzhba nauchnoi informatsii. [Peredovaia]. Pravda, 1967, 12 ianv.

Leont'ev, A. i Panov, D. Chelovek v mire tekhniki. [Problemy inzh.
psikhologii]. Pravda, 1966, 14 okt.

Klavel' Bernar. Proshchai, Bessi! Rasskaz. Per. s frants.: U. Malishevskii.
Ill.: E. Lebedeva. Lit. gaz., 1965, 9 okt.

Arsenal sovetskogo rastenievodstva. [O rabote Vsesoiuz. in-ta rastenievodstva im. Vavilova. Stat'i i zametki] : D. Brezhnev. Dlia obnovleniia zemli. –
K. Budin. Poiski v glubinakh zhizni [i dr.]. Sel. zhizn', 1967, 22 iiulia.

Some changes in the rules have been made for indicating source. In
1936 and 1937, information about source was given in a brief, conventional
form; for example, *Pravda*, 10: 3 IA 10'36 meant *Pravda*, No. 10, p. 3,
10 Jan 1936. In the years 1938-1952, the form was *Sov. iskusstvo*, 22 I 38.
The form of entry that is used today was introduced in 1953.

Arrangement of Material

Material is arranged systematically on the basis of the classification used
in the organs of national bibliography. Within divisions, widely accepted and
up-to-date subject headings are used to group materials dealing with important political, economic, and cultural events in the USSR and abroad, with
international events and with anniversary dates.

In the 1940s, a separate record of materials from local and republic
newspapers of a regional nature was introduced. From 1940 to May 1941,
these materials were recorded in a special monthly supplement to the annals.
During 1947-1950, after the republic newspapers were once again covered,
materials were listed in special monthly appendices bound in with the annals
each month. Since 1951, items from republic newspapers have again been
listed with materials from central newspapers.

Indexes and Other Aids

The *Annals of Newspaper Articles. Auxiliary Indexes* comes out quarterly as a separate publication. It contains name and geographic indexes.

The name index includes names of authors of articles; authors, translators, and illustrators of artistic works; and also the names of persons to whom

articles are dedicated. The geographic index contains physiographic, geological, administrative territorial, economic, and historical geographic entities. Under the administrative territorial headings are topical subheadings corresponding basically to the main divisions of the classification used in the organs of national bibliography.

In each first issue of the annals, the classification and a foreword, "From the Editor," briefly describing the annals, are given. The foreword also provides a list of newspapers cited.

Chronological List of Auxiliary Indexes[2]

Years	Types of Indexes	Frequency
1936-1937	No indexes	
1938	Personalia; corporate; name	Quarterly; Annually
1939	Name; corporate; geographic	Monthly
1940	Name; corporate; subject; geographic	Monthly
1941		
1st half-year	Name; corporate; subject; geographic	Monthly
2nd half-year	Name	Semiannually
1942-1943	Name	Quarterly
1944	Name	Monthly
1945-1948	Name	Quarterly
1949	Name	Quarterly; Annually (for cumulated index)
1950-1955	Name; geographic	Quarterly; Annually (for cumulated index)
1956-1967	Name; geographic	Quarterly

List of Numbers Issued

Gazetnaia letopis' [Newspaper Annals] 1936-1937.

1936 Nos. 1-24	Materials from central and republic newspapers are recorded together.
1937 Nos. 1-24	

Letopis' gazetnykh statei [Annals of Newspaper Articles] 1938-

1938	Nos. 1-36	Materials from central and republic newspapers recorded together.
1939	Nos. 1-60a	In all, 61 issues. Materials from central, republic, territorial, and regional newspapers recorded together.
1940	Nos. 1-56	Only materials from central newspapers are recorded. Materials from republic, territorial, regional, district, and city newspapers are recorded separately in 12 monthly issues (Jan-Dec).
1941	Nos. 1-49/50	In all, 40 issues. Beginning with No. 31/32, all numbers are double. Materials from central newspapers are recorded. Separately, in five monthly issues (Jan-May), materials from republic, territorial, regional, district, and city newspapers are recorded.
1942- 1943	Nos. 1-24 each year	Only materials from central newspapers are recorded.
1944- 1946	Nos. 1-52 each year	Only materials from central newspapers are recorded.
1947- 1948 1949- 1950	Nos. 1-48 each year Nos. 1-52 each year	Materials from central newspapers are recorded separately. Materials from republic newspapers are recorded in special monthly appendices bound in every final number of the month.
1951- 1959	Nos. 1-52 each year	Materials from central and republic newspapers are recorded together.
1960- 1967	Nos. 1-12 each year	Materials from central and republic newspapers are recorded together.

Supplementary Issues

Letopis' gazetnykh statei. Respublikanskie, kraevye, oblastnye, okruzhnye i gorodskie gazety. [Annals of Newspaper Articles. Republic, Territorial, Regional, District, and City Newspapers] 1940-May 1941.

1940	[Nos. 1-12]
1941	[Nos. 1-5 (Jan-May)]

Footnotes

[1] In 1936 and 1937, it was published under the title *Gazetnaia letopis'* [Newspaper Annals].

[2] In 1938, indexes were placed in issue Nos. 9, 18, 27, and 36. Since 1939, they have been issued as separates. Auxiliary indexes were issued quarterly to the supplementary issues of *Annals of Newspaper Articles* for 1940 and 1941.

■ ■ ■

ANNALS OF REVIEWS
(Letopis' retsenzii)

This annals, published since 1935,[1] covers reviews since 1934 and comes out quarterly. In it are entered reviews published in Russian of works issued in the Soviet Union and abroad in the languages of the peoples of the USSR and in foreign languages.

All publications which are covered by the *Annals of Journal Articles* and the *Annals of Newspaper Articles* are used as sources of reviews. Territorial and regional newspapers are also used. However, materials from critical bibliographic journals and bulletins, such as *V mire knig* (In the World of Books) since 1961, and *Novye knigi za rubezhom* (New Books Abroad) since 1965, are chosen selectively.

Over the years, the sources used have varied. In 1934, 45 newspapers were used; in 1966, about 150. The number of periodicals cited has increased as the list of sources in *Annals of Journal Articles* has expanded from about 500 to 2,000 titles.

Reviews, critical articles and notes, literary surveys and other materials of critical analysis or evaluation[2] of publications of various types, such as books, periodicals, newspapers, albums, music and cartographic publications, and also literary and artistic works published in periodicals and newspapers are included.

Announcements and annotations of new publications and reviews of theatrical productions and films are not included. In certain years until 1950, the *Annals of Reviews* did include reviews of theatrical performances and films if they were critical.

During the war years, *Annals of Reviews* was not published, and the resultant gaps in the listing of reviews from 1942 to 1944 were not filled until the annual issues of the annals were published in 1947 and 1948. A gap still remains from the second to the fourth quarters of 1941. The annals for 1942 and 1943 covered only the central and republic newspapers.

Bibliographic Description

In each citation, the work being reviewed is the basis. The entry consists of two parts. In the first is a short description of the work being reviewed: surname of author, title of work, place, publisher, and date of publication or indication of the source in which the reviewed work was published. In the second part, the description of the review is given: surname of reviewer, title of review if it is not the same as the work reviewed, and indication of source in which the review was published.

The entry is given in Russian. Entries for reviewed works which were published aborad in a foreign language and printed in a Latin script are the exception..For these, a Russian translation follows the original language.

Examples of Entries

Mikhailov, A. I. Pavel Korin. [M., "Sov. khudozhnik", 1965]. Zotov, A. Khudozhnik, 1966, No. 3, s. 62.

Grekova, I. Letom v gorode. Rasskaz. V zhurn.: Novyi mir, 1965, No. 4.
Brovman, G. Grazhdanskoe chuvstvo i kharakter sovremennika. Moskva, 1966, No. 4, s. 197-203.
Lobanov, M. Vnutrennii i vneshnii chelovek. Mol. gvardiia, 1966, No. 5, s. 286-302.

Schlesinger, A. M. A thousand days. John F. Kennedy in the White House. [Tysiacha dnei. Dzhon F. Kennedi v Belom dome]. Boston, 1965. Anatol'ev, G. Tysiacha dnei presidentstva Kennedi. Mezhdunar. zhizn', 1966, No. 4, s. 127-129.

Over the years, the form of the entry for reviews has changed. During the period 1934-1937, the entry had a simplified form in the first part and a schematic form in the second. Following the author and title of the reviewed work, a brief description of the review was given. The year of publication of the newspaper or periodical was not shown if it was the same as that of the annals. For example:

Altauzen, D. Izbrannoe − g. KP S 215 (N. Spasskii). This may be read as "Komsomol'skaia pravda", 1937, September, No. 215. Reviewer: N. Spasskii.

Brekht, B. Roman nishchikh. − zh. LS III 244-50 (V Admoni); Rsts. XII 19-20 (O. Nemerovskaia). Here we have two reviews of a work by B. Brecht: one in the periodical "Literaturnyi sovremennik", 1937, No. 3, p. 244-250, reviewed by V. Admoni; the other in the periodical "Rezets" (Leningrad), 1937, No. 12, p. 19-20, reviewed O. Nemerovskaia.

After a series of changes, the form of the bibliographic entry became stabilized in 1952.

Arrangement of Material

Entries of reviews are arranged systematically by the classification scheme used in the organs of national bibliography. Entries for reviews of foreign works are found in a section at the end. In the annals for 1934-1940, entries are arranged alphabetically by author and title of the work being reviewed.

Indexes and Other Aids

In every quarterly issue of the annals, there is an alphabetical index of authors, editors, and titles of works being reviewed and an alphabetical index of reviewers. Soviet and foreign works are treated separately. Indexes cumulate in the final quarterly issue for the year.

In each first issue for the year, there is a foreword, "From the Editor," which briefly describes the annals. Each issue contains a list of newspapers from which reviews cited in the annals are taken. In the periods 1935-1941 and 1948-1965, lists of newspapers examined are given.

Chronological List of Auxiliary Indexes[3]

Years	Types of Indexes	Frequency
1934-1936	Systematic	Annual
1937	Systematic list of surnames of authors and titles of books (without reference numbers)[4]	Annual
1938	Systematic	Annual
1939	Systematic; reviewers	Quarterly
1940	Systematic; reviewers	Annual
1941 1st quarter	Authors and titles of books; reviewers	Quarterly
1942-1944	Authors and titles of books; reviewers	Annual
1945-1952	Authors and titles of books; reviewers	Quarterly and annual (for the cumulated index)
1953-1967	Authors, editors, and titles of books;[5] reviewers	Quarterly and annual (for the cumulated index)

List of Numbers Issued

Letopis' retsenzii [Annals of Reviews] 1934-1938.

1934.	M., 1935. 130 p.
1935.	M., 1936. 163 p.
1936.	M., 1937. 164 p.
1937.	M., 1939. 199 p. Supplement: Tables of statistical data on reviews for 1935-1937.
1938.	Nos. 1, 2, 3, 4.

Bibliografiia retsenzii [Bibliography of Reviews] 1939-1941.

1939.	Nos. 1, 2, 3, 4.
1940.	Nos. 1, 2, 3, 4.
1941.	No. 1. (Nos. 2, 3, 4 were not published)

Letopis' retsenzii [Annals of Reviews] 1942-

1942.	No. 1/4. M., 1948. 75 p.
1943.	No. 1/4. M., 1948. 54 p.
1944.	No. 1/4. M., 1947. 72 p.
1945.	Nos. 1, 2/3, 4.
1946-1967.	Nos. 1, 2, 3, 4 each year.

Information about reviews of theatrical performances, films, concerts, exhibitions, and other cultural and entertainment events is published in the *Annals of Journal Articles* and the *Annals of Newspaper Articles.*

For reviews of the period before 1934, when the special annals of reviews was not yet published, the *Annals of Journal Articles* is useful to some degree because it records important critical articles of various publications. For the period before 1925, lists of reviews can be found in the *Bibliographic Annual,*[6] which came out under the editorship of I. V. Vladislavlev.

Footnotes

[1] In the years 1939-1941, it was published as *Bibliografiia retsenzii* [Bibliography of Reviews].

[2] All these materials are called "reviews" here.

[3] Indexes are found in every issue of the annals, except that in the 1938 and 1940 issues, the indexes are found in the last quarterly issue of the year.

[4] Entries in the annals for 1937 are given without numbering.

[5] Since 1965, the index has separated those works published in the USSR from those published abroad.

[6] *Bibliograficheskii ezhegodnik.*

■ ■ ■

BIBLIOGRAPHY OF SOVIET BIBLIOGRAPHY
(Bibliografiia sovetskoi bibliografii)

This is an annual bibliographic guide to bibliographies published in the Soviet Union and listed in the organs of national bibliography.

Although the annual for 1939 was the first, it was not published until 1941. Following an interruption during the war years, publication was resumed with the issuance of the 1946 annual in 1948. Since then, publication has been regular.

The annual covers bibliographies and lists, whether issued separately or in journals and collections; periodicals devoted to bibliography; bibliographies in books and articles; and historical bibliographic surveys found in scholarly monographs and serial publications.

There are two appendices: "List of Reviews of Bibliographies," published since 1955; and "List of Journals with Regular Sections on Bibliography," published since 1957. Since 1958, review articles which survey the condition of bibliography in the USSR each year have been included.

Not found in the annual are various kinds of materials: indexes to periodical literature and publishers' catalogs with listings for a year or less; book-trade catalogs; listings of new books received in libraries of various types, except the largest general and special research libraries; "Methodological and Bibliographic Materials" aids; lists of cited literature in books and articles; lists found in popular books and mass brochures; lists in works not corresponding to the subject matter of these books; lists found in program-methodological materials, textbooks, and educational handbooks; and references to literature in annotations and footnotes. A few of the types of bibliographies mentioned above were included in the annual in previous years.

Also not included in the annual is information about lists in books and articles having fewer than thirty titles. In the years 1939, 1946, 1947, and 1949, lists in books and articles with fewer than twenty titles were not included. However, in some cases, there are exceptions: regardless of the number of titles, bibliographic lists of the works of various persons and literature about them are recorded. In the selection of such lists of literature on well developed themes, the quantitative requirements are raised.

In 1946-1948, literature on the theory, history, and method of bibliography and related questions of library science[1] was included. From 1946 to 1958, lists of periodical publications and collections and indexes whose contents are covered by *Bibliography of Soviet Bibliography* were published.

Bibliographic Description

Bibliographies and lists published separately or in periodicals and collections and also bibliographic journals are described with certain abbreviations and changes according to the rules used in the annals for describing these types of printed works. The entries are annotated. In annotations of significant bibliographies, the nature of the bibliography (subject, annotated, etc.) and the arrangement of material (classified, chronological, etc.) are indicated. An idea is given of the types of materials in the bibliography (books, articles, periodicals, etc.); the size of the bibliography (number of titles); the time span (except for recommended bibliographies); linguistic scope; and so on. After the annotation, reviews of the bibliography are cited.

Full dexcription of the organs of national bibliography and other periodical bibliographic publications is found in the annual only with the initial entry of these publications. The description of bibliographies in books is given in the following form: author and title of the book; place and year of publication; pages on which the bibliography is found or the general number of pages on which several lists are found (at the end of works, articles, parts, sections, chapters); and, if not in the Russian language, an indication of the language of the text.

An entry for a bibliography attached to an article discloses the author and title of the article and designates the source in which it is published.

Lists from an article found in topical collections or in transactions are entered under the title of the collection in which they are found.

Short annotations usually containing only information about the number of titles or arrangement are given to characterize lists found in books and articles.

Examples of Entries

Separately Published Bibliography

Bibliografiia Afganistana. Lit. na rus. iaz. Sost. T. I. Kukhtina. M., "Nauka", 1965. 272 s. (AN SSSR. In-t narodov Azii). 1,300. 1 r. 56 k.

Included are monographs, articles from periodicals, serial publications and collections, abstracts of theses, newspaper materials issued in Russia—USSR. 5,680 titles (reviewers indicated). Also represented are works on adjacent countries and containing important material about Afghanistan. Literature is arranged systematically and chronologically within the sections. Highlighted are basic Marxist-Leninist works, certain bibliographic materials, and also reviews and comments by native authors on foreign literature about Afghanistan. Appendix: Alphabetic index of names and titles.

Bibliographies in Books and Articles

Kosilov, S. A. Ocherki fiziologii truda. M., 1965, s. 370-375. [Ok. 190 nazv.]

Semenov, I. V. Iz istorii otkrytiia i issledovaniia arkhipelaga Severnaia Zemlia. Problemy Arktiki i Antarktiki, vyp. 16, 1964, S. 10-12. [46 nazv.]

Voprosy fiziologii vegetativnoi nervnoi sistemy i mozshechka. Erevan, 1964. 611 s. [Lit. v kontse statei].

Arrangement of Material

Material is arranged systematically according to the classification used in the organs of national bibliography. Bibliographies of bibliographies and general bibliographies are placed in a special section which has preceded the basic text of the annual since 1958.

Within the systematic divisions, bibliographic works published separately or in periodicals and collections are given first, followed by entries for lists found in books and articles (since 1948).

In the annuals for 1947 and 1948, entries for items on the theory, history, and method of bibliography are found in a separate section at the end.

For the years 1946 and 1947, lists of periodicals and collections whose indexes are recorded in the *Bibliography of Soviet Bibliography* are given as auxiliary indexes with references to the basic text of the annual. For 1948 and the years 1950-1958, indexes covering a time period of over a year are shown in the basic text; and those covering a year are shown only in the appendix.

Indexes and Other Aids

The annual has had a name index since 1939, a title index since 1946, and a geographic index since 1962.

The name index includes surnames of all persons mentioned in the entries (including personalia), as well as reviewers whose works are recorded in the *Annals of Reviews*. In the title index, all titles of bibliographic works are recorded. Until 1960, works described under a title or under a surname of an author not on the title page were shown in the index of titles. In the geographic index are physiographic, administrative-territorial, economic, geological, and historical geographic entities to which bibliographic materials are devoted.

In the annuals for 1948 and for 1950 through 1956, indexes of bibliographic periodicals covered by the *Bibliography of Soviet Bibliography* were published.

List of Numbers Issued

Bibliografiia sovetskoi bibliografii [Bibliography of Soviet Bibliography] 1939, 1946-1965.

1939	M., 1941.	272 p.
1946	M., 1948.	167 p.
1947	M., 1949.	214 p.
1948	M., 1952.	213 p.
1949	M., 1951.	233 p.
1950	M., 1951.	196 p.
1951	M., 1953.	207 p.
1952	M., 1953.	227 p.
1953	M., 1954.	226 p.
1954	M., 1955.	271 p.
1955	M., 1956.	314 p.
1956	M., 1957.	367 p.
1957	M., 1959.	374 p.
1958	M., 1960.	LXIII, 416 p.
1959	M., 1961.	XCII, 509 p.
1960	M., 1962.	LXXX, 512 p.
1961	M., 1962.	LXXXIV, 532 p.
1962	M., 1964.	LXXX, 419 p.
1963	M., 1964.	LXXVI, 443 p.
1964	M., 1965.	LXXIX, 406 p.
1965	M., 1966.	LXXX, 391 p.

Information about bibliographic works published in the USSR for the years which *Bibliography of Soviet Bibliography* does not cover can be found in *Book Annals, Book Annual of the USSR*, and *Annals of Journal Articles*.

It should be remembered that the presence of a bibliography in a book or article is noted in the above-indicated publications in the entries for books and articles. Therefore, in searching for a bibliography in a certain field, it is necessary to look through the appropriate field divisions of these annals. Information about periodical bibliographic publications can be found in the *Annals of Serial Publications of the USSR*.

Information about bibliographic materials for the years 1913-1925 and 1929 can also be found in B. S. Bodnarskii's *Bibliografiia russkoi bibliografii* [Bibliography of Russian Bibliography].

Footnotes

[1] Since 1959, the record of literature on the theory, history, and method of bibliography in the annual has been discontinued because it is now covered by *Bibliotekovedenie i Bibliografiia* [Library Science and Bibliography], which is published by the Lenin Library.

■ ■ ■

PUBLICATIONS OF THE BOOK CHAMBERS
OF THE UNION AND AUTONOMOUS REPUBLICS

UKRAINIAN SSR

The publications* described below are issued by the Book Chamber of the Ukrainian SSR.

Book Annals
(Letopis' knig)

The Ukrainian annals has been published since 1924.[1] It comes out monthly and records books and pamphlets. The material is arranged systematically.

The annals has name and subject indexes as well as an index of series. Also, in some numbers, following the basic text and under current topical headings, there are lists of literature whose publication was timed to coincide with certain events, commemorations, etc. Such lists contain short descriptions of the publications with reference to the full entry in the main text.

The annals was issued monthly in 1924, twice a month in 1925 and 1926, weekly in 1927 and 1928, quarterly in 1929 and 1930, and as an annual for the years 1931-1934. It was issued monthly in 1935 and twice a month during the years 1936-1941. For the years 1942-1944, the annals was published as a single issue in 1951. There was an annual for 1945 which was typewritten, and in 1946 it was issued quarterly.

---

*Titles of republic organs of national bibliography are given in Appendix II in English, Russian, and the original languages.

In various years, in addition to books, the annals recorded music (1924-1941, 1946-1954); pictorial art publications (1924-1925, 1927, 1935-1941); maps (1940-1941, 1946, 1954); periodical publications (1924-1928);[2] and articles and reviews (1930).

From 1954 to 1959, in addition to the indexes published in the annals, cumulative annual indexes, both name and series indexes, came out as separate publications.

Annals of Music Literature
(Letopis' muzykal'noi literatury)

This work has been published since 1954. It comes out twice a year, although in 1954 it was an annual; and it records music publications and musical works published in books and periodicals.

Material is arranged by type of music: vocal, instrumental, vocal-symphonic, and stage music with the means of performance, such as chorus, vocal solo, orchestra, etc., indicated.

Indexes include a name index of composers and authors of literary texts, index of titles, and index of publications in which music is published.

Annals of Pictorial Art
(Letopis' izobrazitel'nogo iskusstva)

The pictorial art annals has been published since 1937.[3] In the years 1939-1951, it was not published. It comes out twice a year and records pictorial art publications: posters, portraits, prints, and so forth. In 1960 and 1961, leaflets were also included.

Material in the annals is arranged by type of publication.

The annals has an alphabetical index of artists, authors of literary texts, and other important persons.

Annals of Journal Articles
(Letopis' zhurnal'nykh statei)

This annals has been published since 1936.[4] It comes out bimonthly and records articles, documentary materials, and belles-lettres found in periodicals and collections. Material is arranged systematically.

It has name and geographic indexes and a list of periodicals and collections used. In some issues, following the main text and under current, topical headings, are found lists of articles devoted to various events. Another list contains short entries of articles with reference to the full entry in the main text.

In the years 1936-1941, the annals was published monthly. In 1949, a cumulative publication for the period 1942-1944 was issued; and, in 1948, an annual for 1945 was published. In 1946 and 1947, the annals came out quarterly, and in the years 1948-1959, monthly.

Annual issues of cumulated auxiliary indexes to the annals were published in the years 1954-1963.

Annals of Newspaper Articles
(Letopis' gazetnykh statei)

This annals began publication in 1937.[5] It was not published in 1942 and 1943. It comes out bimonthly and records articles, documentary material, and belles-lettres published in republic and regional newspapers. Material is arranged systematically.

Auxiliary aids to use consist of name and geographic indexes as well as a list of newspapers covered by the annals.

Newspaper articles devoted to various political events, anniversaries, etc., are listed under current topical headings in some issues of the annals.

The annals has varied in frequency: in 1937 and 1938, it came out bimonthly; in 1939 and 1940, there were 36 issues annually; in 1941, only 21 issues; in 1944 and 1945, it came out annually; and in 1946 and 1947, monthly.

Annals of Reviews
(Letopis' retsenzii)

First published in 1936,[6] the *Annals of Reviews* comes out monthly and records reviews published in periodicals and newspapers. During the period 1942-1947, it was not published.

Material in the annals is arranged systematically. It has an alphabetical index of authors, editors, and titles of works reviewed, an index of reviewers, and a list of periodicals used in compiling the reviews. Since 1955, the indexes have cumulated in the last issue of the year.

Frequency has varied from time to time: only two issues in 1935; twelve issues a year in the period 1936-1940; and six issues in 1941.

Ukrainian SSR in Publications of the Soviet Republics
(Ukrainskaia SSR v izdaniiakh respublik Sovetskogo Soiuza)

This work has been published since 1956. It now comes out annually, although until 1966 it came out twice a year. It covers materials about the Ukraine published in other republics of the USSR: books, periodical and newspaper articles, and reviews. The material is arranged systematically; and, within divisions, entries for books are separated from entries for articles.

Reviews are found in a special section. There is a name index and a list of indexed serial publications.

* * *

Book Annual of the Ukrainian SSR
(Ezhegodnik knigi USSR)

Published for the years 1954 and 1955. Books are arranged systematically, and there are alphabetical indexes for names, titles, and corporate bodies.

* * *

The Ukrainian Book Chamber also issued the following retrospective bibliographies:

Kniga Ukrainskoi SSR. 1917-1923. Bibliografiia [Book of the Ukrainian SSR. 1917-1923. Bibliography] Khar'kov, 1959. 1599 l. (Mimeographed).

Periodicheskie izdaniia USSR. Zhurnaly. 1918-1960. Bibliograficheskii spravochnik [Periodical Publications of the Ukrainian SSR. Journals. 1918-1960. Bibliographic Handbook] Khar'kov, 1956-1964.

1918-1950. [Compiled by N. I. Bagrich and D. Kh. Mazus] 1956. VII, 464 p.

1951-1960. [Compiled by A. I. Kozlova, D. Kh. Mazus, G. D. Ruban, and others] 1964. 181 p.

Periodicheskie izdaniia USSR. Gazety. 1917-1960. Bibliograficheskii spravochnik [Periodical Publications of the Ukrainian SSR. Newspapers. 1917-1960. Bibliographic Handbook] Khar'kov, 1965. 575 p.

Footnotes

[1] Title varies: *Letopis' ukrainskoi pechati* [Annals of the Ukrainian Press] 1924-1930; *Letopis' pechati USSR. Knigi* [Annals of the Ukrainian Press. Books] 1931-1934, 1942-1944; *Letopis' pechati* [Annals of the Press] 1935; *Letopis' pechati. Knigi* [Annals of the Press. Books] 1936-1941, 1945-1953.

[2] The recording of periodicals and newspapers in 1929 was done in the publication *Pressa USSR* (Press of the Ukrainian SSR), which came out with information for the first quarter of 1929 and had three supplements in which materials for the rest of the year were recorded (Supplement Nos. 1-3).

[3] Title varies: *Letopis' pechati. Proizvedeniia izobrazitel'nogo iskusstva* [Annals of the Press. Works of Pictorial Art] 1937-1938, 1952-1953; *Letopis' izobrazitel'nogo iskusstva* [Annals of Pictorial Art] 1954-1959; *Letopis' izobrazitel'nogo iskusstva i listovok* [Annals of Pictorial Art and Leaflets] 1960-1961.

[4] Title varies: *Letopis' pechati. Zhurnal'nye stat'i* Annals of the Press. Journal Articles] 1936-1941, 1946-1953; *Letopis' pechati USSR. Zhurnal'nye stat'i* [Annals of the Ukrainian Press. Journal Articles] 1942-1945.

[5] Title varies: *Letopis' pechati. Gazetnye stat'i* [Annals of the Press. Newspaper Articles] 1937-1941, 1946-1953; *Letopis' pechati USSR. Gazetnye stat'i* [Annals of the Ukrainian Press. Newspaper Articles] 1944-1945.

[6] Title varies: *Letopis' retsenzii* [Annals of Reviews] 1935; *Letopis' pechati. Retsenzii* [Annals of the Press. Reviews] 1936-1939, 1948-1953; *Bibliografiia retsenzii* [Bibliography of Reviews] 1940-1941.

■ ■ ■

BELORUSSIAN SSR

The publications described below are issued by the Book Chamber of the Belorussian SSR, which is attached to the V. I. Lenin State Library of the BSSR.

Annals of Belorussian Publishing
(Letopis' pechati BSSR)

This annals has been published since 1926.[1] It has recorded material since 1925. It comes out monthly and lists books, pamphlets, music, printed pictorial works, periodical articles (since 1934), newspaper articles from republic newspapers (since 1937), regional newspapers (since 1956), and reviews. Since 1946, literature about Belorussia published in other republics of the Soviet Union has been included. Since 1956, literature about Belorussia published in foreign socialist countries has also been included. The first attempt to record literature about Belorussia was made in 1935.

The annals consists of four parts: "Book Annals," "Annals of Music Literature and Pictorial Art," "Annals of Periodical and Newspaper Articles," and "Belorussian SSR in the Publications of the USSR and Foreign Socialist Countries." Reviews are covered, along with periodical and newspaper articles. Entries for books, pamphlets, articles, and reviews are arranged systematically; entries for music, alphabetically; pictorial art publications, by type, i.e., portraits, posters, albums, and so forth.

Collections of "Auxiliary Indexes" have been published separately every year since 1956. The collections contain the following indexes: name indexes to the sections on books, music, and pictorial art publications; subject index; geographic index; series index to the section on books; index of titles of collections; and index of titles and first words of the texts of vocal works to the music section. Also included are annual cumulations of reviews and lists of periodical and serial publications issued in the republic during the year.

The first attempt to publish an annals was made in 1924 with the second issue of the journal *Asveta* [Enlightenment], which contained the "Annals of Belorussian Publishing," listing books and periodicals for the first half of 1924. Also, Issue No. 1 of the "Annals of Belorussian Publishing" for 1924 was printed separately.

The frequency of the annals has varied. A combined issue, No. 1-6, was put out in 1925. It came out bimonthly in 1926-1927. In 1928-1940, it came out monthly, except in 1933 when it was published in two semiannual issues. The years 1941-1945 were covered in two parts in 1948 and 1949. In 1949, 1946 was covered in two parts, while 1947 was published in 1948; and in the period 1948-1954, it came out quarterly.

Over the years, periodicals and reviews have been included in various publications. Periodical publications for the years 1925-1932 and 1947-1955 were listed in *Annals of Belorussian Publishing*; for 1933-1938, in the annual *Belorussian Periodical Press*; for 1956-1958 and since 1961, in the collection of "Auxiliary Indexes"; and for 1959-1960, in the *Book Annual of the Belorussian SSR*. Reviews are regularly recorded in the *Annals of Belorussian Publishing*. In 1956-1958 and 1961, they were also recorded in the annual "Auxiliary Indexes" and in 1959-1960, in the *Book Annual of the Belorussian SSR*.

* * *

Book Annual of the Belorussian SSR
(Ezhegodnik knigi BSSR)

Published for 1959 and 1960, it covered books, periodical and serial publications, and reviews. Books were arranged systematically; periodicals and transactions, alphabetically by type; newspapers, by territory; and reviews, alphabetically by the surnames of the authors of the works reviewed. The annual has name and series indexes.

Belorussian Periodical Press
(Periodicheskaia pechat' BSSR v . . . godu)

This work was published during the years 1933-1938, came out annually, and listed periodicals and newspapers according to their condition on June 1. Entries for periodicals are arranged alphabetically by title; those for newspapers, by type, i.e., central, regional, or district. It contains a place of publication index.

* * *

General retrospective bibliographies were also published by the Book Chamber and other departments of the V. I. Lenin State Library of the BSSR.

Letopis' belorusskoi pechati [Annals of Belorussian Publishing] Pt. [1]-4. Minsk, 1927-1961.

[Pt. 1][2] Bibliographic List of Belorussian Publications of the XVI-XVIII Centuries. [Compiler: G. IA. Golenchenko]. 1961. 132 p. (Duplicated).

Pt. 2. Separate Publications in the Belorussian Language. 1835-1916. (With a Supplement of Proclamations and Leaflets 1863-1905). [Compiler: IU. Bibilo]. 1929. 38 p.

Pt. 3. 1917-1924. First Notebook. Publications in the Belorussian Language. [Compiler: IU. Bibilo]. 1927. 56 p.

Pt. 4. Periodical Publishing in the Belorussian Language. [1917-1926]. [Compiler: IU. Bibilo]. 1927. 36 p.

Knigi Belorusskoi SSR. Svodnaia bibliografiia [Books of Belorussian SSR. Collective Bibliography] 1956-1960. Minsk, 1963. 144 p.

Muzykal'naia literatura BSSR [Music Literature of the BSSR] (Sheet music). Bibliography of Separate Publications. 1917-1961. [Compiler: F. A. Merina]. Minsk, 1963. 199 p.

Periodicheskaia pechat' Belorussii [Periodical Press of Belorussia] 1817-1916. Bibliographic Index. [Compiler: A. A. Sokol'chik]. Minsk, 1960. 138 l. (Duplicated).

Periodicheskaia pechat' Belorusskoi SSR [Periodical Press of the Belorussian SSR] Issues 1-2. [Compiler: V. Adamovich]. Minsk, 1960. (Mimeographed).

Issue 1. Journals. 1917-1958. 168 l.
Issue 2. Newspapers. 1917-1959. 116 l.

Periodicheskaia pechat' Belorusskoi SSR [Periodical Press of the Belorussian SSR] 1959-1963. Pt. 1-2. [Compiler: F. A. Merina]. Minsk, 1964. (Mimeographed).

Part 1. Journals, Transactions, Bulletins. 56 l.
Part 2. Newspapers. 2, 102 l.

Belorusskaia periodicheskaia pechat' [Belorussian Periodical Press] 1917-1927. Systematic Index of Material from Journals and Collections Issued in the BSSR in 1917-1927. [Compiler: IU. Bibilo]. Minsk, 1929. XII, 244 p.

Footnotes

[1] In the years 1926-1935, it was published under the title *Letopis' belorusskoi pechati* [Annals of Belorussian Publishing].

[2] Part 1 has no general title.

■ ■ ■

UZBEK SSR

The following annals are published by the State Book Chamber of the Uzbek SSR:

Book Annals
(Knizhnaia letopis')

Except for 1931, 1933-1936, and 1941-1944, this annals has been published each year since 1928.[1] It comes out monthly and lists books, pamphlets, and, since 1958, music. In the annals for 1928 and 1929, periodical publications, such as newspapers, journals, and bulletins issued in the Uzbek and Tadzhik Soviet Socialist Republics, were also recorded.

Material listed is divided into two parts: in the first part is found literature in Uzbek and other languages of the peoples of the USSR (except Russian) and, in the second part, literature in Russian and foreign languages. In both parts, entries for books and pamphlets are arranged by subject, while entries for music are in alphabetic order.

The annals has a name index and a list of languages in which books are published. Until 1939, there was also an index of corporate bodies and a title index. In some issues, usually in No. 12, an appendix containing entries for books recorded late was inserted.

Until 1956, the frequency of the annals varied. Since then, with few exceptions, the annals has been published monthly.

Annals of Journal Articles
(Letopis' zhurnal'nykh statei)

This annals, published since 1931, comes out monthly and records articles, documentary materials, and belles-lettres found in journals. It was not published in the years 1942-1947 and 1949-1957.

In each issue, articles in Uzbek are given first, followed by those in Russian. Within the language divisions, the arrangement is systematic. The annals has a name index and a list of indexed periodicals and collections.

For the years 1931-1941 and 1948, the annals covered two year, one year, and half year periods. From 1958 to 1961, it was published quarterly. In certain years, some numbers of the annals were not published.

* * *

The Alisher Navoi State Public Library published the following retrospective bibliography:*

Avsharova, M. P. *Russkaia periodicheskaia pechat' v Turkestane* [Russian Periodical Publishing in Turkestan] (1870-1917). Bibliography of the Literature. Tashkent, 1960. 197 p.

Footnotes

[1] In the years 1928-1930 and 1932, it was published as *Knizhnaia letopis' Uzbekistanskoi gosudarstvennoi knizhnoi palaty* [Book Annals of the Uzbek State Book Chamber] and in 1937, as *Letopis' pechati Uzbekskoi SSR* [Publishing Annals of the Uzbek SSR].

■ ■ ■

---

*Editor's note: To the retrospective bibliographies of Uzbekistan may be added the following: *Kniga Sovetskogo Uzbekistana* [The Book of Soviet Uzbekistan] (1917-1927). A Bibliography. [Compilers: M. M. Baisheva, A. T. Tishkina]. Tashkent, 1976. 202 p. (State Book Chamber of the Uzbek SSR).

KAZAKH SSR

The following annals are published by the Book Chamber of the Kazakh SSR:

Publishing Annals of the Kazakh SSR
(Letopis' pechati Kazakhskoi SSR)

This annals, published since 1957, comes out quarterly and records books and pamphlets,[1] music, pictorial art publications (since 1963), periodical publications, articles from periodicals and newspapers, and reviews.

The material is divided into two sections: in one section is literature in the Kazakh and other languages of the peoples of the USSR (except Russian), and in the other is literature in Russian.

Each section consists of the following parts: "Book Annals," "Annals of Periodical and Newspaper Articles," "Annals of Reviews," "Annals of Pictorial Art," and "Annals of Musical Works." Books, articles, and reviews are arranged systematically; music is arranged alphabetically by title; and printed pictorial works, by type, such as portraits, posters, prints, etc.

Statistical information about publishing in Kazakh SSR is included in specific numbers of the annals, as are supplementary listings of books recorded late.

The annals has a name index and a list of indexed periodicals, collections, and newspapers.

* * *

The following were formerly published by the book chamber:

Book Annals
(Knizhnaia letopis')

This annals, published in the periods 1937-1939 and 1946-1956, came out annually. In 1950, there was a cumulative edition for 1946-1948; and there were two issues for 1950. It recorded books and pamphlets.

Books published in Kazakh and other languages besides Russian, as well as those published in Russian, were placed either in different sections or separate issues. Arrangement of material was systematic. There were no indexes up to 1951; since then, only a name index.

Annals of Journal Articles
(Letopis' zhurnal'nykh statei)

This annals was published during the periods 1938-1939 and 1947-1956. Published annually, it recorded articles, documentary materials, and belles-lettres from journals and collections. A cumulative edition for 1947-1948 came out in 1950.

Each issue had two sections: one contained articles in the Kazakh language and the other, articles in Russian. Arrangement of entries was systematic. The annals contained a list of indexed journals and collections. There were no indexes.

Great Patriotic War of the Soviet People.
A Bibliography of Publishing in the Kazakh SSR
(Velikaia Otechestvennaia voina sovetskogo naroda.
Bibliograficheskii ukazatel' pechati Kazakhskoi SSR)

This work was published in the years 1941-1943, 1945, and 1948. It recorded books and articles covering the period June 1941 to March 1942. The material was arranged systematically, but there were no indexes. Issues contained lists of indexed sources.

* * *

General retrospective bibliographies published by the Kazakh Book Chamber include:*

---

*Editor's note: Since 1967, when this guide was published, several additional retrospective bibliographies have been published.

Kniga Sovetskogo Kazakhstana [The Book of Soviet Kazakhstan] 1956-1965. Consolidated Bibliography. Alma Ata, 1970.

Kniga Sovetskogo Kazakhstana [The Book of Soviet Kazakhstan] 1966-1970. Consolidated Bibliography. Alma Ata, 1974.

Pechatnye proizvedeniia izobrazitel'nogo iskusstva Kazakhstana [Pictorial Art Publications of Kazakhstan] 1960-1970. Alma Ata, 1975.

Muzykal'naia literatura Sovetskogo Kazakhstana [Musical Literature of Soviet Kazakhstan] 1938-1965. Alma Ata, 1969.

Notnye proizvedeniia Kazakhskoi SSR [Music Publications of Kazakh SSR] 1966-1974. Alma Ata, 1976.

Gazety Kazakhskoi SSR [Newspapers of the Kazakh SSR] 1917-1975. Alma Ata, 1977.

Ukazatel' retsenzii [Index of Reviews] 1938-1968. Alma Ata, 1971.

Avtoreferaty dissertatsii [Author Abstracts of Dissertations] 1938-1970. Alma Ata, 1974.

Kniga Sovetskogo Kazakhstana [The Book of Soviet Kazakhstan] 1917-1945. Consolidated Bibliography. V. 1-2. Alma-Ata, 1961-1962.

    V. 1. 1962. 446 p.

    V. 2. [Compilers: D. Kazbekova, Z. Kasymova, P. A. Kovaleva, et al.]. 1961. 360 p.

Kniga Sovetskogo Kazakhstana [The Book of Soviet Kazakhstan] 1946-1955. Consolidated Bibliography. [Compilers: P. A. Kovaleva, D. Aksartova, Z. Kasymova, et al.]. Alma-Ata, 1966. 558 p.

Bibliograficheskii ukazatel' pechati Kazakhskoi SSR [Publishing Bibliography of the Kazakh SSR] (1917-1939). Pt. 2. Periodical Press. [Compilers: A. A. Karnaukhova, N. Sabitov, and G. P. Tsarev]. Alma-Ata, 1941. 100 p.

Letopis' periodicheskikh izdanii Kazakhskoi SSR [Annals of Periodicals of the Kazakh SSR] 1940-1955. A Bibliography. [Compilers: Z. Kasymova, E. A. Skurishina]. Alma-Ata, 1957. 61 p.

Letopis' periodicheskikh izdanii Kazakhskoi SSR [Annals of Periodicals of the Kazakh SSR] 1917-1959: Consolidated Bibliography. [Compilers: D. Kazbekova and E. Skurishina]. Alma-Ata, 1963. 75 p.

Izobrazitel'noe iskusstvo Kazakhstana [Pictorial Art of Kazakhstan] A Bibliography. 1938-1959. [Compiler: R. Turogel'dieva]. Alma-Ata, 1963. 75 p.

Letopis' izobrazitel'nogo iskusstva i listovok [Annals of Pictorial Art and Leaflets] No. 1. (January-December). [Compiler: R. Turogel'dieva]. Alma-Ata, 1961.

Footnotes

[1] Books and pamphlets were not listed in *Letopis' pechati Kazakhskoi SSR* for 1962 but were recorded in *Knizhnaia letopis'*.

■ ■ ■

GEORGIAN SSR

The following publications are issued by the Book Chamber of the Georgian SSR:

Book Annals
(Knizhnaia letopis')

Published since 1926, *Book Annals* comes out monthly and records books and pamphlets. The material is organized by language: books in the Georgian language, books in Russian, and books in other languages. Entries for Georgian and Russian books are arranged systematically, while entries in other languages are arranged alphabetically. The annals has a name index, a geographic index since 1959, and a place of publication index since 1964.

In 1926, the annals came out quarterly; in 1927 and 1929-1931, monthly; in 1932, as a single annual issue; in 1933 and 1934, monthly; in 1935 and 1936, bimonthly; and in 1937, as an annual issue only.

The literature for the period 1917-1925 is recorded in issue No. 1 for 1926, which also includes a list of periodicals and newspapers for the same period. In some years, other types of publications were included: periodicals, in 1927 and in Issue No. 3 for 1953; printed pictorial works, in 1941-1956 and 1959;[1] maps, in 1941-1952 and 1959; music, in Issue No. 12 for 1939, 1941-1956, and 1959; and reviews, in 1939-1943 and 1949-1957.

In 1928, the months June to December 1957, and 1958, the annals was not published. The gap for 1928 was partly filled by the publication of *Bibliographia Georgica*; the one for 1957 was filled by a single issue in 1964; and the one for 1958, by a single issue in 1965.

Bibliography of Musical Works
(Bibliografiia muzykal'nykh proizvedenii)

The music bibliography has been published since 1959 with issues recording material for two year periods: for 1957-1958, in 1959; for 1959-1960, in 1961; for 1961-1962, in 1963; for 1963-1964, in 1966. In addition to separate musical works, it also includes works published in books, periodicals, and newspapers.

Entries are arranged by type of music, although musical works found in books, periodicals, and newspapers are arranged alphabetically. The bibliography contains name and title indexes.

Bibliography of Pictorial Art
(Bibliografiia izobrazitel'nogo iskusstva)

Published since 1962, this work covers material for two year periods: 1962 covered 1959-1960, while the year 1964 covered 1961-1962. It records posters, reproductions, postcards, other types of pictorial art works, and graphics out of books.

The material is arranged by type of work. There are name indexes for artists, authors of literary texts, and persons to whom works are dedicated.

Annals of Journal Articles
(Letopis' zhurnal'nykh statei)

Published since 1939, this annals comes out monthly and records articles, documentary materials, and belles-lettres published in magazines. During the months of June to December 1957 and 1958, it was not published.

Materials in Georgian and Russian are recorded separately and arranged systematically. There are several indexes: a name index, a geographic index since 1955, and, since 1943, a list of sources indexed.

Annals of Newspaper Articles
(Letopis' gazetnykh statei)

Published since 1934,[2] this annals comes out bimonthly. However, in the years 1935-1938, it came out monthly; and in 1939-1957 and 1959-1960, there were 36 issues a year. In 1937 and 1958, it was not published. It records articles, documentary materials, and belles-lettres found in newspapers.

Materials in Georgian and Russian are listed separately and arranged systematically. There are several indexes: a name index; since 1959, a geographic index; an index of corporate bodies; and a list of indexed newspapers.

Bibliography of Reviews
(Bibliografiia retsenzii)

Published since 1959, this bibliography has recorded material since 1958. It is issued annually and covers reviews and critical articles and surveys taken from periodicals.

The material is arranged systematically. Within divisions, entries for Georgian publications are given first, followed by those in Russian. The annual has an alphabetical index of authors, editors, translators, and titles of works reviewed; an alphabetical index of reviewers; and a list of sources used.

Georgia and Georgian Leaders in Publications of Sister Republics
(Gruziia i gruzinskie deiateli v izdaniiakh bratskikh respublik)

Issued annually since 1963, this work records books, music, pictorial art publications, and periodical and newspaper articles about Georgia published in other republics of the Soviet Union since 1961.

The material is arranged systematically. There is a name index, an index of languages besides Russian, and a list of sources used.

* * *

Also published by the Book Chamber are the following general retrospective bibliographies:

Gruzinskaia kniga [The Georgian Book] A Bibliography. Vol. 1-3. Tbilisi, 1941-1964.

> Vol. 1. 1629-1920. 1941. XLIV, 560 p. [For supplements to Vol. 1, see the journal *Vestnik bibliografii*, Tbilisi, 1948, No. 4-5, p. 141-196].

> Vol. 2. 1921-1945.
> Issue 1. [Compilers: P. Khundadze and T. Nakashidze]. 1950. XIV, 808, 6 p.
> Issue 2. [Compilers: P. Khundadze, T. Nakashidze, and V. Dzhodzhua]. 1951. 809-1395 p.
> Issue 3. [Compilers: T. Chubinidze, E. Diasamidze, T. Nakashidze, and V. Dzhodshua]. 1954. 162 p.

> Vol. 3. 1946-1950. 1964. VIII, 496 p.

Armianskaia kniga v Gruzii [The Armenian Book in Georgia] A Bibliography. Tbilisi, 1941. 152 p.

Bibliografiia gruzinskoi periodiki [Bibliography of Georgian Periodicals] 1819-1945. Compiler: G. Bakradze. Tbilisi, 1947. XV, 271 p.

Zertsalov, G. B. *Bibliografiia russkoi periodiki Gruzii* [Bibliography of Russian Periodicals of Georgia] Pt. 1. 1828-1920. Tbilisi, 1941. 196 p.

Periodika Gruzii za 1935 g. [Periodicals of Georgia for 1935] Tbilisi, 1936. 80 p.

Dzhodzhua, V. K. *Bibliografiia periodicheskikh izdanii Gruzinskoi SSR* [Bibliography of Periodical Publications of the Georgian SSR] 1946-1947. Tbilisi, 1948. 77 p.

Kutsiia-Gvaladze, T. *Bibliografiia gruzinskikh muzykal'nykh proizvedenii* [Bibliography of Georgian Musical Works] 1872-1946. Tbilisi, 1947. 136 p.

Bibliografiia muzykal'nykh proizvedenii [Bibliography of Musical Works] 1947-1956. [Compiler: N. Sabashvili]. Tbilisi, 1965. 149 p.

Bibliografiia retsenzii. Gruzinskie knigi, zhurnaly i gazety [Bibliography of Reviews. Georgian Books, Periodicals and Newspapers] 1931-1938. Tbilisi, 1941. 58 p.

Bibliographia Georgica. 1928. [Systematic Index of Scientific Literature of Georgia for 1928.] Tbilisi, 1930. 134 p.

Footnotes

[1] Pictorial art works for 1959 were also recorded in the *Bibliography of Pictorial Art,* while music was covered by the *Bibliography of Musical Works.*

[2] In 1934 through 1936, it was issued under the title *Gazetnaia letopis'* [Newspaper Annals].

■ ■ ■

AZERBAIDZHAN SSR

The following publications are issued by the Azerbaidzhan State Book Chamber:

Annals of Azerbaidzhan Publishing
(Letopis' pechati Azerbaidzhana)

Published since 1926,[1] this annals comes out monthly and lists books, pamphlets, music since 1940, pictorial art publications since 1965, and periodical and newspaper articles and reviews since 1960. From 1962 on, literature about Azerbaidzhan published in other Soviet republics has also been listed. Periodical publications were listed in 1926-1931, 1938, and 1940-1941.

The annals is divided into the following parts: "Book Annals," "Annals of Journal Articles," "Annals of Newspaper Articles," "Annals of Music Literature and Pictorial Art," "Annals of Reviews," and "Azerbaidzhan in the Press of the USSR." In each part, material is arranged by language, with literature in Azerbaidzhani first.

Entries for books and articles are arranged systematically. Music and pictorial art works are given alphabetically by title. Reviews are arranged by source, i.e., reviews from newspapers and reviews from periodicals, and then by language, first those in Azerbaidzhani, followed by those in Russian. The annals has had a name index since 1928. There is also a list of indexed periodicals and newspapers. In the last number for the year, statistical data about publishing are provided.

Frequency of the annals varied in different years. Only one issue was published for 1926-1927, but monthly issues came out from 1928 to 1941. In 1951, one issue was published, covering the years 1942-1946. From 1947 through 1958, the annals came out quarterly; and, in 1959, six issues were published.

Book Annual of Azerbaidzhan
(Ezhegodnik knigi Azerbaidzhana)

This work has been published since 1961, listing books and pamphlets since 1960.

Material is arranged in two parts: books and pamphlets in Azerbaidzhani and books in Russian. Within these parts, material is arranged systematically. Each part has a name index.

Much earlier, in 1941, the *Annual of Book Production of the Azerbaidzhan SSR. 1939*[2] was published.

Annals of Journal Articles of Azerbaidzhan
(Letopis' zhurnal'nykh statei Azerbaidzhana)

This annals was published for the periods 1938-1941 and 1947-1959. Frequency varied: until 1941, it was semiannual; in 1941 and from 1947 through 1959, it was quarterly. It listed articles, documentary material, and belles-lettres found in periodicals and collections.

The material is organized into two parts: articles in Azerbaidzhani and those in Russian. Entries are arranged systematically in each part. The annals has had a name index since 1956. Since 1938, some years have included lists of periodicals and collections used as sources.

The listing of periodical articles began with the 1932 edition of the cumulation *Journal Articles of the Azerbaidzhan SSR*,[3] which covered the years 1920-1930. In 1934, two issues of the annals came out for 1931 and 1932.

The gap in the listing of articles for 1933-1937 and 1942-1946 was filled by the following publications: *Annals of Journal Articles. 1931-1938*[4] (Baku, 1965. 172 p.) and *Annals of Journal Articles. 1942-1946*[5] (Baku, 1965. 91 p.).

Annals of Newspaper Articles of Azerbaidzhan
(Letopis' gazetnykh statei Azerbaidzhana)

This annals was published for the years 1938-1941 and 1947-1959.[6]
Its frequency until 1941 was quarterly, in 1941 and since 1947, monthly.
In 1942 and 1946, separate issues came out.

It listed articles, documentary materials, and belles-lettres found in
newspapers. Material in each issue of the annals is divided into two parts:
articles in Azerbaidzhani and articles in Russian. Within each part, arrangement is systematic. Since 1950, it has had a name index, and, until 1954,
a list of newspapers indexed was included in certain years.

* * *

Also published by the Azerbaidzhan State Book Chamber are the
following general retrospective bibliographies:

Knizhnaia letopis' [Book Annals] 1920-1925. Baku, 1962. 67 p. (Azerbaidzhan State Book Chamber).

Azerbaidzhanskaia kniga [The Azerbaidzhan Book] (A Bibliography). Vol.
1. 1780-1920. [Compiler: A. Aliev]. Baku, 1963. 220 p. (Azerbaidzhan
State Book Chamber).*

Azerbaidzhanskaia kniga [The Azerbaidzhan Book] (Bibliography. 1940-
1950). [Compiler: S. Aliev]. Baku, 1951. 196 p. (Azerbaidzhan State Book
Chamber).

Bibliografiia retsenzii [Bibliography of Reviews] (1946-1959). Baku, 1961.
107 p. (Azerbaidzhan State Book Chamber).

Akhundov, N. *Periodicheskaia pechat' v Azerbaidzhane* [Periodical Press
in Azerbaidzhan] (1832-1920). Bibliography. Baku, 1965. 178 p. (AN AzSSR.
Nizami Institute of Literature and Language).

---

*Editor's note: The second volume of *Azerbaidzhanskaia kniga*, covering the
years 1920-1940, was completed in 1969; and a third volume, for the period 1941-1960,
is being compiled.

Footnotes

[1] Title varies: 1926-1927, *Letopis' Azerbaidzhanskoi gosudarstvennoi knizhnoi palaty* [Annals of the Azerbaidzhan State Book Chamber]; 1940-1959, *Knizhnaia letopis' Azerbaidzhana* [Book Annals of Azerbaidzhan].

[2] *Ezhegodnik knizhnoi produktsii Azerbaidzhanskoi SSR. 1939.*

[3] *Zhurnal'naia letopis' Azerbaidzhanskoi SSR.*

[4] *Letopis' zhurnal'nykh statei. 1931-1938.*

[5] *Letopis' zhurnal'nykh statei. 1942-1946.*

[6] A bibliography of newspaper articles for 1930-1938 and one for 1942-1946 are being prepared.

∎ ∎ ∎

LITHUANIAN SSR

The Book Chamber of the Lithuanian SSR publishes the following annals:

Annals of Publishing
(Letopis' pechati)

Published since 1957, this annals comes out monthly and records books, pamphlets, music, pictorial art works, periodicals and other serial publications, maps, periodical and newspaper articles, and reviews. Literature about Lithuania published in other republics of the Soviet Union and in foreign socialist countries is also included.

The *Annals of Publishing* is composed of the following parts: "Book Annals," "Annals of Music Literature," "Annals of Pictorial Art," "Annals of Periodical and Newspaper Articles," "Annals of Reviews," and "Annals of Soviet Lithuanica." Entries for books, articles, and reviews are arranged systematically with literature in Lithuanian given first. Music is arranged alphabetically by title, and printed pictorial works, by type, such as posters, prints, etc. A list of serials covered during the year is given in Issue No. 12. Entries for periodicals, bulletins, and other serial publications are grouped systematically, while entries for newspapers are arranged by area.

Since 1960, indexes to the annals have been published separately on an annual basis under the title *Annals of Publishing. Indexes.*[1] This work contains the following indexes: a name index to all the sections of the annals; a title index to all sections devoted to books, music, and serial publications; a corporate author index to the sections concerning books, periodical and newspaper articles, serials, and Soviet Lithuanica; a geographic index to the sections on books, periodical and newspaper articles, and Soviet Lithuanica; and a place of publication index to the section on serials.

Before 1957, the following works were published by the Book Chamber:

Book Annals
(Knizhnaia letopis')

Published during the years 1947-1956, this annals came out quarterly and listed in separate sections books and pamphlets, music, printed pictorial works, leaflets until 1953, and reviews of books until 1950. From 1951 on, material published outside the republic was listed.

Information about books, pamphlets, leaflets, and reviews is arranged systematically; information about music, alphabetically by title; and information about printed pictorial works, by type. A name index accompanies each section. Furthermore, the section devoted to books has indexes for title, corporate author, and, since 1954, geographic entities.

Annals of Periodical Publications of the LIthuanian SSR
(Letopis' periodicheskikh izdanii Litovskoi SSR)

This annals was published for the years 1949 and 1951-1954, came out annually, and covered newspapers, periodicals, transactions, bulletins, and other periodical and serial publications. Material is arranged as follows: republic, regional, district, MTS, and departmental newspapers; periodicals; transactions; and bulletins. It has a periodical and newspaper title index, a geographic index, and an index for editors' names.

Information about periodical publishing for 1950 was recorded in *Periodicals of the Lithuanian SSR. 1940-1950*[2] (Vilnius, 1952). In the annals for 1952-1954, only newly issued newspapers, periodicals, and serials were recorded.

Annals of Periodical and Newspaper Articles
(Letopis' zhurnal'nykh i gazetnykh statei)

Published during the period 1949-1956, this annals was issued monthly; and it indexed articles, documentary materials, belles-lettres, and reviews of articles found in periodicals, serials, and newspapers.

Arrangement of the material is systematic. Each number has a name index. In the last number of the year, there is a cumulated name index, an index of organizations and institutions, a geographic index, and a list of periodicals and newspapers indexed for the year.

* * *

The following retrospective bibliographies have also been published by the Lithuanian Book Chamber:*

Kniga Litovskoi SSR [The Book in the Lithuanian SSR] 1940-1941, 1944-1946. Vilnius, 1949-1953.

> 1940-1941. (Books and Music). 1953. 128 p.
>
> 1944-1945. (Books). 1952. 51 p.
>
> 1946. (Books and Music). 1949. 52 p.

Pechat' Litovskoi SSR [Publishing in the Lithuanian SSR] National Cumulated Bibliography. Vol. 1. Book 1-2. 1940-1955. Vilnius, 1962-1964.

> Book 1. [Compilers: E. Urnezhiute, T. Chizhas, A. Ul'pis, et al.]. 1962. XII, 816 p.
>
> Book 2. [Compilers: E. Urnezhiute, A. Biliunas, A. Ul'pis, et al.]. 1964. XIX, 414 p.
>
> The first book lists books published in Soviet Lithuania and also literature about Lithuania published in other republics of the USSR. The second book includes serials, dissertation abstracts, music, printed pictorial works, and maps.

Pechat' Litovskoi SSR perioda Velikoi Otechestvennoi voiny [Publishing in the Lithuanian SSR during the Great Patriotic War] 1941-1944. (To the Liberation of the Lithuanian SSR). [Compilers: A. Ul'pis, R. Sharmaitis, V. Aleksandravichius, et al.]. Vilnius, 1955. XIV, 270 p.

> The bibliography lists books and pamphlets, music, leaflets, periodical publications, and articles from periodicals and newspapers.

Periodika Litovskoi SSR [Periodicals of the Lithuanian SSR] 1940-1950. Vilnius, 1952. 80 p.

Stat'i iz zhurnalov i gazet Litovskoi SSR [Articles from Periodicals and Newspapers of the Lithuanian SSR] 1940-1941, 1944-1948. Vilnius, 1954-1958.

> 1940-1941. 1958. 578 p.
>
> 1944-1945. (After the Liberation of the Lithuanian SSR). 1956. 340 p.
>
> 1946. 1955. 239 p.

---

*Editor's note: In 1969, the first volume of *Knigi na litovskom iazyke* [Books in Lithuanian] (1547-1861) was published. The second volume will cover the years 1862-1904; and volume three, 1905-1917.

1947. 1955. 255 p.

1948. 1954. 236 p.

Besides articles, reviews from periodicals and newspapers are covered.

Footnotes

[1] Until 1960, the indexes were found within *Annals of Publishing.*

[2] *Periodika Litovskoi SSR. 1940-1950.*

■ ■ ■

MOLDAVIAN SSR

The following publication is issued by the State Book Chamber of the Moldavian SSR:

Publishing Annals of the Moldavian SSR
(Letopis' pechati Moldavskoi SSR)

Published since 1963, this annals comes out quarterly and lists books and pamphlets, periodical and newspaper articles, and reviews. Since 1964, it has also listed material about the republic published in other republics of the Soviet Union.

The annals is made up of the following parts: "Book Annals," "Annals of Journal Articles," "Annals of Newspaper Articles," "Annals of Reviews," and "Annals of Soviet Moldavia (Soviet Moldavia in Publishing in the USSR)."

Material in each part is arranged systematically with entries in Moldavian listed first. Each part of the annals has a name index. There is also a list of indexed sources to "Annals of Journal Articles" and "Annals of Newspaper Articles."

The following are former publications of the Book Chamber:

Annals of the Book
(Letopis' knig)

Published in the years 1958-1962, this annals came out quarterly and listed books and pamphlets, music, and printed pictorial works in separate sections.

Entries for books are arranged systematically. Music and printed pictorial works are arranged by type. There is a name index.

Annals of Journal Articles
(Letopis' zhurnal'nykh statei)

Published for the years 1958-1962, this index came out quarterly and listed articles from periodicals and collections and, until 1961, reviews.

Entries for articles are arranged systematically and then alphabetically, regardless of the language of the text. There is a name index and a list of sources indexed.

Annals of Newspaper Articles
(Letopis' gazetnykh statei)

This index was published for the years 1958-1962. It came out monthly, although, until 1961, it was quarterly. It recorded articles from newspapers and, until 1961, reviews.

The annals has two sections: "Articles from Newspapers" and "Reviews." The material is arranged systematically and then alphabetically by title, regardless of the language of the text. There is a name index and a list of newspapers indexed.

* * *

The following retrospective bibliographies were published by the N. K. Krupskaia State Republic Library of the Moldavian SSR:

Knigi, izdannye v MSSR [Books Published in the Moldavian SSR] 1944-1957. Compiler: N. K. Sanalatii. Kishinev, 1955-1958.

1944-1950. 1955. 160 p.

1951-1955. 1957. 343 p.

1956-1957. 1958. 191 p.

■ ■ ■

LATVIAN SSR

The following is published by the Book Chamber of the Latvian SSR:

Publishing Annals of the Latvian SSR
(Letopis' pechati Latviiskoi SSR)

Published since 1957, this annals comes out monthly and lists books and pamphlets, music,[1] printed pictorial works, periodicals, and articles and reviews from periodicals and newspapers. Since 1958, it has also listed material about the republic published in other republics of the Soviet Union. In 1961-1963, it also listed material published in foreign socialist countries.

The annals is made up of the following parts: "Books, Pamphlets," "Periodical Publications," "Music," "Printed Graphics," "Periodical and Newspaper Articles," "Reviews," and "Soviet Latvia in the Press of the USSR." Entries for books, articles, and reviews are arranged systematically with literature published in Latvian given first. Music and printed pictorial works are arranged by type. In the part "Periodical Publications," which is found once a year in Issue No. 12, material is divided into two groups: 1) journals, serials, and bulletins, and 2) newspapers.

Indexes and other aids, found at the back of each issue, include a name index, a title index for books and collections of music, and a list of sources indexed for the sections "Periodical and Newspaper Articles" and "Reviews."

Since 1959, an annual cumulative index entitled *Publishing Annals of the Latvian SSR. Supplementary Indexes*[2] has been published. In this annual, there is also an index of series.

Annals formerly published by the Book Chamber include the following:

Publishing Annals
(Letopis' pechati)

Published during the years 1949-1956, this annals came out quarterly and in separate sections listed books, music, printed pictorial works, and periodical publications.

Entries for books are arranged systematically with those in Latvian given first. Music and printed pictorial works are arranged by type. Periodical publications are found in a separate section in Issue No. 4. Each section has a name index. The annual indexes for 1949-1951 are included in Issue No. 4 for the corresponding year; and, while the annual indexes for 1952-1954 came out in separate publications in 1953-1955, there were no annual indexes for 1955 and 1956.

Annals of Journal and Newspaper Articles
(Letopis' zhurnal'nykh i gazetnykh statei)

Published for the years 1949-1956, this annals appeared monthly. For 1949, it came out an an annual in 1950. It recorded articles, documentary materials, belles-lettres, and reviews published in periodicals and newspapers.

Arrangement is systematic. Literature in Latvian is given first, then literature in Russian. Reviews are placed in a separate section entitled "Annals of Reviews." The annals has a name index and a list of indexed periodicals and newspapers. For the years 1950-1953, the indexes were published as separate annual cumulations.

* * *

The following general retrospective bibliographies were also published in the republic:

Ukazatel' knig 1940-1941 gg., izdannykh v Latviiskoi SSR [Index of Books 1940-1941 Published in the Latvian SSR] Riga, 1962. 151 p. (Book Chamber of the Latvian SSR).

Ukazatel' knig Latviiskoi SSR perioda Velikoi Otechestvennoi voiny [Index of Books of the Latvian SSR for the Period of the Great Patriotic War] July 1941-October 1944. (Published in the USSR). Riga, 1964. 34 p. (Book Chamber of the Latvian SSR).

Ukazatel' knig, vyshedshikh v Latviiskoi SSR [Index of Books Issued in the Latvian SSR] 1944-1948. Riga, 1948-1949. (Book Chamber of the Latvian SSR attached to the State Library of the LSSR).

1944-1945. 1948. 112 p.

1944-1945. Supplement. 1949. 25 p.

1946. 1949. 152 p.

1947. 1949. 176 p.

1948. 1949. 190 p.

Ukazatel' (letopis') gazetnykh i zhurnal'nykh statei za 1944-1945 gg. [Index (Annals) of Newspaper and Periodical Articles for 1944-1945] Riga, 1949. 536 p. (Book Chamber of the Latvian SSR attached to the State Library of the LSSR).

Letopis' zhurnal'nykh i gazetnykh statei [Annals of Periodical and Newspaper Articles] 1946-1948. Riga, 1955-1962. (Book Chamber of the Latvian SSR).

1946. 1962.

1947. 1958.

1948. Nos. 1-4. 1955-1957.

Latyshskaia periodika [The Latvian Periodical] 1768-1919. A Bibliography. [Compilers: K. K. Egle, V. A. Lukina, A. IU. Brempele, V. F. IAget] . Riga, 1966. 525 p. (Academy of Sciences of the Latvian SSR. Fundamental Library).

Footnotes

[1] A bibliography of music publications for 1940-1941 and also a bibliography of music from periodicals and newspapers for 1940-1948 are being readied for publication.

[2] *Letopis' pechati Latviiskoi SSR. Vspomogatel'nye ukazateli.*

■ ■ ■

KIRGHIZ SSR

The following annals are published by the Kirghiz State Book Chamber:

Book Annals
(Knizhnaia Letopis')

Published since 1951, this annals has recorded material since 1950. It lists books and pamphlets and comes out quarterly, although, until 1956, it came out annually. In the period 1953-1955, it also recorded periodical publications.

There are two sections: books in Kirghiz and books in Russian. Each section is arranged systematically. Each issue of the annals has a name index and includes statistical data about books published in the Kirghiz Republic for that year.

Annals of Journal and Newspaper Articles
(Letopis' zhurnal'nykh i gazetnykh statei)

Published since 1956, this annals comes out quarterly and covers articles, documentary materials, and belles-lettres found in periodicals and newspapers.[1] It also covers periodical publications and, since 1966, reviews. Since 1965, material about the republic has been placed in the section "Kirghiz SSR in the Periodical Press of the Soviet Union."

Articles are found in two sections, one with materials in Kirghiz and the other with materials in Russian. Reviews are in a separate section. Within the sections, material is arranged systematically. Periodical publications are listed in Issue No. 4 and are arranged by type. Every issue has a name index and a list of indexed periodicals and newspapers.

* * *

The following general retrospective bibliographies have also been published by the Book Chamber:

Kirgiziia v dni Velikoi Otechestvennoi voiny [Kirgizia during the Great Patriotic War] Bibliography of Publishing in the Kirghiz SSR. (Books, Newspaper and Periodical Articles. June 1941-May 1945). Frunze, 1950. 268 p.

Kniga Sovetskoi Kirgizii [The Book in Soviet Kirghizia] Cumulated Bibliography. 1939-1954. Frunze, 1962-1964.

1939-1949. 1962. 158 p.

1950-1954. [Compilers: Kh. Tantasheva, I. S. Sergievskaia, A. A. Andasheva]. 1964. 184 p.

Ukazatel' literatury na dunganskom, karachaevo-balkarskom i checheno-ingushskom iazykakh, izdannoi v Kirgizii [Index of Literature in the Dungan, Karachay-Balkar, and Chechen-Ingush Languages Published in Kirghizia] (1930-1960). [Compilers: I. S. Sergievskaia, Kh. Tantasheva, B. Saatova]. Frunze, 1962. 16 p.

Footnotes

[1] In 1948-1949, two issues of a work entitled *Publishing Annals of Kirghizia* [Letopis' pechati Kirgizii] came out, covering only newspaper articles for the first quarter of 1948 in Russian (Issue No. 1 published in 1948) and in Kirghiz (Issue No. 1 published in 1949). With these publications, *Letopis' pechati Kirgizii* ceased.

■ ■ ■

TADZHIK SSR

The following publication is issued by the Book Chamber of the Tadzhik SSR:

Publishing Annals of the Tadzhik SSR
(Letopis' pechati Tadzhikskoi SSR)

Although the first attempt to publish it was made in 1941, when only two numbers were issued, this annals has been published quarterly since 1950. In 1950, six numbers were issued.

It lists books and pamphlets; since 1964, music; since 1965, printed pictorial works; since 1951, articles from newspapers and periodical articles;[1] since 1961, articles from transactions and other serial publications; and since 1964, reviews. Since 1965, it has also listed literature about the republic published in other republics of the Soviet Union.

The annals has the following parts: "Book Annals," "Annals of Periodical and Newspaper Articles," "Annals of Reviews," and "Tadzhik SSR in the Press of the Soviet Union." Books and pamphlets are listed systematically with division by language into Tadzhik, Uzbek, and Russian. Printed pictorial works are arranged by type; music, alphabetically by title. Music and printed pictorial works are listed in the section "Book Annals." Articles from periodicals and newspapers are arranged by the Tadzhik, Uzbek, and Russian languages and then systematically. Reviews are arranged systematically also. The annals has name indexes and a list of indexed periodicals and newspapers.

Formerly published by the Book Chamber are the following:

Book Annals
(Knizhnaia letopis')

This annals was published for the period 1937-1949. Issue No. 1 was published for 1937-1938; Issue No. 2, for 1939; a cumulated edition was published in 1949 for 1938-1948; and annals were issued for 1947[2] and 1949. It listed books and pamphlets.

The material is divided by language and then arranged systematically within the divisions. The 1949 issue has indexes for authors and titles.

Annals of Newspaper Articles
(Letopis' gazetnykh statei)

This annals was published for the years 1939-1941 and 1948-1949. Frequency varied from annual to six times a year to quarterly. It covers articles, documentary materials, and belles-lettres published in newspapers.

The articles are arranged in three sections by the Tadzhik, Uzbek, and Russian languages. Within each section, arrangement is systematic. There are no indexes.

* * *

The Book Chamber has also published the following general retrospective bibliographies:

Katalog knig Tadzhikskoi SSR [Catalog of Books of the Tadzhik SSR] (1926-1956). [Compilers: R. O. Tal'man, T. I. Poddymnikova, G. IA. IAkubov, et al.]. Dushanbe, 1960. 289, IV p.

Kniga Sovetskogo Tadzhikistana [The Book of Soviet Tadzhikistan] Catalog. (1957-1961). [Compilers: M. Akhmedova, R. Kukushkina]. Dushanbe, 1963. 315 p.*

Footnotes

[1] Periodical articles for 1940 were indexed in the separately published *Annals of Journal Articles* [Letopis' zhurnal'nykh statei]. For 1947, they were indexed in *Book and Journal Annals* [Knizhno-zhurnal'naia letopis'].

[2] Title: *Book and Journal Annals* [Knizhno-zhurnal'naia letopis']. This annals covered books, pamphlets, and periodical articles.

■ ■ ■

*A second catalog entitled *Kniga Sovetskogo Tadzhikistana* has been published for the years 1962-1966. Volumes for the years 1967-1970 and 1971-1975 are in preparation. Also being compiled is *Letopis' periodicheskikh izdanii Tadzhikskoi SSR* [Annals of Serial Publications of the Tadzhik SSR] for the years 1924-1970.

ARMENIAN SSR

The following annals are published by the State Book Chamber of the Armenian SSR:

Book Annals
(Knizhnaia letopis')

Published since 1925,[1] this annals comes out monthly. It lists books and pamphlets and, since 1951, music, printed pictorial works, and reviews. In 1933, it was not published. Frequency has varied from one to twelve issues a year. In 1950, a cumulative edition came out for 1942-1946.

There are four sections in the annals: "Book Annals," "Annals of Music Literature," "Annals of Pictorial Art," and "Annals of Reviews." Books and reviews are arranged systematically with entries in Armenian placed first. Music and printed pictorial works are given alphabetically by title. It has a name index.

In 1925-1932 and 1934, periodical publications were also listed; and in 1930-1932, 1934, 1938, and 1939, periodical articles were included. In 1929-1930 and 1935-1941, there were no indexes.

From 1963 to 1965, it came out in two issues: a basic one and a supplement. In the supplement were listed official documentary, instructional, program-methodological, and informational materials, as well as author abstracts of dissertations. It was published semiannually. Material is arranged systematically, and each issue has name indexes.

Annals of Journal Articles
(Letopis' zhurnal'nykh statei)

Published since 1938, this annals comes out quarterly and covers articles, documentary materials, and belles-lettres published in periodicals and collections. It was not published in the years 1939-1940 and 1942-1947.

It is divided into two sections: an Armenian section and a Russian section. Within each section, arrangement is systematic. Since 1948, there has been a name index and a list of source journals and collections.

Annals of Newspaper Articles
(Letopis' gazetnykh statei)

Published since 1934,[2] it comes out monthly and lists articles, documentary materials, and belles-lettres found in newspapers. It was not published in 1935-1941 and 1943-1948.

It is divided into two sections: one for articles in Armenian and one for those in Russian. Arrangement is systematic in both sections. There is a name index and a list of newspapers indexed.

* * *

Below are listed general retrospective bibliographies that have been published in Armenia.*

Bibliograficheskii ukazatel' armianskoi staropechatnoi knigi [A Bibliographic Index of Early Armenian Books] 1512-1800. [Compilers: G. M. Davtian, A. G. Sil'vanian, N. A. Voskanian, et al.]. Erevan, 1963. 308 p. (State Republic Library of the Armenian SSR Named after A. F. Miasnikiana).

Davtian, G. M. *Knigi na novoarmianskom iazyke s nachala armianskogo knigopechataniia do 1850 goda* [Books in the New Armenian Language from the Beginning of Armenian Book Printing to 1850] Survey and Bibliography. Erevan, 1964. 143 p. (A. F. Miasnikian State Republic Library of the Armenian SSR).

Korkotian, K. *Armianskaia pechatnaia kniga v Konstantinopole* [The Armenian Printed Book in Constantinople] (1567-1850). Erevan, 1964. 153 p. (A. F. Miasnikian State Republic Library of the Armenian SSR).

Bibliografiia sovetskoi kurdskoi knigi [Bibliography of the Soviet Kurdish Book] (1921-1960). Compiler: N. A. Aleksanian. Erevan, 1962. 124 p. (Academy of Sciences of the Armenian SSR. Sector of Oriental Studies).

Petrosian, O. *Bibliografiia armianskoi periodicheskoi pechati* [Bibliography of Armenian Periodical Publishing] Vols. [1], 2. Erevan, 1956-1957. (State Book Chamber of the Armenian SSR).

[Vol. 1]. (1794-1900). 1956. 746 p.

Vol. 2. (1900-1956). 1957. XXV, 624 p.

Petrosian, O. *Bibliografiia armianskoi periodicheskoi pechati. Armianskaia bol'shevistskaia pechat'* [Bibliography of the Armenian Periodical Press. The Armenian Bolshevik Press] 1920-1954. Erevan, 1954. LXIII, 668 p. (State Book Chamber of the Armenian SSR).

---

*Editor's note: To the retrospective bibliographies may be added the following:

Stepanian, M., Kalaidzhian, V. *Sovetskaia Armeniia v pechati SSSR* [Soviet Armenia in USSR Publishing] 1946-1955. Erevan, 1974. 351 p.

Barsegian, Kh. A. *Bibliografiia armianskoi bol'shevistskoi periodicheskoi pechati* [Bibliography of the Armenian Bolshevik Periodical Press] 1900-1920. Erevan, Aipetrat, 1959. 387 p.

Levonian, G. D. *Armianskaia periodicheskaia pechat'. Polnyi katalog armianskikh gazet i zhurnalov* [The Armenian Periodical Press. Complete Catalog of Armenian Newspapers and Periodicals] Erevan, Published by the Melkonian Fund, 1934. 228 p.

Footnotes

[1] Title varies: 1925-1928, 1936, and 1938 (Nos. 1-3), *Book Annals of the Armenian SSR* [Knizhnaia letopis' SSR Armenii] ; 1929-1932, *Publishing Annals of the Armenian SSR* [Letopis' pechati SSR Armenii] ; 1934, 1937, 1938 (Nos. 4-5), *Book Annals of the Armenian SSR* [Knizhnaia letopis' Armianskoi SSR] ; 1938 (Nos. 6-8) and 1941-1946, *Book Annals* [Knizhnaia letopis'] ; 1938 (Nos. 9/10-12)-1940, *Publishing Annals* [Letopis' pechati] ; and in 1935 and 1948, *Annals of the Book* [Letopis' knigi].

[2] Title varies: 1934, *Newspaper Annals* [Gazetnaia letopis'] ; 1942, *Annals of Newspaper Articles of the Armenian SSR* [Letopis' gazetnykh statei Armianskoi SSR].

■ ■ ■

TURKMEN SSR

The following publication is issued by the Book Chamber of the Turkmen SSR:

Publishing Annals of the Turkmen SSR
(Letopis' pechati Turkmenskoi SSR)

Published since 1930, this annals has listed material from 1920. It was not published in the years 1932-1937 and 1941-1950. Presently, it comes out monthly and lists books, pamphlets, music (since 1962), periodical publications (since 1964),[1] periodical articles (since 1939), newspaper articles (since 1941),[2] and reviews (since 1959). In 1939 and 1940, printed pictorial works were also listed. Since 1957, literature about Turkmenia published in other republics of the Soviet Union has been included.

The annals has the following sections: "Book Annals," "Annals of Periodical and Newspaper Articles," "Annals of Reviews," and "Turkmen SSR in the Press of the Soviet Union." Music is not treated separately.

Issue No. 12 contains a list of periodicals published in the republic for the year.

Material is arranged systematically with Turkmen language entries given ifrst. Periodical publications are arranged by type: periodicals, collections, newspapers. Since 1938, the annals has had a name index and, since 1955, a list of periodicals and newspapers cited. Since 1958, statistical data about publishing in the republic has also been included.

In the first years of its existence, this annals came out under a variety of titles and with different frequencies. In 1930-1932, six numbers were issued under the title *Publishing Annals of Turkmenistan*,[3] listing materials for 1920-1921. Books in the Turkmen language were recorded in Nos. 1, 3, and 5; those in Russian, in Nos. 2, 4, and 6. For 1938-1940, semiannual combined issues (Nos. 1/2, 3/4) came out under the title *Publishing Annals*.[4] No. 3/4 for 1940 (published in 1941) was issued under the title *Book and Journal Annals*.[5] Two separate issues in the Turkmen and Russian languages came out under the title *Turkmen Bibliography*[6] in the first and second quarters of 1941. In the years 1951-1957, *Publishing Annals of the Turkmen SSR* came out quarterly, though very late. In 1957, the annual for 1952 (with a quarterly arrangement of material) was published. In Issue No. 12 for 1958, statistical data on book production for 1957 is given.

The gap in the recording of books for 1932-1937 and 1941-1950 was filled by the bibliography *The Book of Soviet Turkmenistan. 1920-1960.* Also, the gap in the publishing record for 1941-1950 was filled by the following publications:

Knizhnaia letopis' [Book Annals] 1941-1945. Ashkhabad, 1951. 83 p. Covers books in the Turkmen language.

Letopis' pechati Turkmenskoi SSR [Publishing Annals of the Turkmen SSR] 1941-1945. M., 1948. 98 p. Covers books and articles in Russian.

Knizhnaia letopis' [Book Annals] 1946-1950. Ashkhabad, 1955. 131 p. Covers books in Turkmen and Russian.

Letopis' zhurnal'nykh statei [Annals of Journal Articles] 1941-1945. Ashkhabad, 1951. 68 p. Covers articles in the Turkmen language.

Letopis' zhurnal'nykh statei [Annals of Journal Articles] 1946-1947. Ashkhabad, 1951. 32 p. Covers articles in Turkmen.

Letopis' zhurnal'nykh i gazetnykh statei [Annals of Journal and Newspaper Articles] 1941-1950. Ashkhabad, 1961. 249 p. Covers material from republic newspapers in Turkmen and Russian for 1941-1950, articles from journals in Turkmen for 1949-1950, and in Russian for 1946-1950.

* * *

General retrospective bibliographies published by the Book Chamber are:*

Kniga Sovetskogo Turkmenistana [The Book of Soviet Turkmenistan] Cumulative Bibliography. Book 1. 1920-1960. [Compilers: M. Kuvadova, V. Panova, A. Perliev]. Ashkhabad, 1965. 707 p.

Periodicheskie izdaniia Turkmenskoi SSR [Periodical Publications of the Turkmen SSR] 1920-1958. Bibliography. [Compilers: M. A. Dolgova, A. Perliev, K. P. Shelevaia]. Ashkhabad, 1962. 73 p.

Footnotes

[1] Periodical publications were also included in 1938, 1939, and 1956.

[2] Newspaper articles for 1939-1940 were listed in the separate publication *Annals of Newspaper Articles* [Letopis' gazetnykh statei]. Issues 1 and 2 came out for 1939; issues 1/2 and 3/4 came out for 1940.

[3] *Letopis' pechati Turkmenistana.*

[4] *Letopis' pechati.*

[5] *Knizhnaia i zhurnal'naia letopis'.*

[6] *Turkmenskaia bibliografiia.*

■ ■ ■

---

*Editor's note: Three volumes of *Kniga Sovetskogo Turkmenistana* were published between 1965 and 1969, and three volumes of *Periodicheskie izdaniia Turmenskoi SSR* were published between 1962 and 1976.

ESTONIAN SSR

The following annals are published by the State Book Chamber of the Estonian SSR:

Book Annals
(Knizhnaia letopis')

Published since 1946,[1] this annals comes out quarterly and lists books, pamphlets, periodical publications, printed pictorial works, music, and maps. In the years 1944-1946, leaflets were also listed; and in 1948-1949, reviews were listed. The annals in 1951 came out as an annual.

Book Annals has four parts: "Books and Pamphlets," "Printed Graphics," "Music," and "Periodical Publications." Entries for books are arranged systematically with those in Estonian given first. Printed pictorial works and music are arranged by type.

Entries for journals, bulletins, collections, and transactions are grouped systematically, while entries for newspapers are grouped by territory. A list of periodical publications is given in the fourth number of the year.

The indexes have come out annually as a separate issue since 1962. There is a name index to the sections devoted to books and music; a title index to books, music, and periodical publications; an index of organizations and institutions; a series index; a geographic index to books; an index of first words of the texts of vocal music; and an alphabetical index of periodical publications. In 1948 and 1949, an index of authors of reviewed works and titles of reviewed anonymous works, together with an index of reviewers, was published in the annals.

Annals of Articles and Reviews
(Letopis' statei i retsenzii)

Published since 1954, this annals comes out monthly and covers periodical and newspaper articles and reviews. In 1954 and 1955, it came out quarterly.

Since 1959, literature about Estonia published in other republics of the Soviet Union has been placed in a special section. Since 1963, this section has also included literature published in various socialist countries.

The annals has three parts: "Annals of Articles," "Annals of Reviews," and "Soviet Estonica." In each part, the arrangement is systematic. The indexes are issued annually as a separate publication and include a name index to all three parts, an index of titles of anonymous works found in the "Annals of Reviews," and a list of sources indexed. Until 1962, the indexes were a part of the annals itself.

* * *

The Book Chamber earlier published the following:

Annals of Articles
(Letopis' statei)

Published in 1952 and 1953, this annals came out quarterly and indexed articles from periodicals, collections, and newspapers. Material is arranged systematically; and there is a name index and a list of periodicals, collections, and newspapers indexed.

Annals of Reviews
(Letopis' retsenzii)

Published during the years 1950-1953, this annals came out quarterly and covered reviews, critical articles, and surveys published in periodicals, newspapers, and collections. The material is arranged systematically. The annals has a name index, an index of titles of anonymous works reviewed, and an index of reviewers.

* * *

General retrospective bibliographies published by the Fr. R. Kreitsval'd State Library of the Estonian SSR are the following:

Kniga Sovetskoi Estonii [The Book of Soviet Estonia] 1940-1954. Cumulative Bibliography. Tallin, 1956. 513 p.

Knizhnaia letopis' Estonskoi SSR [Book Annals of the Estonian SSR] National Bibliography for 1944-1945. Tartu, 1947. 194 p.

Footnotes

[1] In a collective issue published in 1947, literature for 1944-1945 is listed.

■ ■ ■

BASHKIR ASSR

The State Book Chamber of the Bashkir ASSR publishes the following annals:

Book Annals
(Knizhnaia letopis')*

Published since 1935,[1] this annals has listed material since 1934. It comes out annually and lists books, pamphlets, and since 1956, music. Since 1964, works by Bashkir authors, Bashkir folklore, and literature about Bashkiria published in other republics of the Soviet Union have been put in a special section.

The annals has two parts: one devoted to Bashkir and Tatar language materials, the other to material in Russian. In each part, the material is arranged systematically except that music entries are put in alphabetical order. There is a name index and a list of indexed periodicals and newspapers. In the years 1938-1940, there was also an index of organizations and institutions and a series index.

Since 1962, statistical tables concerning books, newspapers, and periodicals published in the republic for the year have been included.

Until 1950, the annals was composed of four quarterly numbers published as combined issues, covering either a year or a half year. For the years 1934-1937 and 1940-1947, it came out as a single issue each year; for 1938-1939 and 1948-1949, as semiannual issues. Some issues were quite late: those for 1941-1943 came out in 1948; for 1944 in 1950; for 1945 in 1951; and for 1946, in 1952.

* * *

The following was issued earlier by the Book Chamber:

Annals of Periodical Publications
(Letopis' periodicheskikh izdanii)

This annals was published for the years 1937-1940, came out annually, and listed periodicals, newspapers, and other periodical and serial publications.

It consists of two parts: periodicals and newspapers. Within these parts, material is arranged by language with Bashkir and Tatar language publications listed first. It has a place of publication index.

---

*Editor's note: Since 1968, the organ of Bashkir national bibliography has been entitled *Letopis' pechati Bashkirskoi ASSR* [Publishing Annals of the Bashkir ASSR].

Footnotes

[1] In the years 1935-1940, it was entitled *Book Annals of the Bashkir Central Book Chamber* [Knizhnaia letopis' Bashkirskoi tsentral'noi knizhnoi palaty].

■ ■ ■

TATAR ASSR

The following annals is published by the State Book Chamber of the Tatar ASSR:

Publishing Annals of Tataria
(Letopis' pechati Tatarii)

Published since 1961, this annals comes out quarterly and lists books, pamphlets, music, periodical and newspaper articles, and reviews. It also covers literature about Tataria published in other republics of the Soviet Union.

It is composed of the following parts: "Book Annals," "Annals of Reviews," "Music," "Annals of Journal and Newspaper Articles," and "Tataria in the Press of the Soviet Union." In each part, Russian language materials are given, following materials in Tatar and other languages. Entries for books, articles, and reviews are arranged systematically. Music is listed alphabetically by title entry. The annals has a name index and a list of periodicals and newspapers indexed.

* * *

Works formerly published by the Book Chamber are the following:

Book Annals
(Knizhnaia letopis')

This annals was published during the periods 1938-1941 and 1945-1960.* It came out annually, although in certain years there were two to four issues. It recorded books, pamphlets, music, and printed pictorial works.

---

*Editor's note: In 1972, an issue of *Knizhnaia letopis'*, covering the war years, 1941-1945, was published.

In the annals for 1960, literature about Tataria published in other republics of the Soviet Union was also included.

The material is arranged by language. Entries for books and pamphlets are arranged systematically; entries for music, alphabetically. The annals has a name index. In the annals for 1938 and 1939, there is also an index of organizations and institutions.

Annals of Periodical Publications of the Tatar ASSR
(Letopis' periodicheskikh izdanii Tatarskoi ASSR)

Published during the years 1938-1948, this annals came out annually and listed periodicals and newspapers. Material is arranged by language. It has an index of cities and districts with the newspapers published in them.

Annals of Journal and Newspaper Articles
(Letopis' zhurnal'nykh i gazetnykh statei)

Published during the years 1955-1960, this annals came out annually (except for 1955, when it was quarterly) and recorded articles and materials from periodicals and newspapers. In Issue No. 1 for 1955, which had the title *Annals of Journal and Newspaper Articles and Reviews*, reviews were also included.

The material is arranged systematically. The annals has a name index and a list of periodicals and newspapers indexed.

In 1958, it was published in two issues, one for Tatar language publications and the other for Russian publications. For 1959 and 1960, only the issues covering Tatar materials came out.

Annals of Reviews
(Letopis' retsenzii)

Published during the years 1953-1959, this annals came out annually and covered reviews of books and articles from journals and newspapers. Reviews for 1960 are in Issue No. 1 of *Publishing Annals of Tataria* for 1963.

Material is arranged by language and then systematically. There is an index of authors, reviewers, and titles of works reviewed.

■ ■ ■

CHUVASH ASSR

The following annals is issued by the Book Chamber of the Chuvash ASSR:

Publishing Annals
(Letopis' pechati)

Published since 1957, this annals comes out quarterly and lists books and pamphlets, music, printed pictorial works (since 1959), periodical publications, periodical and newspaper articles, and reviews. Since 1964, it has also recorded materials about Chuvashia and works of Chuvash authors published in other republics of the Soviet Union.

The annals has the following parts: "Books," "Periodical Articles," "Newspaper Articles," "Music Publications," "Reviews," and "Pictorial Art." Books and articles are arranged systematically with Chuvash language publications given first. Entries for music, reviews, and printed pictorial works are given in alphabetical order. Issue No. 4 includes a list of periodical publications, a section "Chuvashia in the Press of the USSR," and statistical data about publishing in the republic for the year. It has a name index, an index of titles, and a list of periodicals and newspapers indexed.

* * *

Works formerly published by the Book Chamber are the following:

Book Annals
(Knizhnaia letopis')

Published for the years 1950-1956, this annals came out annually. It listed books, pamphlets, and music, and, in the period 1950-1953, periodical publications. Entries for books and pamphlets are arranged systematically; and those for music, alphabetically. It has a name and title index.

Annals of Journal Articles
(Letopis' zhurnal'nykh statei)

Published for the years 1951-1956, this annals came out annually and recorded articles, documentary materials, and belles-lettres from periodicals and collections.

Arrangement of entries is systematic. There is a name index and a list of periodicals and collections cited.

Annals of Newspaper Articles
(Letopis' gazetnykh statei)

Published for the years 1954-1956, this annals came out quarterly and covered articles and other materials from newspapers. Arrangement of entries is systematic. The annals has a name index and a list of newspapers cited.

* * *

The following general retrospective bibliographies have also been published by the Book Chamber:

Knizhnaia letopis' [Book Annals] 1918-1949. Cheboksary, 1949-1964.

  1918-1928. 1960. 95 p.

  1929-1938. 1964. 274 p.

  1939-1940. 1949. 50 p.

  1941-1945. 1949. 96 p.

  1946-1949. 1950. 100 p.

Letopis' muzykal'noi literatury [Annals of Music Literature] 1917-1952. Cheboksary, 1960. 56 p.

■ ■ ■

PUBLICATIONS OF THE REPUBLIC LIBRARIES
OF THE OTHER ASSRs

In the autonomous republics of the Russian Federation which do not have book chambers, the republic libraries carry out the compilation of the state national bibliography. An annals of publishing is issued by each of the state republic libraries of the Buriat, Dagestan, Kabardino-Balkarsk, Karelian, Komi, Mari, Mordovian, North Ossetian, Udmurt, Chechen-Ingush, and Yakut autonomous republics.

These republics began publishing their own annals at different times. The Komi ASSR and the Buriat ASSR published their annals for 1958 in 1959 and 1960, respectively. The Yakut ASSR published a combined annals for 1958-1959 in 1960. In 1960, the Karelian ASSR, Mordovian ASSR, North Ossetian ASSR, and Chechen-Ingush ASSR published their first annals, which covered the year 1959. In 1961, the Kabardino-Balkarsk ASSR and the Mari ASSR published their first annals for the same year. In the Dagestan ASSR and the Udmurt ASSR, the first annals, covering the year 1960, were published in 1961.

As a rule, the annals of the autonomous republics come out once a year. An exception is the *Publishing Annals of the Karelian ASSR,*[1] which comes out semiannually, although it was issued as an annual in 1959.

The selection, description, and classification of material is done according to instructions developed for book chamber publications.

The annals list books, pamphlets, and periodical publications issued in the autonomous republics. In the annals of the Buriat, Karelian, Komi, Mari, and Mordovian ASSRs, music has been included for various years. In the annals of the Buriat, Komi, Mari, Udmurt, and Yakut ASSRs, printed pictorial works have also been included in certain years. In the annals of the Buriat, Karelian, and Mari ASSRs, periodical and newspaper articles and reviews are covered.

183

Material in these annals is divided by type of publication. In sections devoted to books and articles, material in certain annals is arranged systematically with a further subdivision made on the basis of language; in other annals, it is arranged by language and then systematically.

Music and printed pictorial works are basically arranged by type. In certain republic annals, these materials are arranged alphabetically. Periodical publications are arranged by type and alphabetically by title. All annals have name indexes. The *Publishing Annals of the Buriat ASSR*[2] has an alphabetical index of authors and titles.

The annals of the libraries of the autonomous republics in combination with the annals of the book chambers form a complex system of publication which is, in total, the national bibliography of the Soviet Union.

Footnotes

[1] *Letopis' pechati Karel'skoi ASSR.*

[2] *Letopis' pechati Buriatskoi ASSR.*

PART III

APPENDIXES

APPENDIX I
LIST OF BOOK CHAMBERS WITH ADDRESSES

Vsesoiuznaia knizhnaia palata (All-Union Book Chamber)
Moscow, TSentr, Vsesoiuznaia knizhnaia palata

Knizhnaia palata Ukrainskoi SSR (Book Chamber of the Ukrainian SSR)
Khar'kov, ul. Artema, 31

Knizhnaia palata Belorusskoi SSR (Book Chamber of the Belorussian SSR)
Minsk, ul. Krasnoarmeiskaia, 9

Gosudarstvennaia knizhnaia palata Uzbekskoi SSR (State Book Chamber of
the Uzbek SSR)
Tashkent, ul. Navoi, 30

Knizhnaia palata Kazakhskoi SSR (Book Chamber of the Kazakh SSR)
Alma-Ata, ul. K. Marksa, 85

Gosudarstvennaia knizhnaia palata Gruzinskoi SSR (State Book Chamber
of the Georgian SSR)
Tbilisi, ul. Mardzhanishvili, 5

Azerbaidzhanskaia gosudarstvennaia knizhnaia palata (Azerbaidzhan State
Book Chamber)
Baku, ul. Miasnikova, 8

Knizhnaia palata Litovskoi SSR (Book Chamber of the Lithuanian SSR)
Vil'nius, ul. Rashitoiu, 4

Gosudarstvennaia knizhnaia palata Moldavskoi SSR (State Book Chamber of the Moldavian SSR)
Kishinev, ul. Zhukovskogo, 16

Knizhnaia palata Latviiskoi SSR (Book Chamber of the Latvian SSR)
Riga, ul. Bibliotekas, 5

Kirgizskaia gosudarstvennaia knizhnaia palata (Kirghiz State Book Chamber)
Frunze, ul. Pushkina, 78

Knizhnaia palata Tadzhikskoi SSR (Book Chamber of the Tadzhik SSR)
Dushanbe, ul. Ordzhonikidze, 36

Gosudarstvennaia knizhnaia palata Armianskoi SSR (State Book Chamber of the Armenian SSR)
Erevan, ul. Teriana, 91

Knizhnaia palata Turkmenskoi SSR (State Book Chamber of the Turkmen SSR)
Ashkhabad, ul. 1 Maia, 19

Gosudarstvennaia knizhnaia palata Estonskoi SSR (State Book Chamber of the Estonian SSR)
Tallin, ul. Kokhtu, 3

Gosudarstvennaia knizhnaia palata Bashkirskoi ASSR (State Book Chamber of the Bashkir ASSR)
Ufa, ul. Lenina, 4

Gosudarstvennaia knizhnaia palata Tatarskoi ASSR (State Book Chamber of the Tatar ASSR)
Kazan', ul. Lenina, 2

Knizhnaia palata Chuvashskoi ASSR (Book Chamber of the Chuvash ASSR)
Cheboksary, pr. Lenina, 16v

APPENDIX II
REPUBLIC ORGANS OF CURRENT NATIONAL BIBLIOGRAPHY IN ENGLISH, RUSSIAN, AND THE ORIGINAL LANGUAGES

Title in English	Title in Russian	Original Title
	UKRAINIAN SSR	
Book Annals	Letopis' knig	Litopys knyh
Annals of Music Literature	Letopis' muzykal'noi literatury	Litopys muzychnoi literatury
Annals of Pictorial Art	Letopis' izobrazitel'nogo iskusstva	Litopys obrazotvorchoho mystetstva
Annals of Journal Articles	Letopis' zhurnal'nykh statei	Litopys zhurnalnykh statei
Annals of Newspaper Articles	Letopis' gazetnykh statei	Litopys gazetnykh statei
Annals of Reviews	Letopis' retsenzii	Litopys retsenzii
Ukrainian SSR in Publications of the Soviet Republics	Ukrainskaia SSR v izdaniiakh respublik Sovetskogo Soiuza	Ukrainska RSR u vydanniakh respublik Radianskoho Soiuzu

189

Title in English	Title in Russian	Original Title
	BELORUSSIAN SSR	
Annals of Belorussian Publishing	Letopis' pechati BSSR	Letapis druku BSSR
	UZBEK SSR	
Book Annals	Knizhnaia letopis'	Kitob letopisi
Annals of Journal Articles	Letopis' zhurnal'nykh statei	Zhurnal makolalari letopisi
	ARMENIAN SSR	
Book Annals	Knizhnaia letopis'	Grki taregir
Annals of Journal Articles	Letopis' zhurnal'nykh statei	Zhurnalaiin odvatsneri taregir
Annals of Newspaper Articles	Letopis' gazetnykh statei	Lragraiin odvatsneri taregir
	TURKMEN SSR	
Publishing Annals of the Turkmen SSR	Letopis' pechati Turkmenskoi SSR	Turkmenistan SSR-nin metbugat letopisi
	ESTONIAN SSR	
Book Annals	Knizhnaia letopis'	Raamatukroonika
Annals of Articles and Reviews	Letopis' statei i retsenzii	Artiklite ja Retsensioonide Kroonika

Title in English	Title in Russian	Original Title
	BASHKIR ASSR	
Book Annals	Knizhnaia letopis'	Kitap letopise
	TATAR ASSR	
Publishing Annals of Tataria	Letopis' pechati Tatarii	Tatarstan matbugat el"iazmasy
	KAZAKH SSR	
Publishing Annals of the Kazakh SSR	Letopis' pechati Kazakhskoi SSR	Kitap letopisi
	GEORGIAN SSR	
Book Annals	Knizhnaia letopis'	Tsignis matiane
Bibliography of Musical Works	Bibliografiia muzykal'nykh proizvedenii	
Bibliography of Pictorial Art	Bibliografiia izobrazitel'nogo iskusstva	
Annals of Journal Articles	Letopis' zhurnal'nykh statei	Zhurnalis statiebis matiane
Annals of Newspaper Articles	Letopis' gazetnykh statei	Gazetis statiebis matiane
Bibliography of Reviews	Bibliografiia retsenzii	Retsenziebis bibliografia

Title in English	Title in Russian	Original Title
	AZERBAIDZHAN SSR	
Annals of Azerbaidzhan Publishing	Letopis' pechati Azerbaidzhana	Azerbaijan metbuat letopisi
Book Annual of Azerbaidzhan	Ezhegodnik knigi Azerbaidzhana	
	TADZHIK SSR	
Publishing Annals of the Tadzhik SSR	Letopis' pechati Tadzhiksoi SSR	Solnomai matbuoti RSS Tochikston
	CHUVASH ASSR	
Publishing Annals	Letopis' pechati	Pichet letopise
	LITHUANIAN SSR	
Annals of Publishing	Letopis' pechati	Spaudos metrastis
	MOLDAVIAN SSR	
Publishing Annals of the Moldavian SSR	Letopis' pechati Moldavskoi SSR	Kronika presei RSSM
	LATVIAN SSR	
Publishing Annals of the Latvian SSR	Letopis' pechati Latviiskoi SSR	Latvijas PSR Preses hronika

Title in English	Title in Russian	Original Title
	KIRGHIZ SSR	
Book Annals	Knizhnaia letopis'	Kitep letopisi
Annals of Journal and Newspaper Articles	Letopis' zhurnal'nykh i gazetnykh statei	Zhurnal znana gazettik makalalardyn letopisi

APPENDIX III
TRANSLATION OF ENTRIES APPEARING
IN TEXT OF TRANSLATION

BOOK ANNALS

Tsetkin, K. Recollections of Lenin. Moscow, Politzdat, 1966. 3K26
(003) 40 p. 20cm. 100,000 copies. 7 kopecks.

Slavianskoe vozrozhdenie. A collection of articles and materials.
[Edited by S. A. Nikitin (chief editor) and others]. Moscow, "Nauka", 1966.
250 p. with ill. 22cm. (AN SSSR. In-t Slavianovedeniia). 1,500 copies.
1 rouble 10 kopecks. Bound. —Part of text in Bulgarian, Serbian, and French.

Shkvarkin, V. Comedies. [Introduction by I. Shtok. Notes by L.
Nimvitska]. Moscow, "Iskusstvo", 1966. 374 p.; 14 l. of ill. 17cm. 5,000
copies. 1 rouble 4 kopecks. Bound.
Contents: Chuzhoi rebenok. —Vesennii smotr. —Strashnyi sud.
—Prostaia devushka. —Prints Napoleon.   891.71-2

ANNALS OF SERIAL PUBLICATIONS OF THE USSR

District Newspaper

Avangard. Published from 1 July 1932. Klimovo. 3 times/week. 42cm.
4 p. 2,000 copies. 2 kopecks.
1961 No. 1 (2901) — 155 (3055)
1962 No. 1 (3056) — 50 (3105) (1 Jan-25 Apr)
1965 No. 1 (3106) — 116 (3221) 3 Apr-30Dec)
Break in publication: April 26, 1962-April 2, 1965. Title through
No. 50 (25 Apr) 1962 "Kolkhoznyi put' ".

Journal

Aziia i Afrika segodnia. Monthly socio-political magazine of the Institute of the Peoples of Asia and the Institute of Africa of the Academy of Science USSR. Pub. since July 1957. Moscow, "Nauka". Summaries in English.
1961-1965. – Price 30 kopecks.
Title: through No. 2, 1961 "Sovremennyi Vostok".

Bulletin

Biulleten' Tsentral'nogo nauchno-issledovatel'skogo instituta informatsii i techniko-ekonomicheskikh issledovanii chernoi metallurgii. Pub. since 1944. Bimonthly. Moscow.
1961. 5,000-5,200 copies; 1962. 5,000-5,125 copies; 1963. 5,000-5,150 copies; 1964. 4,300-5,000 copies; 1965. 4,050-4,350 copies. – Price 50 kopecks.
Title through No. 9, 1963: "Biulleten' Tsentr. in-ta informatsii chernoi metallurgii". Publisher through No. 7, 1961: Metallurgizdat.

Transactions

Uchenye zapiski. (Tuva Science Research Institute of Language, Literature, and History). Kyzyl.
Issue 9. 1961. 3,000 copies. 90 kopecks; issue 10. 1963. 1,000 copies. 90 kopecks; issue 11. 1964. 1,500 copies. 1 rouble.
Issue 1 – 1953; issue 8 – 1960.

MUSIC ANNALS

Grieg, E. Two symphonic dances. [Opus 64, Nos. 2 and 3]. Instrumentation for the brass band of G. Sal'nikov. Score and voices [25 orchestral parts]. Moscow, "Muzyka", 1966. 59 p. score, 98 p. of parts with separate paginations. 22cm. (Repertuar dukhovogo orkestra). 1,940 copies. 1 rouble 2 kopecks. In a paper folder.

Pesennik. Popular songs of Soviet composers. [66 songs, choruses, solos. Kiev, "Mistetstvo", 1966]. 261 p. 14cm. 30,000 copies. 1 rouble. Bound. Compiler: N. M. Rybal'chenko. Parallel text in Ukrainian and Russian.

ANNALS OF PICTORIAL ART PUBLICATIONS

Poster

Vyshe, dal'she, bystree. [Toward the Day of the Air Force of the USSR]. Artist: V. Viktorov. Moscow, "Sov. Khudozhnik", 1965. 108x54cm. 125,000 copies. 10 kopecks. Color offset.

Reproduction

Serov, V. Zarosshii prud. (GTG). Moscow, "Pravda", 1965. 60x82cm. 16,000 copies. 30 kopecks. Color autotype.

Plate

Zvontsov, V. M. V polovod'e. Leningrad, Kombinat grafich. rabot LOKHF RSFSR, 1966. 30x31cm. 200 copies. 3 roubles. Etching.

Portrait

Rustaveli, Shota. Artist: E. Rakuzin. Moscow, "Sov. Khudozhnik", 1966. 60x47cm. 10,000 copies. 13 kopecks. – Zincograph.

Album

Tantsuet Turkmenistan. State Ensemble of the Folk Dance of Turkmen SSR. [Photo album. Text and photos by S. Ataev. Verses by P. Ionov]. Ashkhabad, "Turkmenistan", 1965. 112 p. of ill. and text. 22cm. 2,000 copies. 95 kopecks. Bound – Autotype.

CARTOGRAPHIC ANNALS

1:4.000.000

Evropa. Physical instructional map. For high school. G-960. By the map compilation-editorial unit of GUGK in 1964. Editor: Kursakov I. V. Moscow, GUGK, 1965. 4 sheets multicol. 23,000 copies. 43 kopecks.

ANNALS OF JOURNAL ARTICLES

Umanskii, L. Who can become an organizer. An essay on the psychology of the organizer. Molodoi kommunist, 1966, No. 9, p. 79-85. Continuation. Begun in Issue No. 8.

Rubinskii, IU. The Latin quarter. [On the status of French students. Essay]. Novoe vremia, 1966, No. 44, p. 29-32.

Rylov, IU. A. and Skuridin, G. A. On the theory of the ionization calorimeter. IAdrenaia fizika, vol. 2, no. 4, 1965, p. 691-704. Resume in English. Bibliography: 9 titles.

Iskander, Fazil'. The constellation Kozlotur. Tale. Novyi mir, 1966, No. 8, p. 3-75.

ANNALS OF NEWSPAPER ARTICLES

Sluzhba nauchnoi informatsii. [Editorial]. Pravda, 1967, 12 Jan.

Leont'ev, A. and Panov, D. Man in the world of technology. [Problems of engineering psychology]. Pravda, 1966, 14 Oct.

Clavel, Bernard. Proshchai, Bessi! Story. Translated from the French by U. Malishevskii. Illustrator: E. Lebedeva. Literaturnaia gazeta, 1965, 9 Oct.

Arsenal sovetskogo rastenievodstva. [On the work of the Vavilov All-Union institute on plant breading. Articles and notes] : D. Brezhnev. For the revewal of the earth. – K. Budin. Searches into the depths of life [and others]. Sel. zhizn', 1967, 22 July.

ANNALS OF REVIEWS

Mikhailov, A. I. Pavel Korin. [Moscow, "Sov. khudozhnik", 1965]. Zotov, A. Khudozhnik, 1966, No. 3, p. 62.

Grekova I. Summer in the city. Story. In Novyi mir, 1965, No. 4.
Brovman, G. Civic feeling and the character of modern man. Moscow, 1966, No. 4, p. 197-203.
Lobanov, M. Inner and outer man. Mol. gvardiia, 1966, No. 5, p.286-302.

Schlesinger, A. M. A thousand days. John F. Kennedy in the White House. [Tysiacha dnei. Dzhon F. Kennedi v Belom dome]. Boston, 1965.
Anatol'ev, G. The thousand days of the Kennedy presidency. Mezhdu-nar. zhizn', 1966, No. 4, p. 127-129.

BIBLIOGRAPHY OF SOVIET BIBLIOGRAPHY

Separately Published Bibliography

Bibliografiia Afganistana. Literature in Russian. Compiled by T. I. Kukhtin. Moscow, "Nauka", 1965. 272 p. (Academy of Sciences USSR. Institute of the Peoples of Asia). 1,300 copies. 1 rouble 56 kopecks.

Bibliographies in Books and Articles

Kosilov, S. A. Essays on the physiology of work. Moscow, 1965, p. 370-375. [Approx. 190 titles].

Semcnov, I. V. From the history of the discovery and exploration of the archipelago Severnaia Zemlia. Problems of the Arctic and Antarctic, Issue 16, 1964, p. 10-12. [46 titles].

Voprosy fiziologii vegetativnoi nervnoi sistemy i mozshechka. Erevan, 1964. 611 p. [Literature at end of article].

APPENDIX IV
MEETINGS OF THE DIRECTORS
OF THE BOOK CHAMBERS

I.	Moscow	20-23 October	1924
II.	Moscow	October	1925
III.	Kharkov	14-17 March	1927
IV.	Moscow	May	1928
V.	Baku	September	1929
VI.	Moscow	21-16 November	1930
VII.	Moscow	27 December	1936
VIII.	(Not Known)		1937
IX.	Moscow	15-19 December	1949
X.	Moscow	20-23 November	1957
XI.	Moscow	20-27 October	1958
XII.	Moscow	16-19 December	1960
XIII.	Kharkov	13-15 June	1962
XIV.	Moscow	16-18 June	1964
XV.	Moscow	8 October	1965
XVI.	Moscow	30 May	1967
XVII.	Moscow	15-17 October	1969
XVIII.	Moscow ?	12-15 October	1971
XIX.	Moscow	2-3 July	1974
	Moscow*	12-14 April	1976

*This meeting, apparently unnumbered, was called a conference-seminar.

APPENDIX V
GLOSSARY OF TERMS

a

avtoreferat

al'bom

al'manakh

annotatsiia

atlas

a

author abstract

album

anthology, almanac

annotation

atlas

b

bibliograficheskaia zapis'

bibliografiia

broshiura

b

bibliographic entry

bibliography

pamphlet, brochure

v

vedomstvennye izdaniia

vozzvanie

vspomogatel'nyi ukazatel'

vypusk

v

government documents

proclamation

auxiliary index

issue, number

g

gazeta	newspaper
geograficheskaia karta	geographic map
god izdaniia	year of publication
gorod	city, town
gosudarstvennaia bibliografiia	national bibliography
graviura	engraving, print
grafik	graph, diagram
grafika	drawing, print

d

diktant	dictation
dissertatsiia	dissertation, thesis
doklad	report, contribution

e

ezhegodnik	annual, yearbook
ezhegodno	annually
ezhednevno	daily
ezhekvartal'no	quarterly
ezhemesiachno	monthly
ezhenedel'no	weekly

zh

zhurnal	journal, periodical, magazine
vypusk zhurnala	number or issue of a journal
nomer zhurnala	number or issue of a journal

z

zaglavie	title
zaglavnyi list	title page

zagolovok	heading, title
zapis'	entry, record

i | **i**

izvestie	proceedings, transactions
izdanie	edition, publication
izdatel'stvo	publisher
izobrazitel'nie iskusstva	pictorial arts, graphic arts
illiustrator	illustrator
illiustratsiia	illustration
imennoi ukazatel'	name index
informatsiia	indormation

k | **k**

kalendarnye stenki	wall calendar
kalendar'	calendar
karta	map, chart
kartina	picture, painting
kinofil'm	movie, film
kniga	book
knizhki—kartinki	picture books
knizhnaia produktsiia	book production
kompozitor	composer
krai	territory, province

l | **l**

letopis'	annals, chronicle
libretto	libretto
list	sheet, leaf
listazh	number of sheets in a book
listovka	leaflet

(Letter l continues on page 206)

litografiia	lithograph
lozung	slogan
lubok	cheap popular print

m	**m**
malotirazhnoe izdanie	small run edition
masshtab	scale
mesto izdaniia	place of publication
mnozhitel'nyi apparat	duplicating machine, copy machine
monografiia	monograph
morskaia karta	nautical chart

n	**n**
nagliadnye posobiia	visual aids
nazvanie	title, name
nomer	number, issue
noty	printed music

o	**o**
oblast'	province, region
obiazatel'nyi ekzempliar	obligatory copy—i.e., legal deposit copy
okrug	district
ofort	etching
opisanie	description, entry
organ	organ—i.e., in the sense of publication
otkrytka	postcard
otkrytoe pis'mo	postcard

p

papka	folder or case for documents
partitura	score (musical)
perevod	translation
perevodchik	translator
perepechatka	reprint
perechen'	list
periodika	periodical
periodicheskie izdaniia	serial publications, periodical publications
periodichnost' (sometimes povtornost')	periodicity, frequency
personaliia	names of persons to whom a work is dedicated
pechatnoe produktsiia	see pechat'
pechat'	publishing, press, printing, print or type
pis'mo	letter
plakat	poster, placard
podzagolovok	subtitle, subheading
podrubrika	subheading
polnoe sobranie sochinenii	complete works
portret	portrait
posobie	aid
pravila	rules
edinye pravila	uniform rules
predislovie	preface, foreword
probel	gap
prodolzhaiushchiesia izdaniia	continuing publications, serials
proizvedenie	work
proizvedenie pechati	publication, printed work
proizvedenie khudozhestvennoi literatury	work of fiction
putevoditel'	guide book
piatigodnik	quinquennial

r

raion	district
redaktor	editor
glavnyi redaktor	editor-in-chief
otvetstvennyi redaktor	managing editor
reproduktsiia	reproduction (of a painting, drawing, etc.)
respublika	republic
retsenzent	reviewer
retsenziia	review
risunok	drawing, picture
rotator	duplicating machine, such as mimeograph machine
rubrika	heading
rukovodstvo	guide, manual, handbook

s

sbornik	collection
svodnaia bibliografiia	collective bibliography, cumulative bibliography
seriia	series
izdatel'skaia seriia	publisher's series
slovar'	dictionary
sobranie sochinenii	collected works
sol'fedzhio	solfeggio
sostavitel'	compiler, author
sostavlenie	compilation
sochinenie	work
spisok	list
spravochnik	reference work, handbook
ssylka	reference
stat'ia	article
stranitsa	page
skhema klassifikatsii	classification scheme

t

tabel'	table
tabel'-kalendari	tabular calendar
tablitsa	table
tablitsa logarifmov	table of logarithms
tematicheskii	topical, subject
tirazh	press run
trudy	transactions, proceedings

u

ukazatel'	index
alfavitnyi ukazatel'	alphabetic index
vspomogatel'nyi ukazatel'	auxiliary index
geograficheskii ukazatel'	geographic index
imennoi ukazatel'	name index
predmetnyi ukazatel'	subject index
sistematicheskii ukazatel'	systematic or classified index
tematicheskii ukazatel'	topical index
ukazatel' zaglavii	title index
ukazatel' kollektivov	corporate author index
uslovnyi znak	conventional sign
uchebnik	textbook
uchebnoe posobie	textbook
uchenye zapiski	contributions, proceedings

f

familiia	surname
format	size
fotograviura	photogravure
fotograficheskii snimok	photograph
fotosnimok	photograph

kh

chrestomatiia

khudozhestvennaia literatura

khudozhnik, -itsa

kh

reader

belles-lettres, fiction

artist

ts

tsena

ts

price

ch

chast'

ch

part

e

ekzempliar

entsiklopediia

estamp

e

copy

encyclopedia

print, plate

APPENDIX VI
BIBLIOGRAPHY

GENERAL

Chandler, George. *Libraries, Documentation and Bibliography in the USSR 1917-1971: Survey and Critical Analysis of Soviet Studies 1967-1971.* London: Seminar Press, 1972. 183 p. (International Bibliographical and Library Series).

Gorokhoff, Boris I. *Publishing in the U.S.S.R.* Bloomington: Indiana University Publications, 1959. 306 p. (Slavic and East European Series, vol. 19).

Horecky, Paul L. *Libraries and Bibliographic Centers in the Soviet Union.* Bloomington: Indiana University Publications, 1959. 287 p. (Slavic and East European Series, vol. 16).

Kaldor, Ivan. "National Libraries and Bibliographies in the U.S.S.R." In *Comparative and International Librarianship Essays on Themes and Problems.* Westport, CT: Greenwood, 1970. Pp. 167-197.

Ruggles, Melville J., and Vaclav Mostecky. *Russian and East European Publications in the Libraries of the United States.* New York: Columbia University Press, 1960. 396 p. (Columbia University Studies in Library Service, no. 11).

Ruggles, Melville J., and Raynard C. Swank. *Soviet Libraries and Librarianship: Report of the Visit of the Delegation of U.S. Librarians to the Soviet Union, May-June, 1961, under the U.S.–Soviet Cultural Exchange Agreement.* Chicago: American Library Association, 1962. 147 p.

ARCHIVES

"Tipovoe polozhenie ob Arkhive pechati respublikanskoi knizhnoi palaty [Standard Regulation on the Archives of the Press of the Republic Book Chambers]." *Sovetskaia bibliografiia* 4 (1967): 20-22.

AUTOMATION

Gruzinskaia, N. N., and I. S. Teliatitskii. "O putiakh sovershenstvovaniia gosudarstvennoi bibliografii na baze vnedreniia avtomatizirovannoi sistemy vo Vsesoiuznoi knizhnoi palate [Means of Improving National Bibliography on the Basis of Introducing an Automated System in the All-Union Book Chamber]." *Sovetskaia bibliografiia* 4 (1976): 3-9.

Panterov, S. S. "O sozdanii avtomatizirovannoi sistemy podgotovki i vypuska izdanii gosudarstvennoi bibliografii vo Vsesoiuznoi knizhnoi palate [On the Creation of an Automated System for the Preparation and Publication of the National Bibliography at the All-Union Book Chamber]." *Sovetskaia bibliografiia* 5 (1974): 3-8.

BIBLIOGRAPHY

Alferova, Lidiia Nikolaevna, and B. N. Kasabova. *Sovetskaia bibliografiia: sistematicheskii ukazatel' soderzhaniia (1933-1970)* [Soviet Bibliography: A Systematic Index of Contents (1933-1970)]. Moskva: "Kniga," 1972. 209 p.

Briskman, M. A., and A. D. Eikhengol'ts, eds. *Bibliografiia: obshchii kurs* [Bibliography: a Short Course]. Moskva: "Kniga," 1969. 560 p.

Masanov, IU. I. *Teoriia i praktika bibliografii: ukazatel' literatury, 1917-1958* [Theory and Practice of Bibliography: Index of the Literature, 1917-1958]. Moskva: Izd-vo Vsesoiuznoi knizhnoi palaty, 1960. 479 p.

Mikhlina, I. I., and I. B. Chisheiko. "O sootnoshenii tekushchikh posobii gosudarstvennoi i kraevedcheskoi bibliografii v avtonomnykh respublikakh [On the Correlation of Current Aids of National and Regional Bibliography in the Autonomous Republics]." *Sovetskaia bibliografiia* 4 (1974): 25-32

Sokurova, M. V. *Obshchie bibliografii russkikh knig grazhdanskoi pechati, 1708-1955: annotirovannyi ukazatel'* [General Bibliography of Russian Books of the Civil Press, 1708-1955: An Annotated Index]. Izd. 2-e, perer. i dop. Leningrad: 1956. 283 p. (Bibliografiia russkoi bibliografii: annotirovannye ukazateli).

Zdobnov, N. V. *Sinkhronisticheskie tablitsy russkoi bibliografii, 1700-1928, so spiskom vazhneishikh bibliograficheskikh trudov* [Synchronic Tables of Russian Bibliography, 1700-1928, with a List of the Most Important Works]. Moskva: Izd-vo Vsesoiuznoi knizhnoi palaty, 1962. 190 p.

BIBLIOGRAPHY—HISTORY

Choldin, Marianna Tax. "Grigorii Gennadi and Russian Bibliography: A Reexamination." *Libri* 25 (1975): 13-33.

Choldin, Marianna Tax. "A Nineteenth Century Russian View of Bibliography." *Journal of Library History, Philosophy, and Comparative Librarianship* 10 (October 1975): 311-322.

Choldin, Marianna Tax. "The Russian Bibliographical Society: 1889-1930." *Library Quarterly* 46 (January 1976): 1-20.

Choldin, Marianna Tax. "Some Developments in Nineteenth Century Bibliography: Russia." *Libri* 27 (June 1977): 108-115.

Choldin, Marianna Tax. "Three Early Russian Bibliographers." *Library Quarterly* 44 (January 1974): 1-28.

Mashkova, M. V. *Istoriia russkoi bibliografii nachala XX veka (do oktiabria 1917 goda)* [History of Russian Bibliography at the Beginning of the Twentieth Century (until October 1917)]. Moskva: "Kniga," 1969. 492 p.

Mashkova, M. V. "Izuchenie istorii dorevoliutsionnoi i sovetskoi bibliografii v Sovetskom Soiuze [A Study of the History of Prerevolutionary and Soviet Bibliography in the Soviet Union]." *Sovetskaia bibliografiia* 3 (1973): 3-23.

Reiser, S. A. *Khrestomatiia po russkoi bibliografii s XI veka po 1917 g.* [Reader in Russian Bibliography from the Eleventh Century through 1917]. Moskva: Gos. izd-vo kul'turno-prosvetitel'noi lit-ry, 1956. 447 p.

Zdobnov, N. V. *Istoriia russkoi bibliografii do nachala XX veka* [History of Russian Bibliography to the Beginning of the Twentieth Century]. Izd. 2. Moskva: Izd-vo Akademii nauk SSSR, 1951. 511 p.

CATALOGING

Buist, Eleanor. "Soviet Centralized Cataloging: A View from Abroad." *Library Trends* 16 (July 1967): 127-42.

Guseva, A. V. "Pechatnoi kartochke na knigi—40 let [Forty Years of Printed Cards for Books]." *Sovetskaia bibliografiia* 1 (1967): 62-67.

Nemchenko, V. V. "O tsentralizovannoi katalogizatsii knig na sovremennom etape [On Centralized Cataloging Today]." *Sovetskaia bibliografiia* 5 (1975): 3-9.

Rabin, A. E. *Ispol'zovanie pechatnykh kartochek Vsesoiuznoi knizhnoi palaty* [Use of the Printed Cards of the All-Union Book Chamber]. Moskva: Izd-vo Vsesoiuznoi knizhnoi palaty, 1960. 65 p.

Serebrennikov, A. I. "Tsentralizovannaia katalogizatsiia—vazhneishii uchastok deiatel'nosti knizhnykh palat [Centralized Cataloging— A Most Important Element in Book Chamber Activities]." *Sovetskaia bibliografiia* 3 (1967): 25-50.

Vsesoiuznaia knizhnaia palata. *Katalogi Vsesoiuznoi knizhnoi palaty* [Catalogs of the All-Union Book Chamber]. Moskva: 1958. 24 p. (Metodicheskie materialy po gosudarstvennoi bibliograficheskoi registratsii, vyp. XV).

CLASSIFICATION

Biskup, Peter. "Marx-Leninism and Soviet Classification: Some Thoughts on Classification Theory and Practive in the U.S.S.R." *Australian Library Journal* 12 (March 1963): 28-34.

Reynolds, Dennis J. "The Introduction and Use of Decimal Classification in Russia, 1895-1921: UDC, DDC, and the Normal Plan." *Library Quarterly* 47 (October 1977): 431-450.

Rozhdestvenskaia, V. I. "K vykhodu v svet novogo izdaniia skhemy klassifi- katsii literatury v organakh gosudarstvennoi bibliografii [Publication of the New Edition of the Classification Scheme for the Organs of National Bibliography]." *Sovetskaia bibliografiia* 4 (1972): 16-24.

Vsesoiuznaia knizhnaia palata. *Klassifikatsiia literatury v organakh gosudarst- vennoi bibliografii* [Classification of Literature in the Organs of National Bibliography]. Izd. 5-e, pererab. i dop. Moskva: "Kniga," 1971. 308 p. (Metodicheskie materialy po gosudarstvennoi bibliografii, vyp. XXVI).

Whitby, Thomas J. "Evolution and Evaluation of a Soviet Classification." *Library Quarterly* 26 (April 1956): 118-27.

CONFERENCES

"XVIII soveshchanie direktorov knizhnykh palat [Eighteenth Conference of Book Chamber Directors]." *Sovetskaia bibliografiia* 6 (1971): 77-82.

Gruzinskaia, N. N. "Soveshchanie-seminar direktorov knizhnykh palat [Conference-Seminar of Book Chamber Directors]." *Sovetskaia bibliografiia* 6 (1976): 87-91.

Gvizhiani, L. A., I. IU. Bagrova, and IU. I. Fartunin. "Mezhdunarodnyi kongress po natsional'noi bibliografii [International Congress on National Bibliography]." *Sovetskaia bibliografiia* 1 (1978): 96-107

"19-e soveshchanie direktorov knizhnykh palat [Nineteenth Conference of the Book Chamber Directors]." *Sovetskaia bibliografiia* 5 (1974): 97-101.

"XVII soveshchanie direktorov knizhnykh palat [Seventeenth Conference of Book Chamber Directors]." *Sovetskaia bibliografiia* 6 (1969): 58-66.

"XVI soveshchanie direktorov knizhnykh palat [Sixteenth Conference of Book Chamber Directors]." *Sovetskaia bibliografiia* 4 (1967): 9-15.

LEGAL DEPOSIT

Godkevich, M. A. "Obiazatel'nyi ekzempliar na sluzhbu sotsialisticheskomu stroitel'stvu [The Obligatory Copy in the Service of Socialist Construction]." *Sovetskaia bibliografiia* 1/2 (1935): 35-56.

Godkevich, M. A. "Sovetskoe zakonodatel'stvo ob obiazatel'nom ekzempliare [Soviet Legislation on the Obligatory Copy]." *Sovetskaia bibliografiia* 1 (1940): 78-102.

Grigor'ev, IU. V. "Puti uluchsheniia sistemy besplatnogo obiazatel'nogo ekzempliara [Means of Improving the System of the Free Obligatory Copy]." *Sovetskaia bibliografiia* 2 (1947): 3-18.

Grigor'ev, IU. V. "Sistema besplatnogo obiazatel'nogo ekzempliara proizvedenii pechati na sovremennom etape [The System of the Obligatory Copy of Publications Today]." *Sovetskaia bibliografiia* 44 (1956): 3-11.

Grigor'ev, IU. V. "Sistema obiazatel'nogo ekzempliara v 1905-1907 godakh [The System of the Obligatory Copy in the Years 1905-1907]." *Sovetskaia bibliografiia* 38 (1955): 32-37.

Grigor'ev, IU. V. "Sistema obiazatel'nogo ekzempliara v SSSR za 30 let [The System of the Obligatory Copy in the USSR for Thirty Years]." *Sovetskaia bibliografiia* 4 (1947): 32-49.

Kukharkov, N. "Copyright Deposit and Related Services: The All-Union Book Chamber of the U.S.S.R." *Unesco Bulletin for Libraries* 11 (January 1957): 2-4.

Whitby, Thomas J. "Development of the System of Legal Deposit in the U.S.S.R." *College and Research Libraries* 15 (October 1954): 398-406.

NATIONAL BIBLIOGRAPHY–USSR

Alekperov, A. P. "Novoe 'Tipovoe polozhenie o gosudarstvennoi knizhnoi palate soiuznoi respubliki' [The New 'Standard Regulation about the State Book Chamber of the Union Republic']." *Sovetskaia bibliografiia* 5 (1971): 78-81.

Bodnarskii, B. S. "Petrogradskaia 'Knizhnaia letopis' ' [The Petrograd 'Book Annals']." *Sovetskaia bibliografiia* 1 (1940): 153-161.

Chisheiko, I. B., and N. V. Kuznetsova. "Uchetno-registratsionnaia bibliografiia v avtonomnykh respublikakh RSFSR [National Bibliography in the Autonomous Republics of the RSFSR]." *Sovetskaia bibliografiia* 1 (1968): 3-8.

Dunaeva, T. G. "Vozniknovenie i razvitie gosudarstvennoi bibliografii v avtonomnykh respublikakh RSFSR [Origin and Development of National Bibliography in the Autonomous Republics of the RSFSR]." *Sovetskaia bibliografiia* 5 (1972): 13-29.

"Dvadtsat' let Leninskogo dekreta o bibliografii [Twentieth Anniversary of the Lenin Decree on Bibliography]." *Sovetskaia bibliografiia* 1 (1940): 5-12.

Eikhengol'ts, A. D. "Sorok let sovetskoi bibliografii [Forty Years of Soviet Bibliography]." *Sovetskaia bibliografiia* 48 (1957): 3-30.

Fartunin, IU. I. "60 let Vsesoiuznoi knizhnoi palate–tsentru gosudarstvennoi bibliografii [The Sixtieth Anniversary of the All-Union Book Chamber]." *Sovetskaia bibliografiia* 5 (1977): 6-13.

Frantskevich, V. N. "U istokov sovetskoi gosudarstvennoi bibliografii [On the Sources of Soviet National Bibliography]." *Sovetskaia bibliografiia* 1 (1970): 114-122.

Gruzinskaia, N. N. "Osnovnye napravleniia nauchnoi i nauchno-metodicheskoi deiatel'nosti Vsesoiuznoi knizhnoi palaty v oblasti gosudarstvennoi bibliografii [Basic Directions in the Scientific and Methodological Activity of the All-Union Book Chamber in National Bibliography]." *Sovetskaia bibliografiia* 2 (1977): 6-13.

"Knizhnaia palata v pervye gody Sovetskoi vlasti, 1917-1920 gg. [The Book Chamber in the First Years of Soviet Power, 1917-1920]." *Sovetskaia bibliografiia* 3 (1967): 211-243.

Kukharkov, N. N. "Gosudarstvennaia bibliografiia v SSSR [National Bibliography in the USSR]." *Sovetskaia bibliografiia* 1 (1961): 3-10.

Kuznetsova, N. V. "Gosudarstvennaia uchetno-registratsionnaia bibliografiia SSSR na sovremennom etape [National Bibliography in the USSR Today]." *Sovetskaia bibliografiia* 3 (1967): 10-24.

Kuznetsova, N. V. "Sorokaletie Vsesoiuznoi knizhnoi palaty [Fortieth Anniversary of the All-Union Book Chamber]." *Sovetskaia bibliografiia* 4 (1960): 109-111.

Maio-Znak, E. O. "Vsesoiuznaia knizhnaia palata na sovremennoi etape [The All-Union Book Chamber Today]." *Sovetskaia bibliografiia* 4 (1974): 10-24.

Martynov, I. F. "Nachalo gosudarstvennoi bibliograficheskoi registratsii v Sovetskoi Sibiri v 1919-1922 gg. [Origin of National Bibliographic Registration in Soviet Siberia in 1919-1922]." *Sovetskaia bibliografiia* 6 (1966): 55-61.

Martynov, I. F. "O nachale gosudarstvennoi bibliograficheskoi registratsii na territorii Evropeiskoi chasti RSFSR (1918-1920 gg.) [On the Origin of National Bibliographic Registration in the European Part of the RSFSR (1918-1920)]." *Sovetskaia bibliografiia* 4 (1969): 33-49.

Masanov, IU. I. "Bibliograficheskaia i nauchno-metodicheskaia rabota Vsesoiuznoi knizhnoi palaty [Bibliographic and Research Work of the All-Union Book Chamber]." *Sovetskaia bibliografiia* 4 (1960): 3-15.

Masanov, IU. I. "35 let raboty Vsesoiuznoi knizhnoi palaty [Thirty-five Years' Work of the All-Union Book Chamber]." *Sovetskaia bibliografiia* 40 (1955): 3-10.

Masanov, IU. I. "Za dal'neishee uluchshenie raboty knizhnykh palat [Toward Further Improvement in the Work of the Book Chambers]." *Sovetskaia bibliografiia* 45 (1957): 3-16.

Polozhenie o Vsesoiuznoi knizhnoi palate [Regulation Concerning the All-Union Book Chamber]. In *Sovetskaia bibliografiia* 2 (1936): 111-113.

Pontovich, E. E. "Leninskii dekret o bibliografii i ego razvitie v posleduiushch zakonodatel'stve [The Lenin Decree on Bibliography and Its Development in Subsequent Legislation]." *Sovetskaia bibliografiia* 4 (1935): 41-47.

"Programmnyi document (K 50-letiiu Leninskogo dekreta o bibliografii) [Program Document (To the Fiftieth Anniversary of the Lenin Decree on Bibliography)]." *Sovetskaia bibliografiia* 4 (1970): 3-6.

Ruggles, Melville J. "The All-Union Book Chamber of the U.S.S.R." *Libri* 9 (1959): 117-24.

Serebrennikov, A. I. "Zadachi gosudarstvennoi bibliografii i problema polnoty otbora izdanii [Aims of National Bibliography and the Problem of Completeness in the Selection of Publications]." *Sovetskaia bibliografiia* 6 (1975): 3-16.

Shamurin, E. I. "Gosudarstvennaia tsentral'naia knizhnaia palata za 15 let [The State Central Book Chamber for Fifteen Years]." *Sovetskaia bibliografiia* 4 (1935): 7-40.

Shamurin, E. I. "30 let sovetskoi gosudarstvennoi bibliografii [Thirty Years of Soviet National Bibliography]." *Sovetskaia bibliografiia* 4 (1947): 3-31.

Sikorsky, N. M., and E. O. Maio-Znak. *National Bibliography in the USSR and Problems of Bibliographic Control.* International Federation of Library Associations, 39 Session, Grenoble, 1973. 18 p. (Mimeographed)

Tolkachev, N. T. "Gosudarstvennaia bibliografiia v soiuznykh respublikakh [National Bibliography in the Union Republics]." *Sovetskaia bibliografiia* 5 (1948): 58-72.

Utesheva, R. A. "Uchenyi sovet Vsesoiuznoi knizhnoi palaty [Learned Council of the All-Union Book Chamber]." *Sovetskaia bibliografiia* 4 (1969): 85-88.

"V knizhnykh palatakh Sovetskogo Soiuza [In the Book Chambers of the Soviet Union]." *Sovetskaia bibliografiia* 1 (1946): 91-99.

Verevkina, A. N. "Leninskii dekret ob organizatsii bibliograficheskoi dela v strane i razvitie sovetskoi bibliografii [Lenin Decree on the Organization of Bibliographic Affairs in the Country and the Development of Soviet Bibliography]." *Sovetskaia bibliografiia* 3 (1960): 67-77.

Verevkina, A. N., and R. IA. Zverev. "Gosudarstvennaia uchetno-registratsionnaia bibliografiia SSSR (1917-1958) [National Bibliography in the USSR (1917-1958)]." In *Sovetskaia bibliografiia: sbornik statei.* Moskva: Min. kul'tura RSFSR, 1960. Pp. 39-60.

Vesirova, L. A. *National Bibliography in a Multi-national State as Accomplished in the USSR.* International Federation of Library Associations, 36th Session, Moscow, 1970. 16 p. (Mimeographed)

Vsesoiuznaia knizhnaia palata. *Sorok let sovetskoi gosudarstvennoi bibliografii (1920-1960); sbornik statei* [Forty Years of Soviet National Bibliography (1920-1960): A Collection of Articles]. Moskva: 1960. 269 p.

"Vsesoiuznoi knizhnoi palate—50 let [The All-Union Book Chamber—50 Years]." *Sovetskaia bibliografiia* 4 (1967): 3-8.

Whitby, Thomas J. "National Bibliography in the U.S.S.R." *Library Quarterly* 23 (January 1953): 16-22.

Zdobnov, N. B. "Gosudarstvennaia bibliograficheskaia registratsiia pri tsarizme [National Bibliographic Registration under Tsarism]." *Sovetskaia bibliografiia* 4 (1935): 75-95.

Zverev, R. IA. "Razvitie gosudarstvennoi bibliografii v soiuznykh i avtonomnykh respublikakh SSSR [The Development of National Bibliography in the Union and Autonomous Republics of the USSR]." In Gosudarstvennaia ordena Lenina biblioteka SSSR imeni V. I. Lenina. *Trudy* [Transactions]. t. V. Moskva: 1961. Pp. 112-130.

NATIONAL BIBLIOGRAPHY–ARMENIA

Dzhabian, L. M. " 'Sovetskaia Armeniia v pechati SSSR' ['Soviet Armenia in USSR Publishing']." *Sovetskaia bibliografiia* 3 (1975): 110-111.

NATIONAL BIBLIOGRAPHY–AZERBAIDZHAN

Akhundli, F. G. "Knizhnoi palate Azerbaidzhanskoi SSR–50 let [The Fiftieth Anniversary of the Azerbaidzhan Book Chamber]." *Sovetskaia bibliografiia* 4 (1975): 13-15.

Mirzoeva, V. D. "Nauchnaia konferentsiia, posviashchennaia sostoianiiu i razvitiiu gosudarstvennoi bibliografii v Azerbaidzhane [Conference on the Status and Development of National Bibliography in Azerbaidzhan]." *Sovetskaia bibliografiia* 5 (1973): 92-97.

NATIONAL BIBLIOGRAPHY–BASHKIRIA

Khabirova, F. A. "40 let Gosudarstvennoi knizhnoi palate Bashkirskoi ASSR [The Fortieth Anniversary of the State Book Chamber of the Bashkir ASSR]." *Sovetskaia bibliografiia* 3 (1969): 21-22.

NATIONAL BIBLIOGRAPHY–BELORUSSIA

Adamovich, V. S., and N. B. Batatsi. "Bibliograficheskaia deiatel'nost' Gosudarstvennoi biblioteki BSSR im. V. I. Lenina i Knizhnoi palaty BSSR za 50 let [The Bibliographic Activity of the Lenin State Library of the BSSR and the Book Chamber of the BSSR for Fifty Years]." *Sovetskaia bibliografiia* 1 (1973): 13-25.

NATIONAL BIBLIOGRAPHY–CHUVASHIA

Petrova, M. I. "40 let Knizhnoi palate Chuvashskoi ASSR [The Fortieth Anniversary of the Book Chamber of the Chuvash ASSR]." *Sovetskaia bibliografiia* 2 (1972): 32-36.

NATIONAL BIBLIOGRAPHY–ESTONIA

Khel'm, I. A. "25 let Knizhnoi palaty Estonskoi SSR [The Twenty-fifth Anniversary of the Book Chamber of the Estonian SSR]." *Sovetskaia bibliografiia* 3 (1966): 78-79.

NATIONAL BIBLIOGRAPHY—GEORGIA

Nakashidze, T. E. "Piatidesiatiletie Knizhnoi palaty Gruzinskoi SSR [The Fiftieth Anniversary of the Book Chamber of the Georgian SSR]." *Sovetskaia bibliografiia* 1 (1975): 34-37.

NATIONAL BIBLIOGRAPHY—KAZAKHSTAN

IAzberdiev, A. "Problemy otrazheniia natsional'noi pechati v izdaniiakh knizhnykh palat Srednei Azii i Kazakhstana [Problems of Showing National Literature in the Publications of the Book Chambers of Central Asia and Kazakhstan]." *Sovetskaia bibliografiia* 6 (1974): 3-14.

Kasymova, Z. "Novoe bibliograficheskoe izdanie Knizhnoi palaty Kazakhskoi SSR [A New Bibliographic Publication of the Book Chamber of the Kazakh SSR]." *Sovetskaia bibliografiia* 4 (1972): 103-104.

Kasymova, Z. "Sorok let raboty knizhnoi palaty Kazakhskoi SSR [Forty Years of Work of the Book Chamber of the Kazakh SSR]." *Sovetskaia bibliografiia* 4 (1977): 59-65.

NATIONAL BIBLIOGRAPHY—KIRGIZIA

"Knizhnaia palata Kirgizskoi SSR [The Book Chamber of the Kirgiz SSR]." *Sovetskaia bibliografiia* 1 (1946): 96-97.

Momunbaeva, R. M., and V. A. Chevelev. "40-letie Gosudarstvennoi knizhnoi palaty Kirgizskoi SSR [The Fortieth Anniversary of the State Book Chamber of the Kirgiz SSR]." *Sovetskaia bibliografiia* 1 (1978): 31-39.

NATIONAL BIBLIOGRAPHY—LITHUANIA

Bartninkas, A. "Kontrol' za dostavkoi proizvedenii pechati v Knizhnoi palate Litovskoi SSR [Control of the Supply of Publications to the Book Chamber of the Lithuanian SSR]." *Sovetskaia bibliografiia* 6 (1972): 23-26.

Ul'pis, A. IU. "30 let deiatel'nosti Knizhnoi palaty Litovskoi SSR [Thirty Years' Activity of the Book Chamber of the Lithuanian SSR]." *Sovetskaia bibliografiia* 4 (1975): 16-20.

NATIONAL BIBLIOGRAPHY–MOLDAVIA

Kozanak, G. E. "V Knizhnoi palate Moldavskoi SSR [The Book Chamber in the Moldavian SSR]." *Sovetskaia bibliografiia* 6 (1962): 12-13.

NATIONAL BIBLIOGRAPHY–TADZHIKISTAN

Mirov, S. M., and R. A. Kukushkina. "40 let Knizhnoi palate Tadzhikskoi SSR [The Fortieth Anniversary of the Book Chamber of the Tadzhik SSR]." *Sovetskaia bibliografiia* 5 (1975): 17-21.

Musheev, G. "Iz istorii gosudarstvennoi bibliografii v Tadzhikistane [From the History of National Bibliography in Tadzhikistan]." *Sovetskaia bibliografiia* 2 (1974): 32-40.

NATIONAL BIBLIOGRAPHY–TATARIA

Khisamova, A. M. "K 50-letiiu Knizhnoi palaty Tatarskoi ASSR [On the Fiftieth Anniversary of the Book Chamber of the Tatar ASSR]." *Sovetskaia bibliografiia* 1 (1977): 27-30.

NATIONAL BIBLIOGRAPHY–TURKMENIA

IAzberdiev, A. "Knizhnoi palate Turkmenskoi SSR-50 let [The Fiftieth Anniversary of the Book Chamber of the Turkmen SSR]." *Sovetskaia bibliografiia* 4 (1976): 36-37.

NATIONAL BIBLIOGRAPHY–UKRAINE

Roskopyt, A. G. "Gosudarstvennoi bibliografii na Ukraine 50 let [Fifty Years of National Bibliography in the Ukraine]." *Sovetskaia bibliografiia* 5 (1972): 87-92.

Skachkov, V. N. "Gosudarstvennaia bibliografiia na Ukraine [National Bibliography in the Ukraine]." *Sovetskaia bibliografiia* 2 (1972): 24-31.

NATIONAL BIBLIOGRAPHY–UZBEKISTAN

Khaidarova, N. Kh., and V. V. Seliverstova. "Gosudarstvennoi knizhnoi palate Uzbekskoi SSR-50 let [Fifty Years of the State Book Chamber of the Uzbek SSR]." *Sovetskaia bibliografiia* 6 (1976): 29-31.

PUBLICATIONS

Beletskaia, Z. G. " 'Letopis' zhurnal'nykh statei' na sovremennom etape
[The 'Annals of Journal Articles' Today]." *Sovetskaia bibliografiia*
5 (1976): 3-8.

Deev, A. N. "Izdaniia Vsesoiuznoi knizhnoi palaty [Publications of the
All-Union Book Chamber]." *Sovetskaia bibliografiia* 1 (1959): 65-69.

Deev, A. N. "Izdatel'skaia deiatel'nost' Vsesoiuznoi knizhnoi palaty [Pub-
lishing Activity of the All-Union Book Chamber]." *Sovetskaia
bibliografiia* 5 (1960): 88-95.

"40 let sborniku 'Sovetskaia bibliografiia' [The Forty Year Collection
'Soviet Bibliography']." *Sovetskaia bibliografiia* 4 (1974): 84-91.

Golitsyna, M. I. " 'Letopis' retsenzii' [The 'Annals of Reviews']." *Sovskaia
bibliografiia* 5 (1975): 10-16.

Gudovshchikova, I. V. "O 'Bibliografii sovetskoi bibliografii' [On the
'Bibliography of Soviet Bibliography']." *Sovetskaia bibliografiia* 3
(1973): 24-41.

Khenkina, I. A. "K 40-letiiu 'Letopisi gazetnykh statei' [The Fortieth
Anniversary of the 'Annals of Newspaper Articles']." *Sovetskaia
bibliografiia* 3 (1976): 45-47.

Medvedev, IU. B. "Bibliografirovanie zhurnal'nykh statei v Knizhnoi palate
USSR [The Bibliography of Journal Articles in the Book Chamber of
the Ukrainian SSR]." *Sovetskaia bibliografiia* 6 (1976): 32-36.

"Novye zadachi [New Tasks]." *Sovetskaia bibliografiia* 1 (1978): 3-5.

PUBLISHING AND BOOK TRADE

Abruzov, M. F. *Knizhnaia torgovlia v SSSR* [The Book Trade in the USSR].
Moskva: "Kniga," 1976. 155 p.

Arest, IA., and V. Dobrushin. *Bibliotechnye kollektory: zadachi, organizatsiia
i opyt raboty* [Library Collectors: Tasks, Organization, and Experi-
ence]. Moskva: Izd-vo "Kniga," 1973.

Grigor'ev, IU. V. *Sistema knigosnabzheniia sovetskikh bibliotek* [The System
of Book Supply to Soviet Libraries]. Moskva: Gos. izd-vo kul'turno-
prosvetitel'noi lit-ry, 1956. 46 p.

Monastyrskii, I. M. "Nauchno-issledovatel'skaia i informatsionnaia rabota
palaty po problemam knigoizdaniia i knigorasprostraneniia [Research
and Information Work by the Chamber on Problems of Book Publishing and Distribution]." *Sovetskaia bibliografiia* 2 (1977): 14-26.

"TSentral'noe biuro nauchno-tekhnicheskoi informatsii i tekhniko-ekonomicheskikh issledovanii v oblasti poligraficheskoi promyshlennosti,
izdatel'skogo dela, knigovedeniia, gosudarstvennoi bibliografii,
knizhnoi torgovli (TSBNYI po pechati) sozdano v 1967 g. vo Vsesoiuznoi knizhnoi palate [Central Bureau on Scientific and Technical Information and Technical-Economic Research in the Fields of Printing,
Publishing, Bibliology, National Bibliography, and the Book Trade
Created in 1967 at the All-Union Book Chamber]." *Sovetskaia
bibliografiia* 2 (1968): 85.

STANDARDIZATION

Barsuk, A. I. "Standartizatsiia bibliograficheskoi terminologii–trebovanie
vremeni [Standardization of Bibliographic Terminology–a Require-
ment of the Time]." *Sovetskaia bibliografiia* 6 (1974): 15-28.

Gudovshchikova, I. V. "O poniatii 'natsional'naia bibliografiia' [On the
Concept 'National Bibliography']." *Sovetskaia bibliografiia* 5 (1959):
78-88.

Morgenshtern, I. G., and B. T. Utkin. "Unifikatsiia terminologii–vazhneishee
uslovie ee sovershenstvovaniia [Unification of Terminology–a Most
Important Condition for Its Improvement]." *Sovetskaia bibliografiia*
3 (1974): 18-23.

Reshetinskii, I. I. "Pervyi gosudarstvennyi standart na bibliograficheskuiu
terminologiiu [The First State Standard on Bibliographic Terminology]."
Sovetskaia bibliografiia 3 (1970): 11-16.

Semenovker, B. A. "O kakikh standartakh sleduet znat' bibliografu [Stan-
dards the Bibliographer Must Know]." *Sovetskaia bibliografiia* 1
(1978): 52-55.

Semenovker, B. A. "Sovremennoe sostoianie standartizatsii v bibliografii
[Current Status of Standardization in Bibliography]." *Sovetskaia
bibliografiia* 4 (1975): 3-12.

"Sovershenstvovat' i vnedriat' standarty [Improvement and Introduction
of Standards]." *Sovetskaia bibliografiia* 1 (1973): 97-108.

Vodka, G. N., and M. IA. Serebrianaia. "O primenenii GOSTa na bibliograficheskuiu terminologiiu [On the Application of GOST in Bibliographic
Terminology]." *Sovetskaia bibliografiia* 2 (1973): 66-68.

STATISTICS

Maio-Znak, E. O. "Evoliutsiia statistiki pechati v SSSR [Evolution of Publishing Statistics in the USSR]." *Sovetskaia bibliografiia* 3 (1975): 3-23.

Reiser, S. A. "Ob istochnikakh russkoi knizhnoi statistiki [On Sources of Russian Book Statistics]." *Sovetskaia bibliografiia* 1 (1946): 75-90.

Samuilov, V. S. "Sovetskaia statistika pechati [Soviet Publishing Statistics]." *Sovetskaia bibliografiia* 3 (1967): 50-61.

Semenovker, B. A. "Issledovanie sostoianiia i dinamiki razvitiia tekushchego ucheta mirovoi pechatnoi produktsii [Investigation of the Status and Dynamics of Developing a Current Account of World Printed Production]." *Sovetskaia bibliografiia* 5 (1972): 30-38.

Vsesoiuznaia knizhnaia palata. *Gosudarstvennaia bibliografiia i statistika pechati v SSSR* [National Bibliography and Publishing Statistics in the USSR]. Moskva: 1960. 25 p.

Zdobnov, N. V. *Russkaia knizhnaia statistika: iz istorii vozniknoveniia i razvitiia* [Russian Book Statistics: Origin and Development]. Moskva: Izd-vo "Sovetskaia Rossiia," 1959. 53 p.

INDEX

Titles of the currently published annals of national bibliography, principally those of the USSR, are given twice, in Russian and in English translation. Details of the numerous title changes for each annals are provided in the text of the translation in Part II. The transliteration system used is that of the Library of Congress without diacritical marks. The only abbreviation used in this index is *n* for footnote.

225

(continues on page 228)

Music Annals (cont'd)
  mentioned, 30, 73
  types of indexes in, 109-10

Narkompros
  See People's Commissariat of
    Education
National bibliography
  automation, 56-58
  chief aim of, 5
  importance of, 69, 74-75
  in the autonomous republics,
    183-84
  in the republics, 30, 71
  instructions for compiling organs
    of, 71-73
  organs of, 30, 45-46, 73-184
  republic centers of, 35-38, 70
  systems in United States and Soviet
    Union contrasted, 8
  terminology of, 203-10
  Third World acceptance, 8
National Information Systems (NATIS),
  7
National System of Scientific and
  Technical Information (GSNTI), 57
NATIS, 7
NAVKP, 48
Newspapers of the USSR, 46, 74, 105,
  107n
Nikitenko, A. V., 18
Notnaia letopis', 107-13

Obligatory copy
  basis of national bibliography,
    62, 70
  delivery of, 27, 29
  types of, 45
  See also Depository libraries; Legal
    deposit
Organs of national bibliography
  See National bibliography

People's Commissariat of Education,
  26, 28-31 *passim*
Periodical literature
  opinions of Admiral Shishkov and
    S. S. Uvarov, 17
Publishing statistics, 46-48
Publishing USSR in 1976, 46
Pushkin, Alexander, 16, 23

Research Archives of the All-Union
  Book Chamber (NAVKP), 48

Rossica, 16, 77
Royal Society of London, 7
*Rules of Bibliographic Description of
  Publications*, 50
"Russian Bibliographic Index for 1855,"
  19, 23
Russian Book Chamber
  early difficulties, 26-28
  founding of, 21, 69
  location of, 28
  See also Russian Central Book Chamber
Russian Central Book Chamber
  bibliographic center of RSFSR, 30
  formation of, 28, 70
  See also Russian Book Chamber; State
    Central Book Chamber
Russische Bibliothek, 15, 23
Russkaia beseda, 19, 23

Saltykov-Shchedrin State Public Library,
  50, 53
Secrets Law of 1956, 44
Serbinovich, K. S., 17-18
Smirdin, Alexander, 16
Son of the Fatherland, 16
Sovetskaia bibliografiia, 34
Soviet Bibliography, 34
Sovremennik, 16
Standardization, 55-56
State bibliographic registration, 16-22
State Central Book Chamber
  formation of, 31
  See also All-Union Book Chamber
State Public Scientific and Technical
  Library (GPNTB), 50, 56
State Publishing House, 29, 31
Statistics of publishing, 46-48
Syn otechestva, 16

Tadzhik SSR
  organs of national bibliography in,
    169-70, 192
Tatar ASSR
  organs of national bibliography in,
    179-80, 191
Teleskop, 17
Terminological problems
  in international bibliographic control,
    9-10
  in statistics, 48
Third Section, 17
Toropov, A. D., 21
TSBNTI, 56
Turkmen SSR
  organs of national bibliography in,
    173-75, 190